PRACTICAL ILLUSTRATIONS

OF THE

PRINCIPLES OF SCHOOL ARCHITECTURE.

BY HENRY BARNARD.

CONTENTS.

PRACTICAL ILLUSTRATIONS

OF THE

PRINCIPLES OF SCHOOL ARCHITECTURE.

In treating of School Architecture, it will be convenient to present—

I. Common Errors to be avoided.
II. General Principles to be observed.
III Plans and directions for erecting and fitting up school-houses adapted to the varying circumstances of country and city, of a small, and a large number of scholars, of schools of different grades and of different systems of instruction.

I. COMMON ERRORS IN SCHOOL ARCHITECTURE.

Under this head it will be sufficient to enumerate the principal features of school-houses as they are.

They are, almost universally, badly located, exposed to the noise, dust and danger of the highway, unattractive, if not positively repulsive in their external and internal appearance, and built at the least possible expense of material and labor.

They are too small. There is no separate entry for boys and girls appropriately fitted up; no sufficient space for the convenient seating and necessary movements of the scholars; no platform, desk, or recitation room for the teacher.

They are badly lighted. The windows are inserted on three or four sides of the room, without blinds or curtains to prevent the inconvenience and danger from cross-lights, and the excess of light falling directly on the eyes or reflected from the book, and the distracting influence of passing objects and events out of doors.

They are not properly ventilated. The purity of the atmosphere is not preserved by providing for the escape of such portions of the air as have become offensive and poisonous by the process of breathing, and by the matter which is constantly escaping from the lungs in vapor, and from the surface of the body in insensible perspiration.

They are imperfectly warmed. The rush of cold air through cracks and defects in the doors, windows, floor and plastering is not guarded against. The air which is heated is already impure from having been breathed, and made more so by noxious gases arising from the burning of floating particles of vegetable and animal matter coming in contact with the hot iron. The heat is not equally diffused, so that one portion of a school-room is frequently overheated, while another portion, especially the floor, is too cold.

They are not furnished with seats and desks, properly made and adjusted to each other, and arranged in such a manner as to promote the comfort and convenience of the scholars, and the easy supervision on the part of the teacher. The seats are too high and too long, with no suitable support for the back, and especially for the younger children. The desks are too high for the seats, and are either attached to the wall on three sides of the room, so that the faces of the scholars are turned from the teacher, and a portion of them at least are tempted constantly to look out at the windows,—or the seats are attached to the wall on opposite sides, and the scholars sit facing each other. The aisles are not so arranged that each scholar can go to and from his seat, change his position, have access to his books, attend to his own business, be seen and approached by the teacher, without incommoding any other.

They are not provided with blackboards, maps, clock, thermometer, and other apparatus and fixtures which are indispensable to a well regulated and instructed school.

They are deficient in all of those in and out-door arrangements which help to promote habits of order, and neatness, and cultivate delicacy of manners and refinement of feeling. There are no verdure, trees, shrubbery and flowers for the eye, no scrapers and mats for the feet, no hooks and shelves for cloaks and hats, no well, no sink, basin and towels to secure cleanliness, and no places of retirement for children of either sex, when performing the most private offices of nature.

Lest the author should be thought to exaggerate the deficiencies of school-houses as they have been heretofore constructed, and as they are now almost universally found wherever public attention has not been earnestly, perseveringly, and judiciously called to their improvement, the following extracts from recent official school documents are inserted, respecting the condition of school-houses in states where public education has received the most attention.

CONNECTICUT.

Extract *from the " First Annual Report of the Secretary of the Board of Commissioners of Common Schools for* 1838–39.

"In the whole field of school improvement there is no more pressing need of immediate action than here. I present with much hesitation, the result of my examinations as to several hundred school-houses in different parts of the State. I will say, generally, that the location of the school-house, instead of being retired, shaded, healthy, attractive, is in some cases decidedly unhealthy, exposed freely to the sun and storm, and in nearly all, on one or more public streets, where the passing of objects, the noise and the dust, are a perpetual annoyance to teacher and scholar, —that no play-ground is afforded for the scholar except the highway,— that the size is too small for even the *average* attendance of the scholars, —that not one in a hundred has any other provision for a constant supply of that indispensable element of health and life, pure air, except the rents and crevices which time and wanton mischief have made; that the seats and desks are not, in a majority of cases, adapted to children of different sizes and ages, but on the other hand are calculated to induce physical deformity, and ill-health, and not in a few instances (I state this on the authority of physicians who were professionally acquainted with the cases,) have actually resulted in this—and that in the mode of warming rooms, sufficient regard is not had either to the comfort and health of the scholar, or to economy.

That I have not stated these deficiencies too strongly, I beg leave to refer you to the accompanying returns, respecting the condition of school-houses in more than eight hundred districts in the State, and in more than forty particulars in each. These returns were made from actual inspection and measurement of school-houses by teachers and others. An abstract of them in part will be found annexed, together with extracts from letters received from school officers on the subject. I might accumulate evidence of the necessity of improvement here for every district in the State. Without improvement in many particulars which concern the health, the manners and morals of those who attend school, it is in vain to expect that parents who put a proper estimate, not only on the intellectual, but the physical and moral culture of their children, will send to the district school.

The following extracts are taken from official documents, published in 1846 and 1847, and fair specimens of the manner in which school-houses are spoken of, in the reports of local committees, from different parts of the State.

"In one district the school-house stands on the highway, with eighty pupils enrolled as in attendance, in a room nineteen and a half feet square, without any outbuildings of any kind.

In another in the same town, the school-house is less than seven feet high, and the narrow slab seats are twenty-one inches high, (four inches higher than ordinary chairs.) The walls, desks, &c., are cut and marked with all sorts of images, some of which would make heathens blush.

In another, the room is fourteen feet square, and six feet five inches high. The walls are very black."

"In this town there is one of the most venerable school servants in the State. The room is small, and less than seven feet high. Slab seats extend around three sides of the room, and are too high for men. The skill of several generations must have been expended in illustrating the walls with lamp smoke and coal images. The crevices of the floor will admit any quantity of cold air. The door sill and part of the house sill have rotted away. The day I visited it, the teacher and pupils were huddled around the stove."

"In one district, the house stands near the travelled road, is low and small, being only seventeen feet by seventeen, and seven feet two inches high, for the accommodation of sixty or seventy pupils. The seats on the outside are from seventeen to eighteen inches. The walls, door, and sides of the house are disfigured with obscene images."

"There are only three good school-houses in the society; only three that have any out-houses. The rest of the school-houses are in a miserable condition. One is thirty-five or forty years old. Most of them have only slab seats, with the legs sticking through, upwards, like hatchel-teeth, and high enough to keep the legs of the occupants swinging. They are as uncomfortable to little children as a pillory. Seats and desks are adorned with every embellishment that the ingenuity of professional whittlers can devise."

"Two of our school-houses, those in the two largest districts, are in a bad condition, old, unpainted and inconvenient. They are built and constructed *inside* on the old Connecticut plan. Only one row of desks, and that fastened to the wall of the school-room, running quite around it; and long forms, without backs to rest on, the scholars sitting with their backs to the centre of the room. The other two are in better condition, though one is constructed on the same plan as above. The out-buildings are in bad condition generally. One school-house has no out-building nor wood-house. One school-house only is painted outside."

"Of the nine school-houses in this society, not one is really what they all ought to be, for the morals, health, and intellectual improvement of the pupils. Four of them are considered tolerably good, having one out-building, the other five are hardly passable. The desks in most or all of them are where they never ought to be, against the sides of the room and against one end, and with few exceptions, all of a height, with poor accommodations for those clothes, hats, &c.; all located on or near some highway; no play-ground attached to any of them, except the highway."

"A part of our school-houses are comfortable buildings, but destitute of every thing like taste or ornament in the grounds, structure, or the furniture of the rooms. Being generally built in the public highway or close by its side, they are, one and all, without enclosures, ornamental or shade trees. But the want of ornament is by no means the greatest defect of our school-houses; a majority of them are not convenient. Although there has been some improvement in those recently built, yet they are not so good as would be desirable. The out-buildings in too many cases are in a neglected condition, and in some districts are not provided at all, indicating an unpardonable neglect on the part of parents and guardians."—*East Windsor.*

"It appears that a great proportion of the school-houses are in a sad condition and of bad architecture. Architectural drawings should, therefore, be scattered over the state, so that in the buildings to be erected those abominations may be avoided which are now so abundant."—*Glastenbury.*

"The internal construction of most of our school-houses is bad, and occasions great inconvenience and hindrance to the prosperity of our schools. Let as much be done as can be, to remove those miserable prison-houses for our children, and in their stead let there be good, large, and convenient school-houses."—*Suffield*, 2*d.*

"None of our school-houses have play-grounds attached; they generally stand in the highway, and some on a corner where several roads meet."—*Bethany.*

"Another evil is the poor, cold, inconvenient and gloomy school-houses which we find in many districts. There is one in this society not more attractive than a barn, for comfort and accommodation in a cold day: the best I can say about it is, it is thoroughly ventilated."—*Lebanon*, 4*th.*

"The houses and the internal arrangement are inconvenient; a slanting board the whole length of the house for a desk, and a slab-board for a seat so high that the scholars cannot reach the floor with their feet, constitute the conveniences of half of the schools in this society."—*Easton.*

"We see many a school-house which looks more like some gloomy, dilapidated prison, designed for the detention and punishment of some desperate culprit, than a place designed for the intellectual training of the children of an enlightened and prosperous nation. Instead of being rendered pleasant and attractive to the youthful mind, they are almost as cold and cheerless as an Indian wigwam."—*Chaplin.*

"Many of our school-houses are in a miserable condition, possessing less attractions outwardly than our prisons, while within they are dark, gloomy and comfortless. They are all destitute of an appearance of any out-house."—*Warren.*

"The general plan of all the school-houses is the same. Writing desks are placed around the room against the walls; these are generally so high that it would be inconvenient for adults, much more for children to use them. The seats stand in front of these, so that the pupil has his option to sit with his face or his back to the teacher. In the former case, he has the edge of the writing desk to support his back; in the latter, nothing. An arrangement like this is the worst possible. Of the five school-houses in the society, two may be warmed so as to be comfortable at all times; a third needs nothing but a good stove; but the remaining two cannot be made fit for a school to occupy without thorough repairs. There is but one out-building of any kind connected with the school-houses of this society, and this is entirely unfit for use."—*Winchester.*

"Throughout Middlesex county the school-houses, taken as a whole, are several degrees below respectability—rarely ever painted within or without, and if painted at all, they ever afterward show a worn and weather-beaten coat, like the half starved, half clothed outcast of society. Yet these houses are owned by the public, worth its tens of thousands, and they groan grievously if a small tax is levied to improve them. Of the four locations of school-houses in this town, not one has sufficient land for a private dwelling, and all the land combined would be less than an acre. One stands wholly on the highway; another stands on a bleak and rocky elevation, and during some portions of the winter, almost inaccessible. This location was chosen probably because it was cheaper than the pleasant field on the opposite side of the way. Why should the public school-house which accommodates from thirty to fifty pupils, ten and eleven months in the year, five and a half days of each week, not require as much land as a church or private dwelling?"—*Chester.*

"Our school-houses are not what they ought to be either in their location or construction. In their location they are generally found upon some barren knoll, or too near the highway, forming part of the fence between the highway and the adjoining proprietor, alike destitute of ornament or shade calculated to render them pleasing or attractive. The desks are almost always too high and continuous, instead of single, nor is there generally a gradation in reference to the size of the scholar. Few school-rooms are well ventilated; not more than one or two properly or healthfully warmed; the consequence is unnecessary frequency of colds, head-aches and ill health."—*Tolland.*

The Superintendent (Hon. Seth P. Beers) of Common Schools, thus introduces the subject in his Annual Report for 1848.

"The reports of school visitors from every part of the state speak in strong terms of condemnation of the deplorable condition of many district school-houses. The progress of renovation and improvement in this department has not been as rapid or as thorough, during the past year, as in other sections of New England, or as the true interests of the common schools imperiously demand. Badly located school-houses still "encumber the highway,"—"without shrub or shade-tree around,"—"without play-ground, yard, or out-house, mat or scraper,"—without means of ventilation and uniform temperature,"—"with seats too high and destitute of support for the back,"—"with desks attached to three sides of the room," "with windows destitute of glass,"—"clapboards hanging loose,"—"blinds propped up to be kept in their places,"—"the wood without shelter," and "the stove without a door." These are specimens of the language used by school visitors in describing the places where the children of Connecticut are receiving their early training in taste, manners, morals, and health,—language which it is hoped will touch the pride of the districts, and lead to some efficient action on the subject."

"How surprising and disgraceful is the fact, that a very large proportion of the school-houses of our state present vastly fewer attractions, in point of comfortable arrangement and tastefulness, than are seen about our poor-houses, our jails, and our state penitentiary! This remark is too true of the school-houses in this society. They are all located directly on the road or in it, with hardly a shrub or shade-tree around any one of them; and with no play-ground except the highway, which the children, in several districts, have to share in common with geese and swine. Of their external condition nothing very creditable or gratifying can be said. Six, of the nine school-houses in this society, are wooden ones, and they generally bear a time-honored, weather-beaten aspect. Unpainted and blindless, with clapboards agape to catch the winds of winter, and window-panes rattling, or fallen from the decayed sash, they present a most forlorn and gloomy aspect, which, to say the least, is not very well suited to woo the youthful mind, and fill it with pleasant fancies. One, unacquainted with their original design, might mistake them for the abodes of the evil genii, which would naturally be supposed to haunt the dreary solitudes which surround them.

The internal condition of these school-houses is in perfect keeping with the external. In several of them, the plastering is broken and missing, to say nothing of the dark and dingy color of what remains. The stoves are smoky, and the benches and desks are so high as to be better adapted to the children of a race of giants, than to those of the present generation; and these are hacked and gashed by the pupils, as if in retaliation for the torture suffered from them. My compassion has been deeply moved as I have frequently entered these abodes of suffering, and seen their unhappy inmates—the children of protestant parents—doing penance upon their high seats, with no support to their backs but the soft edge of the projecting board which forms the desk, and with their feet dangling in mid-air several inches from the floor. And when I have looked upon these youthful sufferers, thus seated and writhing with pain, the question has often arisen in my mind, what have these ill-starred children done that they should be doomed to so excruciating torture? What rank offenses have they committed that they should thus be suspended between the heavens and earth for six hours each day? And from deep-felt pity for the innocent sufferers, I have sometimes wished (perhaps it was cruel) that their parents had to sit for one hour in a similar position, that they might learn how to pity their children, and be prompted to attend to their health and comfort in the internal arrangement of the school-room.

Add to all this the fact, so outrageous to common decency, that most of these school-houses have no out-buildings whatever attached to them; and does not the case appeal movingly to the friends of humanity, and demand prompt and decisive measures of reform? Is it not passing strange, that while many parents incur considerable expense in providing themselves with cushioned and carpeted slips in church, where they ordinarily spend, perhaps, but three hours each week, they should be so utterly regardless of the comfort and happiness of their offsprings in the school-room?"—*Bloomfield.*

"Three of the houses are located in the highway; an excellent device for saving land, but a miserable one for the comfort, safety and improvement of children. In selecting sites for the new houses, recently erected, a good degree of space fronting was provided for. Only two houses have blinds or shutters; all the others give full scope for the sun to see what is going on in the school-room, often to the manifest annoyance of the children and teacher; unless, perchance, the latter has genius enough to convert a stray newspaper, or some other available article, into a temporary curtain to shut him out."—*Manchester.*

"Our school-houses, though not cold and leaky, are very badly constructed within, and are therefore very inconvenient. Two of them stand mostly in the highway, so that one passing in a carriage or on horseback may look in upon the whole school, and as a matter of course the scholars will look at whatever passes. When the school-house is so exposed, it would seem, that *modesty* in our children would require the convenience of good out-houses; but this is not the case with any two school-houses in the town. We have urged the importance of these things, but with poor success."—*Suffield,* 2*d.*

"There are some houses unfit for their purpose; the weather-boards are starting off, "and the wind enjoys quite freely the luxury of coming in and being warmed by the fire; and the dear children suffer much between a cold northwester and a red-hot stove." It is very common to find the school-houses mutilated by the cuttings of obscene figures; this should draw forth the unqualified censure of proprietors and teachers. Further, there are cases where there are no out-houses for the use of children. This is a sore evil, and ought to be remedied immediately."—*Groton.*

"Among the ten school-houses in this district are several very good buildings; but, taking in view the size and proportions of the edifices, the internal arrangement, the fitness of the seats and desks for the object designed, we feel impelled to say, that in our opinion there are no very good school-houses. In some of the districts it is said the people are obliged to go among strangers to procure teachers, on account of the shabbyness of the school-houses."—*Brooklyn.*

"Not more than one-half of our school-houses in this society are very good, if, indeed, they can be termed more than comfortable. The remainder are bad, some of them very bad, exhibiting nothing of comfort or convenience. In some of them, there are no desks fit to be used for writing purposes. The seats are so constructed as to afford no place to rest the back, or, in some cases, even the sole of the foot. Many of the schools are destitute of out-houses. Some of them have no conveniences for hanging up the hats or clothes of the children, or even to shelter the wood from the weather. And more than half our school-houses are destitute of black-boards, a fact alike discreditable to the district and to the teachers who have served in them."—*Stafford,* 1*st.*

"It appears from the superintendent's report for 1847, that of 1663 school-houses in the state, 873 have out-houses, and 745 have none! This fact is, undoubtedly, a burning shame and a deep disgrace to the state. It is unworthy of a civilized country, and indicates a state of things that ought to exist only among savages. The committee are happy to say that we have little or no share in this shameful fact: but our school-houses are by no means what they should be, and call for improvement.

They are generally *on* or *in* the street, whereas every building devoted to such a purpose ought to be in a retired situation, with suitable yards for play-grounds, and convenient fixtures. The windows in some do not let down from the top, and therefore are not properly ventilated. In only two out of eight school-houses are the benches what they should be. Large desks running around the room for the older scholars ought to be wholly discarded as intolerable nuisances. The scholars are of necessity always looking into the street; the windows can be opened only by climbing over the benches and desks. The scholars' backs are turned toward the teacher; they sit close together, and of course are often whispering. Large girls can leave their seats only by placing their feet on a level with their hips, which it is not always best that females should do. The smaller benches often have backs that are so *low* as to be of little service. Every school-house ought to be provided with a single desk for each pupil, and every pupil ought to have a slate and books to keep in the desk."—*Vernon.*

The following extracts are taken from the Annual Reports for 1849.

"The *school-houses* are not what they should be. Some of them are decidedly bad. They are neither convenient nor pleasant. The benches and desks are inconvenient. Some of the small scholars are reduced to the miserable necessity of swinging in the air, without being able to either get a foothold or a place to rest their backs against. *Ventilation* is not attended to. Every school-room should be so constructed that it can be freely ventilated, so that the scholars may have pure atmospheric air to breathe. This every one must appreciate, who knows the value of health, and does not wish to see a generation of sickly drones coming on to the stage. As a general thing, the external appearance of the school-houses is bad. A stranger passing through a district, can easily select the school-house. If you see a very unique-looking building, a "squatter" in the highway, or standing by permission on the side of some lot, in a corner rendered useless by a location on the border of some swampy moor, or on some arid field, where no vestige of life is—*that* you may conclude is the district school-house. *That* is the place where our children are to resort, during three-fourths of the first sixteen years of their lives, to get an education. *Such* are the associations with their early, perhaps *all* their education! Why is not the district school the place where correct taste should be demonstrated? Impressions *will* be made, and if they ever yield to good taste, school-house associations, in their present state, will not deserve the credit."—*Enfield.*

"Our school-houses are in a bad condition. Look into the school some warm, comfortable day, when the children are more likely to be in attendance, and if you please, walk in and breathe a specimen of the air in a New England unventilated school-house. If you are a well-bred man, you must do violence to your kind feelings, when you take a seat and look around and find that the teacher has nothing left for his accommodation but a standee; our school-houses are literally jammed full, i. e. the seats—any attempt at improvement is voted down on account of the cost."—*South Windsor, Wapping.*

"One district, for a wonder, occupied a new school-house; but while it is *excellent, compared with the old one*, it is *contemptible*, if not *wicked*, compared with what it *ought* to be. The only plan about it seems to be, the *minimum scale of expenditure.* Its dimensions are too limited even for so small a school. The desk or counter is uniform, and attached to three sides of the room, and almost out of *the tallest scholar's reach!* I have protested to the district, and possibly they will lower the counter, *some time or other.* The other districts *need* new school-rooms, and some *talk* of building."—*Wolcott.*

"In regard to the school-houses in our five districts, only one can be said to be very good. Another, recently repaired, may be called good in a qualified sense; while the remaining three are quite ordinary, if not bad. This neglect to provide neat and comfortable school-houses, doubtless has a tendency to dampen the ardor of children in literary pursuits, and in various ways to retard their progress."—*Plainfield.*

"The school-room in the third district presents the same unsightly appearance which it has in years past; and from the height to which the writing desks, and slabs used for seats, are elevated, some persons would naturally infer that they were originally designed for a race of giants."—*Pomfret, Abington.*

"Most of the school-*houses* are in a bad condition, being old, ill-constructed, and inconvenient. Especially is this the case with regard to the interior of some of them, the seats of which are too high for the comfort of the scholars, with nothing to rest the back against, except the sharp edge of a plank or board, which serves as a writing desk, and this placed so high as to bring the arm to an unnatural and uneasy position when attempting to write. The school-houses, too, with one or two exceptions, stand in the highway, many within a few feet of the traveled path, with windows looking directly upon it, so that the attention of the scholar is necessarily attracted to every passer-by, thus diverting his attention from his studies, retarding his progress, and annoying his teacher."—*Litchfield, Milton.*

The Annual Report of the Superintendent of Common Schools for 1850 contains the following remarks on the condition of the school-houses.

"If any reliance can be placed on the representations made by teachers and school visitors from two hundred and four out of the two hundred and seventeen school societies in the state, as collected from written communications to this department in the course of the last four years, a majority of our school-houses are badly located, badly ventilated, imperfectly warmed in winter, having uncomfortable seats and desks, without apparatus except a black-board, and destitute of the most ordinary means of cleanliness and convenience. To this overwhelming mass of testimony (Appendix G) as to the necessity of immediate and thorough improvement in this portion of the educational field, I will here add an extract from a communication by a teacher of much experience and distinction, who received his education and commenced his experience in teaching in the district schools of this state. His remarks refer to the condition of school-houses in a single county—to three-fourths of which he had just made a personal visit."

"OLD SCHOOL-HOUSES.—These are the Antiquities of Connecticut, rude monuments of art, that must have had their origin coeval with the pyramids and catacombs, for aught we can learn to the contrary, save by the uncertain information of tradition. "It always stood there," says "the oldest inhabitant," when asked the date of the erection of one of them. Little brown structures of peculiar aspect, meek, demure, burrowing in some lone, damp and depressed spot, or perchance perched on the pinnacle of a rock, as if too contemptible and abject to occupy a choice piece of earth,—exposed to the remorseless winds of winter, and the fervid rays of summer,—at one end a narrow and dingy entry, the floor covered with wood, chips, stones, hats, caps, odd mittens, old books, bonnets, shawls, cloaks, dirt, dinner baskets, old brooms, ashes, &c., all thrown together in the order as here catalogued,—the principal room retaining its huge stone chimney, which for generations boasted its ghastly fire-place, affording a ready oblivion to annual piles of green and snow-soaked wood,—the burnt, smoked, scratched and scrawled wainscoting,—the battered and mutilated plastering,—the patched windows,—the crippled and ragged benches,—the desks which have endured a short eternity of whittling,—the masses of pulverized earth in constant agitation, filling the throat, eye and nostrils of the inmates,—the unmistakable compound of odors which come not from "Araby the blest"—all point to the remote antiquity of these buildings, and intimate the veneration in which they are held. That some of these structures are always to remain, does not seem to admit of a "reasonable doubt." The records of their origin, as we have seen, are gone, and the testimony of the past few generations is conclusive that no change has been effected in their appearance from a remote period; hence the deduction that they are among the "things to remain," and never to pass away. Though the "annual miracle of nature" may not be vouchsafed to preserve them, yet, like the monuments of the American Indians which receive their annual votive offering of stones, and are thus rendered imperishable, so these "antiquities," receiving their semi-occasional patches upon windows, upon clapboards, roofs and floors, together with the autumnal embankment of earth around their base, and all these given and received obsequious to the *annual solemn* votes of the district,—stand, despite the advance of public opinion, the "war of elements," and "the tooth of time."

Modern School Architecture.—It is much to be regretted that a work similar to "Barnard's School Architecture" had not been issued and circulated throughout the state some ten years ago, that such as have since that time erected new houses, (that are to stand forever,) might have consulted approved models for the size and forms of their structures, and improved plans for their internal arrangements. It would seem, however, that enough had been said by the author of that work in his annual reports, and occasional addresses in the state, to have excited interest sufficient in those intending to build new houses, to extend their inquiries and observations beyond the limits of their own district, and beyond the pattern of their own recently condemned school-house, and at least to select suitable locations for houses and necessary out-buildings, if not for a yard and play-ground.

The material changes observed in the construction of new houses about the county, consist in placing the *end* of the building toward the street instead of the *side*, and giving a very narrow entry across the end of the building,—affording, in some instances, two entrances into the school-room, with only one into the entry. A portion of the entry is used for wood, which being thrown against the plastering, lays bare the lathing, making the building, while yet new, bear the tokens of age. In a few instances only have two outside doors been observed, giving separate entrances to boys and girls.

In most instances where the building is not erected on the line of the highway, it is placed only so far back as to allow a straggling wood pile just outside the traveled path. An instance is not now remembered where the generosity of the district has given a play-ground to the school, aside from the *public common* or the *traveled highway*.

The internal arrangements of the new houses are, in *many instances*, exactly like those of their immediate predecessors, save that in all cases it is believed the old movable slab benches, are superseded by permanent benches with backs. The windows, in all cases perhaps, in the new houses, have made a sensible step *downward* toward the floor; and the desks and seats of the larger scholars, have also been brought down from their inconvenient and dizzy heights, that their occupants may not be "while *in*, above the world."

Where change has been wrought in the fixtures of the room, the desks are almost always clumsy, occupying unnecessary portions of the room, and rendering them inconvenient for the evolutions of the school.

Ventilation has received a passing thought in the erection of most of the new houses, yet its importance is not probably fully appreciated, nor the best methods of securing it clearly understood. Some ventilate from the windows so successfully, as to part with the warm air almost entirely, and at the same time to retain the offensive gases and odors of the room. Some ventilators are placed in the ceiling in the corners of the rooms, others are placed immediately over the stove pipe,—some are movable, and moved with a cord,—others are simply a scuttle, expected to rise by the expansive power of the gases, as safety valves of engines operate by accumulation of steam.

The substitution of stoves (mainly box stoves,) for the engulphing fire place, as a means of warming school-rooms, is noticed in the new houses.

Of School-Houses generally.—To ascertain if improvement has been effected in this class of structures in the state, we must resort to one or two devices of the astronomer, in observing the motions of the heavenly bodies, viz., to notice their respective positions at different and remote periods of time. The progress of improvement has been so slow, (if improvement has been made in school-houses,) that an observer from year to year only, might be at a loss to know that such was the fact; but a comparison of the structures fifteen or twenty years ago, with the buildings now occupied for schools, will doubtless enable one to say that *progress has been made.* It is stated on very creditable authority that in *some* societies and some towns, *one*, and in some instances, more *than* one house has been built, and one or more has been *painted.*

The contributions upon old hats, upon writing books that are "writ through," &c., &c., are levied less frequently than formerly to repel the winds at the windows; fewer clapboards are now seen swinging gaily by a single nail, than in bye-gone days; the asthmatic wheezing of the winds through the uncounted apertures is hushed, and the pupils enjoy an irrigation through the roof less frequently than formerly. Curtains are occasionally found to protect the eyes of the pupils from the blinding rays of the sun; the comfort of the smaller children is materially increased by the addition of backs to their hard seats; the desks and seats of the larger pupils have descended toward the floor; the use of stoves giving a comfortable temperature to the rooms, instead of the former equatorial heat and the polar cold; in rare instances the ingenious designs in chalk and charcoal upon the walls and ceiling have retired behind a coating of whitewash, and the yawning fire-place has been plastered over. All these movements distinctly indicate that vitality at least exists among the people of this commonwealth, and that *the best good of their children, as they tell us, lies nearest their hearts.*

It is earnestly hoped that all persons will be open to conviction and receive the above statement of facts as a perfect demonstration of the earnestness of the community for the well being of the schools.

When we come to the *et ceteras* of the school-rooms, such as shovel and tongs, brooms, brushes, bells, globes, sinks, wash-basins, towels, pegs, hooks and shelves for hats, clothing, &c., it is feared such great, such momentous changes, such rapid advances, will not appear to have been made; probably not three districts in the county have gone so fast, or so far in advance of the others as to have procured all these articles; probably not more than half a dozen districts have supposed it important, that even a mat and scraper are necessary for pupils to use after walking, perhaps a mile in the mud; yet we should be doing them injustice in not supposing that they really feel this quenchless interest, which they represent themselves as possessing for their children, and should greatly misjudge them if we supposed them not doing all in their power to encourage their children in obtaining useful knowledge, and in cultivating the minor virtues while in school.

OUT-BUILDINGS.—An appalling chapter might be written, on the evils, the almost inevitable results of neglecting to provide these indispensable appendages to school-houses in our state. Who can duly estimate the final consequences of the first shock given to female delicacy, from the necessary exposure, to which the girls in the public schools are inevitably subjected; and what must be the legitimate results of these frequent exposures during the school-going years of youth? What quenchless fires of passion have been kindled within the bosom of the young of both sexes by these exposures, fires that have raged to the consuming of personal happiness, to the prevention of scholastic improvement, and to the destruction of personal character? again, what *disgust* has been created in both sexes by the results of not having the appropriate retirements which nature imperiously demands? and finally, may not the disinclination, the aversion of large numbers of families, of mothers especially, to sending their daughters to the public schools, have been created by the sufferings they themselves have endured, from the above cause; and an unwillingness to subject the delicacy of their daughters to the obnoxious trial? Were the question not so peculiar as almost to defy examination, it is apprehended this would be found to be the truth. Will it not seem incredible, even to Connecticut men, to be informed that less than one-half of the school-houses in this commonwealth are without these necessary buildings? yet such is probably the fact; thus dooming thousands of girls to bear a loathsome burden of mortification, which they cannot remove without withdrawing from the schools. I have no *exact* data for the above estimate, yet it is probably not far below the truth, if indeed it is at all. So filthy are *most* of those that are provided, that they are not only quite useless, but disgusting in the extreme. In one society of nine schools but one out-house was provided, and that, I was informed, could only be reached in *dry* weather, such was its *location;* nor could it be used even then, such was its *condition.* This state of things, it would seem, should be utterly changed, and that speedily."

MASSACHUSETTS.

EXTRACTS *from the "Report of the Secretary (Hon. Horace Mann) of the Board of Education for* 1846."

"For years the condition of this class of edifices, throughout the State, taken as a whole, had been growing worse and worse. Time and decay were always doing their work, while only here and there, with wide spaces between, was any notice taken of their silent ravages; and, in still fewer instances, were these ravages repaired. Hence, notwithstanding the improved condition of all other classes of buildings, general dilapidation was the fate of these. Industry and the increasing pecuniary ability which it creates, had given comfort, neatness, and even elegance to private dwellings. Public spirit had erected commodious and costly churches. Counties, though largely taxed, had yet uncomplainingly paid for handsome and spacious court-houses and public offices.

In 1837, not one third part of the Public School-houses in Massachusetts would have been considered tenantable by any decent family, out of the poor-house, or in it. As an incentive to neatness and decency, children were sent to a house whose walls and floors were indeed painted, but they were painted, all too thickly, by smoke and filth; whose benches and doors were covered with carved work, but they were the gross and obscene carvings of impure hands; whose vestibule, after the oriental fashion, was converted into a veranda, but the metamorphosis which changed its architectural style, consisted in laying it bare of its outer covering. The modesty and chastity of the sexes, at their tenderest age, was to be cultivated and cherished, in places, which oftentimes were as destitute of all suitable accommodations, as a camp or a caravan. The brain was to be worked amid gases that stupefied it. The virtues of generosity and forbearance were to be acquired where sharp discomfort and pain tempted each one to seize more than his own share of relief, and thus to strengthen every selfish propensity.

At the time referred to, the school-houses in Massachusetts were an opprobrium to the State; and if there be any one who thinks this expression too strong, he may satisfy himself of its correctness by inspecting some of the few specimens of them which still remain.

The earliest effort at reform was directed towards this class of buildings. By presenting the idea of taxation, this measure encountered the opposition of one of the strongest passions of the age. Not only the sordid and avaricious, but even those, whose virtue of frugality, by the force of habit, had been imperceptibly sliding into the vice of parsimony, felt the alarm. Men of fortune, without children, and men who had reared a family of children, and borne the expenses of their education, fancied they saw something of injustice in being called to pay for the education of others; and too often their fancies started up into spectres of all imaginable oppression and wrong. The school districts were the scene where the contending parties arrayed themselves against each other; the school-house itself their arena. From time immemorial, it had been the custom to hold school district meetings in the school-house. Hither, according to ancient usage, the voters were summoned to come. In this forum, the question was to be decided, whether a new edifice should be erected, or whether the ability of the old one to stand upon its foundations for another season, should be tried. Regard for the health, the decent manners, the intellectual progress and the moral welfare of the children, common humanity, policy, duty, the highest worldly interests of the race, were marshalled on one side, demanding a change; selfishness, cupidity, insensibility to the wants and the welfare of others, and that fallacious plea, that because the school-house had answered the purpose so long, therefore it would continue to answer it still longer,—an argument which would make all houses, and roads, and garments, and every thing made by human hands, last forever,—resisted the change. The disgraceful contrast between the school-house and all other edifices, whether public or private, in its vicinity; the immense physical and spiritual sacrifices which its condition inflicted upon the rising generation, were often and unavailingly urged; but there was always one argument which the advocates for reform could use with irresistible effect,—the school-house itself. Cold winds, whistling through crannies and chinks and broken windows, told with merciless effect upon the opponents. The ardor of opposition was cooled by snow-blasts rushing up through the floor. Pain-imparting seats made it impossible for the objectors to listen patiently even to arguments on their own side; and it was obvious that the tears they shed were less attributable to any wrongs which they feared, than to the volumes of smoke which belched out with every gust of wind from broken funnels and chimneys. Such was the case in some houses. In others, opposite evils prevailed; and the heat and stifling air and nauseating effluvia were such as a grown man has hardly been compelled to live in, since the time of Jonah.

Though insensible to arguments addressed to reason and conscience, yet the senses and muscles and nerves of this class of men were less hardened than their hearts; and the colds and cramps, the exhaustion and debility, which they carried home, worked mightily for their conversion to truth. Under such circumstances, persuasion became compulsory.

Could the leaders of the opposition have transferred the debate to some commodious public hall, or to their own spacious and elegant mansions, they might have bid defiance to humanity and remained masters of the field. But the party of reform held them relentlessly to the battle-ground; and there the cause of progress triumphed, on the very spot where it had been so long dishonored.

During the five years immediately succeeding the report made by the Board of Education to the Legislature, on the subject of school-houses, the sums expended for the erection or repair of this class of buildings fell but little short of *seven hundred thousand dollars.* Since that time, from the best information obtained, I suppose the sum expended on this one item to be about *one hundred and fifty thousand dollars annually.* Every year adds some new improvement to the construction and arrangement of these edifices.

In regard to this great change in school-houses,—it would hardly be too much to call it a *revolution,*—the school committees have done an excellent work,—or rather, they have begun it;—it is not yet done. Their annual reports, read in open town meeting, or printed and circulated among the inhabitants, afterwards embodied in the Abstracts and distributed to all the members of the government, to all towns and school committees have enlightened and convinced a State.

NEW-YORK.

EXTRACT *from the "Annual Report of the Superintendent (Hon. Samuel Young) of Common Schools, made to the Legislature, January* 13, 1844."

"The whole number of school-houses visited and inspected by the county superintendents during the year was 9,368: of which 7,685 were of framed wood; 446 of brick; 523 of stone, and 707 of logs. Of these, 3,160 were found in good repair; 2,870 in ordinary and comfortable repair, and 3,319 in bad repair, or totally unfit for school purposes. The number furnished with more than one room was 544, leaving 8,795 with one room only. The number furnished with suitable play-grounds is 1,541; the number not so furnished, 7,313. The number furnished with a single privy is, 1,810; those with privies containing separate apartments for male and female pupils, 1,012; while the number of those not furnished with *any privy* whatever, is 6,423. The number suitably furnished with convenient seats, desks, &c., is reported at 3,282, and the number not so furnished, at 5,972. The number furnished with proper facilities for ventilation is stated at 1,518; while the number not provided with these essential requisites of health and comfort is 7,889.

No subject connected with the interests of elementary instruction affords a source of such mortifying and humiliating reflections as that of the condition of a large portion of the school-houses, as presented in the above enumeration. One-third only of the whole number visited, were found in good repair; another third in ordinary and comfortable condition only in this respect—in other words, barely sufficient for the convenience and accommodation of the teachers and pupils; while the remainder, consisting of 3,319, were to all intents and purposes unfit for the reception of man or beast.

But 544 out of 9,368 houses visited, contained more than one room; 7,313 were destitute of any suitable play-ground; nearly six thousand were unfurnished with convenient seats and desks; nearly eight thousand destitute of the proper facilities for ventilation; and upwards of six thousand without a privy of any sort; while of the remainder but about one thousand were provided with privies containing different apartments for male and female pupils! And it is in these miserable abodes of accumulated dirt and filth, deprived of wholesome air, or exposed without adequate protection to the assaults of the elements, with no facilities for necessary exercise or relaxation, no convenience for prosecuting their studies; crowded together on benches not admitting of a moment's rest in any position, and debarred the possibility of yielding to the ordinary calls of nature without violent inroads upon modesty and shame; that upwards of two hundred thousand children, scattered over various parts of the State, are compelled to spend an average period of eight months during each year of their pupilage! Here the first lessons of human life, the incipient principles of morality, and the rules of social intercourse are to be impressed upon the plastic mind. The boy is here to receive the model of his permanent character, and to imbibe the elements of his future career; and here the instinctive delicacy of the young female, one of the characteristic ornaments of the sex, is to be expanded into maturity by precept and example! Is it strange, under such circumstances, that an early and invincible repugnance to the acquisition of knowledge is imbibed by the youthful mind; that the school-house is regarded with unconcealed aversion and disgust, and that parents who have any desire to preserve the health and the morals of their children, exclude them from the district school, and provide instruction for them elsewhere?

If legislation could reach and remedy the evil, the law-making power would be earnestly invoked. But where the ordinary mandates of humanity, and the laws of parental feeling written by the finger of heaven on the human heart, are obliterated or powerless, all statutory provisions would be idle and vain. In some instances during the past year, comfortable school-houses have been erected to supply the place of miserable and dilapidated tenements which for years had been a disgrace to the inhabitants. Perhaps the contagion of such worthy examples may spread; and that which seems to have been beyond the influence of the ordinary impulses of humanity, may be accomplished by the power of example or the dread of shame.

NEW HAMPSHIRE.

EXTRACTS *from the "Report of the Commissioner, (Prof. Haddock, of Dartmouth College) of Common Schools, to the Legislature of New Hampshire, June Session,* 1847."

"The success of our whole system depends as much on a thorough reform in the construction and care of school-houses as upon any other single circumstance whatever.

It is wonderful, and when their attention is called to it, strikes the inhabitants of the Districts themselves as really unaccountable, that careful and anxious parents have been content to confine their children for so many hours a day through a large part of the severest and most trying seasons of the year, in houses so ill constructed, so badly ventilated, so imperfectly warmed, so dirty, so instinct with vulgar ideas, and so utterly repugnant to all habits of neatness, thought, taste, or purity. There are multitudes of houses in the State, not only inconveniently located, and awkwardly planned, but absolutely dangerous to health and morals.

And it has struck me with the greater surprise, that this is true not only of the thinly-peopled parts of the State, but of flourishing villages. In one

VERMONT.

EXTRACT *from the "First Annual Report of the State Superintendent (Hon. Horace Eaton,) of Common Schools, October,* 1846," *made to the Legislature.*

"It might occur to any one in travelling through the State, that our school-houses are almost uniformly located in an uninteresting and unsuitable spot, and that the buildings themselves too generally exhibit an unfavorable, and even repulsive aspect. Yet by giving some license to the imagination it might be supposed that, notwithstanding their location and external aspect were so forbidding, the internal appearance would be more cheerful and pleasant—or at least, that the arrangement and construction within would be comfortably adapted to the purposes which the school-house was intended to fulfil. But an actual inspection of by far the greatest number of the school-houses in the State, by County Superintendents, discloses the unpleasant fact, that ordinarily the interior does but correspond with the exterior, or is, if possible, still worse. A very large proportion of these buildings throughout the State must be set down as in a miserable condition. The melancholy fact is established by the concurrent report of all our County Superintendents, that in every quarter of the State they are, as a class, altogether unsuited to their high purposes. Probably nine-tenths of them are located upon the line of the highway; and as the geographical centre of the district usually determines their situation, aside from the relation with the road, it is a rare chance that one is not placed in an exposed, unpleasant and uncomfortable spot. In some cases—especially in villages—their location seems to be determined by the worth, or rather by the *worthlessness* of the ground on which they stand—that being selected which is of the least value for any other purpose. Seldom or never do we see our school-houses surrounded by trees or shrubbery, to serve the purpose which they might serve so well—that of delighting the eye, gratifying the taste, and contributing to the physical comfort, by shielding from the scorching sun of summer, and breaking the bleak winds of winter. And from buildings thus situated and thus exposed, pupils are turned out into the streets for their sports, and for other purposes still more indispensable. What better results could be expected under such a system than that our 'girls should become hoydens and our boys blackguards?' Indeed it would be a happy event, if in no case results still more melancholy and disastrous than this were realized.

MAINE.

EXTRACT *from a special "Report of the Secretary of the Board of Education, upon the subject of School-Houses."*

"It is worthy of note, and of most serious consideration, that a majority of the returns speak of ill-constructed school-houses as one of the most prominent 'defects in the practical operation of the law establishing common-schools.' The strength and uniformity of the language made use of, as well as the numerous applications to the members of the board, and their secretary, for information upon this subject, leave no room for doubt as to the existence of a wide-spread evil; an evil, the deleterious influence of which, unless it is reformed, and that speedily, is not to be confined to the present generation, but must be entailed upon posterity. In remarking upon this subject, as long ago as 1832, it was said by the board of censors of the American Institute of Instruction, that 'if we were called upon to name the most prominent defect in the schools of our country; that which contributes most, directly and indirectly, to retard the progress of public education, and which most loudly calls for a prompt and thorough reform, it would be the want of spacious and convenient school-houses.' From every indication, there is reason to believe that the remark is applicable to our school-houses, in their present condition, as it was when made."

RHODE ISLAND.

EXTRACTS *from "Report on the condition and improvement of the Public Schools of Rhode Island, submitted Nov.* 1, 1845, *by Henry Barnard, Commissioner of Public Schools.*"

"Of these, (three hundred and twelve school-houses visited,) twenty-nine were owned by towns in their corporate capacity; one hundred and forty-seven by proprietors; and one hundred and forty-five by school districts. Of two hundred and eighty school-houses from which full returns were received, including those in Providence, twenty-five were in very good repair; sixty-two were in ordinary repair; and eighty-six were pronounced totally unfit for school purposes; sixty-five were located in the public highway, and one hundred and eighty directly on the line of the road, without any yard, or out-buildings attached; and but twenty-one had a play-ground inclosed. In over two hundred school-rooms, the average height was less than eight feet, without any opening in the ceiling, or other effectual means for ventilation; the seats and desks were calculated for more than two pupils, arranged on two or three sides of the room, and in most instances, where the results of actual measurement were given, the highest seats were over eighteen inches from the floor, and the lowest, except in twenty-five schools, were ever fourteen inches for the youngest pupils, and these seats were unprovided with backs. Two hundred and seventy schools were unfurnished with a clock, black-board, or thermometer, and only five were provided with a scraper and mat for the feet."

MICHIGAN.

EXTRACTS *from "Annual Report of the Superintendent (Hon. Ira Mayhew) of Public Instruction of the State of Michigan, submitted December* 10, 1847."

"In architectural appearance, school-houses have more resembled barns, sheds for cattle, or mechanic shops, than Temples of Science,—windows are broken—benches are mutilated—desks are cut up—wood is unprovided—out-buildings are neglected—obscene images and vulgar delineations meet the eye without and within—the plastering is smoked and patched—the roof is so open as to let in a flood of water in a storm, sufficient to drown out a school, were not the floor equally open."

We close this mass of testimony as to the deplorable condition of the common, or public school-houses in States where public instruction has received the most attention, with an extract from a "*Report on School-houses, published by order of the Directors of the Essex County Teachers' Association in* 1833."

"There is one subject more to which we must be permitted to refer. One in which the morals of the young are intimately connected, one in which parents, instructors, and scholars, should unite their efforts to produce a reform; there should be nothing in or about school-houses, calculated to defile the mind, corrupt the heart, or excite unholy and forbidden appetites; yet considering the various character of those brought together in our public schools, and considering also how inventive are corrupt minds, in exhibiting openly the defilement which reigns within, we do not know but we must expect that school-houses, as well as other public buildings, and even fences, will continue to bear occasional marks both of lust and profaneness. But we must confess that the general apathy which apparently exists on this subject, does appear strange to us. It is a humbling fact, that in many of these houses, there are highly indecent, profane, and libidinous marks, images and expressions, some of which are spread out in broad characters on the walls, where they unavoidably meet the eyes of all who come into the house, or being on the outside, salute the traveler as he passes by, wounding the delicate, and annoying the moral sensibilities of the heart. While there is still a much greater number in smaller character, upon the tables and seats of the students, and even in some instances, of the instructors, constantly before the eyes of those who happen to occupy them. How contaminating these must be, no one can be entirely insensible. And yet how unalarmed, or if not entirely unalarmed, how little is the mind of community directed to the subject, and how little effort put forth to stay this fountain of corruption. We will mention as evidence of the public apathy, one house which we suppose is this day, it certainly was a few months since, defiled by images and expressions of the kind referred to, spread out in open observation upon its walls, which are known to have been there for eight or ten years. In this building during all this time, the summer and winter schools have been kept; here the district have held their business meetings; here frequently has been the singing-school; here, too, religious meetings have often been held; here, too, the school committee, the fathers, mothers, and friends of the children, have come to witness the progress of their children in knowledge and virtue; all of whom must have witnessed, and been ashamed of their defilement, and yet no effectual effort has been put forth to remove them. Such things ought not to be; they can, to a considerable extent, be prevented. The community are not therefore altogether clear in this matter.

We will close these remarks by observing that after an extensive and careful examination of the state of a great number of school-houses in this and other States, we are constrained to believe, that in regard to accommodation, the convicts in the State Prisons, except those condemned to solitary and perpetual confinement, and we are not certain that in all cases these should be excepted, are better provided for, than the dear children of New England, the glory of the present, and the hope of the coming age. And when we regard the deleterious effect which the want of accommodation and other imperfections in and about these buildings, must have upon the growth, health, and perfectness of the bodily system, upon the mental and moral power, upon the tender and delicate feeling of the heart, we must suppose there is as pressing a call for the direct interference of the wise and benevolent, to produce an improvement, as there is for the efforts of the Prison Discipline Society, or for many of the benevolent exertions of the day. And we do most solemnly and affectionately call upon all, according to their situation in life, to direct their attention to the subject; for the bodies, the minds, the hearts of the young and rising generation require this. It is a service due to the present and future generation. A service due to their bodies and souls."

II. GENERAL PRINCIPLES OF SCHOOL ARCHITECTURE.

1. A location, healthy, accessible from all parts of the district; retired from the dust, noise, and danger of the highway; attractive, from its choice of sun and shade, and commanding, in one or more directions, the cheap, yet priceless educating influences of fine scenery.

2. A site large enough to admit of a yard in front of the building, either common to the whole school or appropriated to greensward, flowers and shrubbery, and two yards in the rear, one for each sex, properly inclosed, and fitted up with rotary swings, and other means of recreation and exercise, and with privies, which a civilized people never neglect.

3. Separate entrances to the school-room for each sex; each entrance distinct from the front door, and fitted up with scraper, mats, and old broom for the feet; with hooks, shelves, &c., for hats, overcoats, over-shoes, and umbrellas; with sink, pump, basin and towels, and with brooms and duster, and all the means and appliances necessary to secure habits of order, neatness and cleanliness.

4. School-room, in addition to the space required by aisles and the teacher's platform, sufficient to accommodate with a seat and desk, not only each scholar in the district who is in the habit of attending school, but all who may be entitled to attend; with verge enough to receive the children of industrious, thoughtful, and religious families, who are sure to be attracted to a district which is blessed with a good school-house and a good school.

5. At least one spare room for recitation, library, and other uses, to every school-room, no matter how small the school may be.

6. An arrangement of the windows, so as to secure one blank wall, and at the same time, the cheerfulness and warmth of the sunlight, at all times of the day, with arrangements to modify the same by blinds, shutters, or curtains.

7. Apparatus for warming, by which a large quantity of pure air from outside of the building can be moderately heated, and introduced into the room without passing over a red-hot iron surface, and distributed equally to different parts of the room.

8. A cheap, simple, and efficient mode of ventilation, by which the air in every part of a school-room, which is constantly becoming vitiated by respiration, combustion, or other causes, may be constantly flowing out of the room, and its place filled by an adequate supply of fresh air drawn from a pure source, and admitted into the room at the right temperature, of the requisite degree of moisture, and without any perceptible current.

9. A desk with at least two feet of top surface, and in no case for more than two pupils, inclined towards the front edge one inch in a foot, except two to three inches of the most distant portion, which should be level, and covered with cloth to prevent noise—fitted with an ink-pot (supplied with a lid and a pen-wiper,) and a slate, with a pencil-holder and a sponge attached, and supported by end-pieces or

stanchions, curved so as to be convenient for sweeping, and to admit of easy access to the seat—these of varying heights for small and large pupils, the front edge of each desk being from seven to nine inches (seven for the lowest and nine for the highest,) higher than the front edge of the seat or chair attached.

10. A chair or bench for each pupil, and in no case for more than two, unless separated by an aisle, with a seat hollowed like an ordinary chair, and varying in height from ten to seventeen inches from the outer edge to the floor, so that each pupil, when properly seated, can rest his feet on the floor without the muscles of the thigh pressing hard upon the front edge of the seat, and with a support for the muscles of the back, rising above the shoulder-blades.

11. An arrangement of the seats and desks, so as to allow of an aisle or free passage of at least two feet around the room, and between each range of seats for two scholars, and so as to bring each scholar under the supervision of the teacher.

12. Arrangements for the teacher, such as a separate closet for his overcoat, &c., a desk for his papers, a library of books of reference, maps, apparatus, and all such instrumentalities by which his capacities for instruction may be made in the highest degree useful.

13. Accommodations for a school library for consultation and circulation among the pupils, both at school and as a means of carrying on the work of self-education at their homes, in the field, or the workshop, after they have left school.

14. A design in good taste and fit proportion, in place of the wretched perversions of architecture, which almost universally characterize the district school-houses of New England.

15. While making suitable accommodation for the school, it will be a wise, and, all things considered, an economical investment, on the part of many districts, to provide apartments in the same building, or in its neighborhood, for the teacher and his family. This arrangement will give character and permanence to the office of teaching, and at the same time secure better supervision for the school-house and premises, and more attention to the manners of the pupils out of school. Provision for the residence of the teacher, and not unfrequently a garden for his cultivation, is made in connection with the parochial schools in Scotland, and with the first class of public schools in Germany.

16. Whenever practicable, the privies should be disconnected from the play-ground, and be approached from a covered walk. Perfect seclusion, neatness and propriety should be strictly observed in relation to them.

17. A shed, or covered walk, or the basement story paved under feet, and open for free circulation of air for the boys, and an upper room with the floor deafened and properly supported for calisthenic exercises for the girls, is a desirable appendage to every school.

As many of the houses described are provided with very inadequate means of warming and ventilation, the following summary of the principles, which ought to be regarded in all arrangements for these objects, is given as the result of much observation, reflection, and experience.

1. The location of the school-house must be healthy, and all causes,—such as defective drains, stagnant water, decaying animal or vegetable substances, and manufactures, whose operations evolve offensive and deleterious gases,—calculated to vitiate the external atmosphere, from which the air of the school-room is supplied, must be removed or obviated.

2. The means provided for ventilation must be sufficient to secure the object, independent of doors and windows, and other lateral openings, which are intended primarily for the admission of light, passage to and from the apartment, and similar purposes. Any dependence on the opening of doors and windows, except in summer, will subject the occupants of the room near such points to currents of cold air when the pores of the skin are open, and when such extreme and rapid changes of temperature are particularly disagreeable and dangerous.

3. Any openings in the ceiling for the discharge of vitiated air into the attic, and hence to the exterior of the building, or by flues carried up in the wall, no matter how constructed or where placed, cannot be depended on for purposes of ventilation, unless systematic arrangements are adopted to effect, in concert with such openings, the introduction and diffusion of a constant and abundant supply of pure air, in the right condition as to temperature and moisture.

4. All stoves, or other heating apparatus, standing in the apartment to be warmed, and heating only the atmosphere of that apartment, which is constantly becoming more and more vitiated by respiration and other causes, are radically defective, and should be altogether, without delay, and forever discarded.

5. Any apparatus for warming pure air, before it is introduced into the school-room, in which the heating surface becomes *red-hot*, or the air is warmed above the temperature of boiling water, is inconsistent with true ventilation.

6. To effect the combined objects of warming and ventilation, a large quantity of moderately heated air should be introduced in such a manner as to reach every portion of the room, and be passed off by appropriate openings and flues, as fast as its oxygen is exhausted, and it becomes vitiated by carbonic acid gas, and other noxious qualities.

7. The size and number of the admission flues or openings will depend on the size of the school-room, and the number of persons occupying the same; but they should have a capacity to supply every person in the room with at least five cubic feet of air per minute. Warm air can be introduced at a high as well as a low point from the floor, provided there is an exhaustive power in the discharging flues sufficient to secure a powerful ascending current of vitiated air from openings near the floor.

8. Openings into flues for the discharge of vitiated air, should be made at such points in the room, and at such distances from the openings for the admission of pure warm air, that a portion of the

warm air will traverse every part of the room, and impart as much warmth as possible, before it becomes vitiated and escapes from the apartment.

These openings can be made near the floor, at points most distant from the admission flues, provided there is a fire draught, or other power operating in the discharging flues, sufficient to overcome the natural tendency of the warm air in the room to ascend to the ceiling; otherwise they should be inserted in or near the ceiling.

Openings at the floor are recommended, not because carbonic acid gas, being heavier than the other elements of atmospheric air, settles to the floor, (because, owing to the law of the diffusion of gazes among each other, carbonic acid gas will be found equally diffused through the room,) but because, when it can be drawn off at the floor, it will carry along with it the cold air which is admitted by open doors, and at cracks and crevices, and also the offensive gases sometimes found in school-rooms.

9. All openings, both for the admission and discharge of air, should be fitted with valves and registers, to regulate the quantity of air to pass through them. The quantity of air to be admitted should be regulated before it passes over the heating surface; otherwise, being confined in the air chamber and tubes, the excessive heat will cause much injury to the pipes and the woodwork adjoining.

10. All flues for ventilation, not intended to act in concert with some motive power, such as a fan, a pump, the mechanism of a clock, a fire-draught, a jet of steam, &c., but depending solely on the spontaneous upward movement of the column of warm air within them, should be made large, (of a capacity equal to at least 18 inches in diameter,) tight, (except the openings at the top and bottom of the room;) smooth, (if made of boards, the boards should be seasoned, matched, and planed; if made of bricks, the flue should be round, and finished smooth,) and carried up on the inside of the room, or in the inner wall, with as few angles and deviations from a direct ascent as possible, above the highest point of the roof.

11. All flues for the discharge of vitiated air, even when properly constructed and placed, and even when acting in concert with a current of warm air flowing into the room, should be supplied with some simple, reliable exhaustive power, which can be applied at all seasons of the year, and with a force varying with the demands of the season, and the condition of the air in the apartment.

12. The most simple, economical, and reliable motive power available in most school-houses is heat, or the same process by which the natural upward movements of air are induced and sustained. Heat can be applied to the column of air in a ventilating flue,

1. By carrying up the ventilating flue close beside, or even within the smoke flue, which is used in connection with the heating apparatus.

2. By carrying up the smoke-pipe within the ventilating flue, either the whole length, or in the upper portion only. In a small school-room, the heat from the smoke-pipe carried up for a few feet only in the ventilating flue before it projects above the roof, is a

motive power sufficient to sustain a constant draught of cool and vitiated air, into an opening near the floor.

3. By kindling a fire at the bottom, or other convenient point in the ventilating flue

If the same flue is used for smoke from the fire, and vitiated air from the apartment, some simple self-acting valve or damper should be applied to the opening for the escape of the vitiated air, which shall close at the slightest pressure from the inside of the flue, and thus prevent any reverse current, or down draught, carrying smoke and soot into the apartment.

4. By discharging a jet of steam, or a portion of warm air from the furnace, or other warming apparatus, directly into the ventilating flue.

Any application of heat by which the temperature of the air in the ventilating flue can be raised above the temperature of the apartment to be ventilated, will cause a flow of air from the apartment to sustain the combustion, (if there is a fire in the flue,) and to supply the partial vacuum in the flue, which is caused by the rarefaction of the air in the same.

In all school buildings, when several apartments are to be ventilated, the most effectual, and, all things considered, the most economical, mode of securing a motive power, is to construct an upright brick shaft or flue, and in that to build a fire, or carry up the smoke-pipe of the stove, furnace, or other warming apparatus; and then to discharge the ventilating flues from the top or bottom of each apartment, into this upright shaft. The fire draught will create a partial vacuum in this shaft, to fill which, a draught will be established upon every room with which it is connected by lateral flues. Whenever a shaft of this kind is resorted to, the flues for ventilation may be lateral, and the openings into them may be inserted near the floor.

13. With a flue properly constructed, so as to facilitate the spontaneous upward movement of the warm air within it, and so placed that the air is not exposed to the chilling influence of external cold, a turncap, constructed after the plan of Emerson's Ejector, or Mott's Exhausting Cowl, will assist the ventilation, and especially when there are any currents in the atmosphere. But such caps are not sufficient to overcome any considerable defects in the construction of the ventilating flues, even when there is much wind.

14. The warming and ventilation of a school-room will be facilitated by applying a double sash to all windows having a northern and eastern exposure.

15. In every furnace, and on every stove, a capacious vessel well supplied with fresh water, and protected from the dust, should be placed.

16. Every school-room should be furnished with two thermometers placed on opposite sides in the room, and the temperature in the winter should not be allowed to attain beyond 68° Fahrenheit at a level of four feet from the floor, or 70° at the height of six feet.

17. The necessity for ventilation in an occupied apartment is not obviated by merely reducing the atmosphere to a low temperature.

In the following pages will be found plans and descriptions of a few of the best school-houses, which have been recently erected in Rhode Island and Connecticut, for schools of different grades, from designs or directions furnished by the author of this treatise. They are not presented as faultless specimens of school architecture, but as embracing, each, some points of excellence, either in style, construction, or arrangement. Although the author, as Commissioner of Public Schools for Rhode Island, was consulted in almost every instance by the local building committee, and was always gratified in having opportunities to furnish plans, or make suggestions,—yet he was seldom able to persuade the committee, or the carpenters, to carry out his plans and suggestions thoroughly. Something would be taken from the height, or the length, or the breadth;—some objections would be made to the style of the exterior or the arrangement of the interior;—and particularly the plans recommended for securing warmth and ventilation were almost invariably modified, and in very many instances entirely neglected. He desires, therefore, not to be held responsible for the details of any one house as it now stands,—for being thus held responsible, he should probably receive credit for improvements which others are as much entitled to as himself, and should in more instances be held accountable for errors of taste, and deficiencies in internal arrangements, against which he protested with those having charge of the building. He wishes the reader to bring all the plans published in this volume, no matter by whom recommended, or where erected, to the test of the principles which have just been briefly set forth. If in any particular they fall short of the standard therein established, so far they differ from the designs which the author would try to see followed in houses erected under his own eye. But with some reservation, most of the school-houses recently erected in Rhode Island can be pointed to as embracing many improvements in school architecture. Although the last state in New England to enter on the work of establishing a system of common schools, it is believed, she has now a system in operation not inferior in efficiency to any of her sister states. Be that as it may, Rhode Island can now boast of more good school-houses, and fewer poor ones, in proportion to the whole number, than any other State—more than one hundred and fifty thousand dollars having been voluntarily voted for this purpose in less than three years, by school districts, not including the city of Providence. The few poor houses which remain, if they can resist much longer the attacks of the elements, cannot stand up against the accumulating weight of public condemnation.

To Mr. Thomas A. Teft, of Providence, much credit is due for the taste which he has displayed in the designs furnished by him, and for the elevations which he drew for plans furnished or suggested by the Commissioner. He should, not, however, be held responsible for the alterations made in his plans by the committees and carpenters having charge of the erection of the buildings after plans furnished by him.

III. PLANS OF SCHOOL-HOUSES.

In determining the details of construction and arrangement for a school-house, due regard must, of course, be had to the varying circumstances of country and city, of a large and a small number of scholars, of schools of different grades, and of different systems of instruction.

1. In by far the largest number of country districts as they are now situated, there will be but one school-room, with a smaller room for recitations and other purposes needed. This must be arranged and fitted up for scholars of all ages, for the varying circumstances of a summer and of a winter school, and for other purposes, religious and secular, than those of a school, and in every particular of construction and arrangement, the closest economy of material and labor must be studied. A union of two or more districts for the purpose of maintaining in each a school for the younger children, and in the center of the associated districts a school for the older children of all or, what would be better, a consolidation of two or more districts into one, for these and all other school purposes, would do away with the almost insuperable difficulties which now exist in country districts, in the way of comfortable and attractive school-houses, as well as of thoroughly governed and instructed schools.

2. In small villages, or populous country districts, at least two school-rooms should be provided, and as there will be other places for public meetings of various kinds, each room should be appropriated and fitted up exclusively for the use of the younger or the older pupils. It is better, on many accounts, to have two schools on the same floor, than one above the other.

3. In large villages and cities, a better classification of the schools can be adopted, and, of course, more completeness can be given to the construction and arrangement of the buildings and rooms appropriated to each grade of schools. This classification should embrace at least three grades—viz. Primary, with an infant department; Secondary, or Grammar; Superior, or High Schools. In manufacturing villages, and in certain sections of large cities, regularly organized Infant Schools should be established and devoted mainly to the culture of the morals, manners, language and health of very young children.

4. The arrangement as to supervision, instruction and recitations, must have reference to the size of the school; the number of teachers and assistants; the general organization of the school, whether in one room for study, and separate class rooms for recitation, or the several classes in distinct rooms under appropriate teachers, each teacher having specified studies; and the method of instruction pursued, whether the mutual, simultaneous, or mixed.

Since the year 1830, and especially since 1838, much ingenuity has been expended by practical teachers and architects, in devising and perfecting plans of school-houses, with all the details of construction and fixtures, modified to suit the varied circumstances enumerated above, specimens of which, with explanations and descriptions, will be here given.

Plans of School-Houses with one School-room.

The largest number of school-houses which are erected with but one school-room, are intended for District, or for Primary Schools.

District School.

By a District School, in this connection, is understood a public school open to all the children of the district, of both sexes, and of the school age recognized by the practice of the district, or the regulations of the school committee of the town to which such district belongs. It is an unclassified school, and is taught in one apartment, by one teacher, usually without any assistance even from older pupils of the school. It varies in the character of its scholars, and its methods of instruction, from summer to winter, and from winter to summer. In summer, the younger children and classes in the elementary studies predominate, and in the winter the older pupils, and classes in the more advanced studies, whilst some of both extremes, as to age and studies, are to be found in both the winter and summer session of the district school. This variety of ages and studies, and consequent variety of classes, increased by the irregularity of attendance, is not only a serious hinderance to the proper arrangement, instruction and government of the school, but presents almost insuperable obstacles to the appropriate construction and furniture of the school-house, which is too often erected on the smallest possible scale of size and expense. A vast amount of physical suffering and discomfort to the pupils is the necessary result of crowding the older and younger pupils into a small apartment, without seats and furniture appropriate to either, and especially when no precaution has been taken to adapt the supply and arrangements of seats and desks according to the varying circumstances of the same school in winter and summer. In every district, or unclassified school, the school-room should be fitted up with seats and desks for the older and younger pupils, sufficient to accommodate the maximum attendance of each class of scholars at any season of the year. And if this cannot be effected, and only a sufficient number of seats can be secured to accommodate the highest number of both sexes in attendance at any one time, then in winter the seats and desks for the smaller children should be removed to the attic, and their place supplied by additional seats and desks for the older pupils; and in summer this arrangement should be reversed.

Primary Schools.

By a Primary School, in our American School Systems, is understood, not generally an Elementary School, embracing a course of instruction for the great mass of the children of the community under fourteen years of age—but specifically, that class or grade of schools which receive only the youngest pupils, and those least advanced in their studies.

Any scheme of school organization will be imperfect which does not include special arrangements for the systematic training and instruction of very young children, especially in all cities, manufacturing villages, and large neighborhoods. Among the population of such places, many parents are sure to be found, who, for want of intelligence or leisure, of constancy and patience, are unfitted to watch the first blossoming of the souls of their children, and to train them to good physical habits, virtuous impulses, and quick and accurate observations ; to cleanliness, obedience, openness, mutual kindliness, piety, and all the virtues which wise and far-seeing parents desire for their offspring. The general result of the home training of the children of such parents, is the neglect of all moral culture when such culture is most valuable ; and the acquisition of manners, personal habits, and language, which the best school training at a later period of life can with difficulty correct or eradicate. To meet the wants of this class of children, Halls of Refuge and Infant Schools were originally instituted by Oberlin, Owen, and Wilderspin, and now constitute under these names, or the names of Primary Schools, or Primary Departments, a most important branch of elementary education, whether sustained by individual charity, or as part of the organization of public instruction.

No one at all acquainted with the history of education in this country, can doubt that the establishment of the Primary School for children under six years of age, in Boston, in 1818, as a distinct grade of schools, with the modifications which it has since received there, and elsewhere, from the principles and methods of the Infant School system, has led to most important improvements in the quality and quantity of instruction in our public schools, and the sooner a Primary School properly organized, furnished and managed, can be established in every large neighborhood, and especially in the "infected districts" of cities and manufacturing villages, the more rapid and more thorough will be the progress of education. Its doors should stand wide open to receive such children as are abandoned by orphanage, or, worse than orphanage, by parental neglect and example, to idle, vicious, and pilfering habits, before the corruptions incident to their situation have struck deep into their moral nature, and before they have fallen under the alluring and training influences and instruction of bad boys who infest such regions, polluting the atmosphere by their profane and vulgar speech, and participating in every street brawl and low-bred riot. From all such influences, the earlier the children of the poor and the ignorant are withdrawn, and placed under the care and instruction of an Infant or Primary School, the better it will be for them and for society. But in every locality the Primary School should be established, and brought as near as possible to the homes of the children, in order to secure their early and regular attendance, and to relieve the anxiety of parents for their safety on their way to and from school. The peculiarities of play-ground, school-room, and teachers required for this class of schools, should be carefully studied, and promptly and liberally provided. The school-room should be light, cheerful, and large enough for the evolutions of large classes,—furnished with appropriate seats, furniture, apparatus, and means of visible illustration, and having a retired, dry, and airy play-ground, with a shelter to resort to in inclement weather, and with flower borders, shrubbery, and shade-trees, which they should be taught to love and respect. The play-ground is as essential as the school-room for a Primary School, and is indeed the uncovered school-room of physical and moral education, and the place where the manners and personal habits of children can be better trained than elsewhere. With them, the hours of play and study, of confinement and recreation, must alternate more frequently than with older pupils.

To teach these schools properly, to regulate the hours of play and study so as to give variety, vivacity, and interest to all of the exercises, without over-exciting the nervous system, or overtasking any faculty of mind or body,—to train boys and girls to mild dispositions, graceful and respectful manners, and unquestioning obedience,—to preserve and quicken a tenderness and sensibility of conscience as the instinctive monitor of the approach of wrong,—to cultivate the senses to habits of quick and accurate observation and discrimination,—to prevent the formation of artificial and sing-song tones,—to teach the use of the voice, and of simple, ready, and correct language, and to begin in this way, and by appropriate exercises in drawing, calculation, and lessons on the properties and classification of objects, the cultivation of the intellectual faculties,—to do all these things and more, require in the teacher a rare union of qualities, seldom found in one in a hundred of the male sex, and to be looked for with the greatest chance of success among females, "in whose own hearts, love, hope, and patience have first kept school," and whose laps seem always full of the blossoms of knowledge, to be showered on the heads and hearts of infancy and childhood. In the right education of early childhood, must we look for a corrective of the evils of society in our large cities and manufacturing villages, and for the beginning of a better and higher civilization than has yet blessed our world. The earlier we can establish, in every populous district, primary schools, under female teachers, whose hearts are made strong by deep religious principle,—who have faith in the power of Christian love steadily exerted to fashion anew the bad manners, and soften the harsh and self-willed perverseness of neglected children,—with patience to begin every morning, with but little, if any, perceptible advance beyond where they began the previous morning,—with prompt and kind sympathies, and ready skill in music, drawing, and oral methods, the better it will be for the cause of education, and for every other good cause.

THE following plan of a Play Ground for an Infant or Primary School is copied from "*Wilderspin's Early Education.*" We should prefer to see an accomplished female teacher presiding over the scene.

Play-Ground for an Infant or Primary School.

The chief requisites in an infant-school play-ground are the following: A Climbing Stand; a Horizontal Bar; Parallel Bars; Wooden Swings; a Double Inclined Plane.

The Climbing Stand consists essentially of a frame-work of poles, which support ropes for climbing. One of the most simple and economical is made of two ordinary scaffold poles, planed smooth and painted, which support a transverse beam having hooks, to which the ropes are attached.

The dimensions may be as follows: Length of perpendicular poles, 15 feet, of which 4 feet are sunk in the ground; circumference of poles at the surface of the ground, 14 inches; length of transverse beam at top, 9 feet. To this beam are attached, by screwing in, two iron hooks, which support the ropes; these are 1½ inches in diameter, to afford a firm grasp to the hand. In order that the ropes may not wear through where attached to the hooks, they are spliced round an iron ring, which is grooved on the outer surface to give a firmer hold to the rope. Both the ropes should be attached to the bottom of the poles so as to hang loosely: if not fastened at the bottom, the children use them as swings while clinging to them, and are apt to injure themselves by falling, or others by coming violently in contact with them.

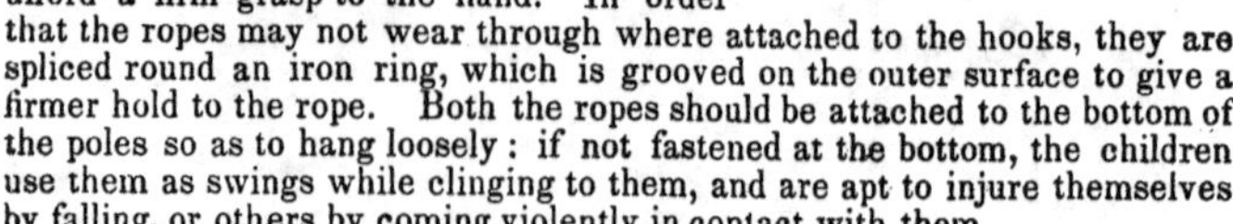

No apparatus is more advantageous: it is economical in its erection, and not liable to get out of order; it affords exercise to a number of children at the same time, a succession being constantly engaged in climbing and descending the ropes and poles; the muscular exertion is not violent, but decidedly beneficial, expanding the chest, and giving power and freedom of motion to the arms. This exercise is also quite free from danger, the children never advancing higher up the ropes than they feel themselves secure. During the seven years the Home and Colonial Infant-school has been established, 200 children have been the average attendance, but no accidents have occurred from the use of the climbing-stand.

The Horizontal Bar consists of a wooden bar formed of beech, red deal, or some other tough wood not apt to splinter or warp, about three inches in diameter, and usually six feet long, turned or planed round and smooth, in order that the hands may not be blistered by the friction.

Every play-ground should possess two or three of these useful additions; one 6 feet from the ground, another 5 feet, and a third 4 feet high,—each one being supported and fixed firmly by a post at both ends. Or they may be arranged so that four posts will support the three bars. The exercises performed on the horizontal bars consist in the child remaining suspended by the arms and hands; in drawing the body up so as to look over the bar several times in succession; in traversing from one end of the bar to the other (suspended by the hands,) both backwards and forwards; in swinging the body whilst suspended from the bar.

The Parallel Bar consists of two bars placed parallel with one another, each being from 6 to 8 feet long, 4 inches deep by 2 inches wide, with the corners rounded off. The posts that support these bars in their position should be 18 inches apart. The bars should project four inches beyond the post. Two sets of parallel bars are advantageous, one being 2 feet 9 inches high for the younger children, the other 4 feet high for the elder.

The exercises on these bars consist in supporting the body on the arms, one hand resting on each bar, and by moving each hand alternately, proceeding forwards and backwards along the bars; in swinging the body between the arms; and in springing over the bar on each side, both backwards and forwards.

The Wooden Springs afford a kind of exercise extremely popular with the younger children, who are not sufficiently active to take part in the other exercises. Each swing consists of two distinct parts: 1. A piece of 2-inch deal, 1 foot wide and 3 feet long, one end of which is sunk firmly in the ground, the other projecting 18 inches above the surface. At each edge of this piece is screwed on an iron plate, with an eye to receive the iron pivot on which the upper piece works. The upper, or horizontal piece, is made of 2-inch plank, 1 foot wide and 12 feet long. At each end of this piece three handles, formed of 1½-inch deal, are strongly mortised in, 1 foot apart, thus forming seats for three children at each end. Between the handles the plank should be rounded at the edges, so as to form an easy seat. At the under surface of each end a small block of wood is fixed, to prevent the plank wearing by striking the ground.

The above directions should be adhered to. If the support be made lower, the motion of the swing is much lessened; if the plank be made shorter, or the support higher, the swing approaches too nearly to the perpendicular, and serious accidents may ensue from the children being thrown violently from the seats. The whole should be made as stout as recommended, otherwise it is apt to break from the violent action.

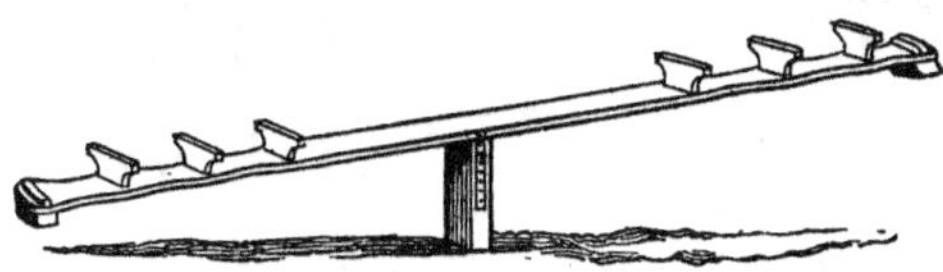

The Double Inclined Plane is adapted more especially for the younger children. It consists merely of a support of two-inch deal, 1 foot wide, and projecting 3 feet from the ground. On this is laid the ends of two planks, each 12 feet long, 1 foot wide, and 1½ inch in thickness. On the upper surface of each plank may be nailed, at intervals of eight or ten inches, small cross-pieces, to prevent the feet slipping.

The use of the inclined plane is, that by ascending and descending it, children acquire a facility in balancing themselves. The exercise is beneficial, as it calls into action the muscles of the legs and even of the body. It also furnishes an excellent situation to jump from, as the children can themselves vary the height of the leap at pleasure.

The general use of all these various exercises is, that the different muscles of the body may be strengthened, and the children thus fitted for a future life of labor, and better prepared to escape in case of accidents.

The house should stand in a dry and airy situation, large enough to allow a spacious play ground. No pains should be spared on this principal and paramount department of a proper infant school. The more extensive the ground may be, the better; but the smallest size for 200 children ought to be 100 feet in length, by at least 60 in breadth. It should be walled round, not so much to prevent the children from straying, as to exclude intruders upon them, while at play: for this purpose, a wall or close paling, not lower than six feet high, will be found sufficient. With the exception of a flower border, from four to six feet broad all round, lay the whole ground, after leveling and draining it thoroughly, with small *binding* gravel, which must be always kept in repair, and well swept of loose stones. Watch the gravel, and prevent the children making holes in it to form pools in wet weather; dress the flower border, and keep it always neat; stock it well with flowers and shrubs, and make it as gay and beautiful as possible. Train on the walls cherry and other fruit trees and currant bushes; place some ornaments and tasteful decorations in different parts of the border—as a honeysuckle bower, &c., and separate the dressed ground from the graveled area by a border of strawberry plants, which may be protected from the feet of the children by a skirting of wood on the outside, three inches high, and painted green, all round the ground. Something even approaching to elegance in the dressing and decking of the playground, will afford a lesson which may contribute to refinement and comfort for life. It will lead not only to clean and comfortable dwellings, but to a taste for decoration and beauty, which will tend mainly to expel coarseness, discomfort, dirt, and vice, from the economy of the humbler classes.

For the excellent and safe exercise afforded by the *Rotary Swing*, erect, at the distance of thirty feet from each other, two posts or masts, from sixteen to eighteen feet high above the ground; nine inches diameter at the foot, diminishing to seven and a half at top; of good well-seasoned, hard timber; charred with fire, about three feet under ground, fixed in sleepers, and bound at top with a strong iron hoop. In the middle of the top of the post is sunk perpendicularly a cylindrical hole, ten inches deep, and two inches in diameter, made strong by an iron ring two inches broad within the top, and by a piece of iron an inch thick to fill up the bottom, tightly fixed in. A strong pivot of iron, of diameter to turn easily in the socket described, but with as little lateral play as possible, is placed vertically in the hole, its upper end standing 4 inches above it. On this pivot, as an axle, and close to the top of the post, but so as to turn easily, is fixed a wheel of iron, twenty-four inches diameter, strengthened by four

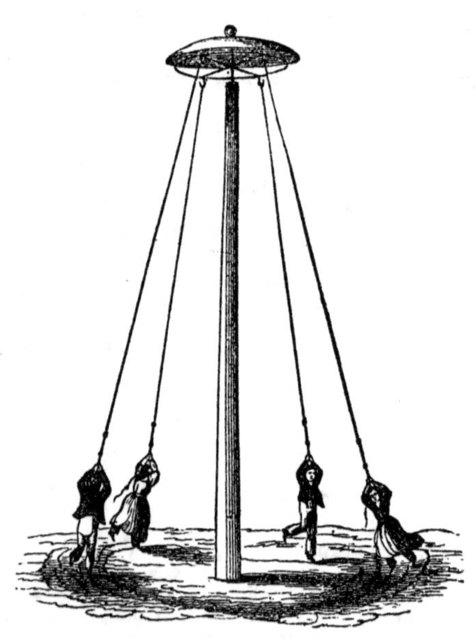

Rotary Swing.

spokes, something like a common roasting-jack wheel, but a little larger. The rim should be flat, two inches broad, and half an inch thick. In this rim are six holes or eyes, in which rivet six strong iron hooks, made *to turn in the holes*, to prevent the rope from twisting. To these hooks are fixed six well-chosen ropes, an inch diameter, and each reaching down to within two feet of the ground, having half-a-dozen knots, or small wooden balls, fixed with nails, a foot from each other, beginning at the lower extremity, and ascending to six feet from the ground. A tin cap, like a lamp cover, is placed on the top of the whole machine, fixed to the prolongation of the pivot, and a little larger than the wheel, to protect it from wet. To this, or to the wheel itself, a few waggoners' bells appended, would have a cheerful effect on the children. The operation of this swing must, from the annexed cut, be obvious. Four, or even six children, lay hold of a rope each, as high as they can reach, and, starting at the same instant, run a few steps in the circle, then suspend themselves by their hands, drop their feet and run again when fresh impulse is wanted; again swing round, and so on. A child of three or four years old, will often fly several times round the circle without touching the ground. There is not a muscle in the body which is not thus exercised; and to render the exercise equal to both halves of the body, it is important that, after several rounds in one direction, the party should stop, change the hands, and go round in the opposite direction. To prevent fatigue, and to equalize the exercise among the pupils, the rule should be, that each six pupils should have thirty or forty rounds, and resign the ropes to six more, who have counted the rotations.

Toys being discarded as of no use, or real pleasure, the only *plaything* of the playground consists of bricks for building, made of wood, four inches by two and one and a-half. Some hundreds of these, very equally made, should be kept in a large box in a corner of the ground, as the quieter children delight to build houses and castles with them; the condition, however, always to be, that they shall correctly and conscientiously replace in the box the full complement or *tale* of bricks they take out; in which rule, too, there is more than one lesson.

In a corner of the playground, concealed by shrubbery, are two water closets for the children, with six or eight seats in each; that for the boys is separate from, and entered by, a different passage from that for the girls. Supply the closets well with water, which, from a cistern at the upper end, shall run along with a slope under all the seats, into a sewer, or a pit in the ground. See that the closets are in no way misused, or abused. The eye of the teacher and mistress should often be here, for the sake both of cleanliness and delicacy. Mr. Wilderspin recommends the closets being built adjoining the small class-room, with small apertures for the teacher's eye in the class-room wall, covered with a spring lid, and commanding the range of the place. There is nothing in which children, especially in the humbler ranks, require more training.

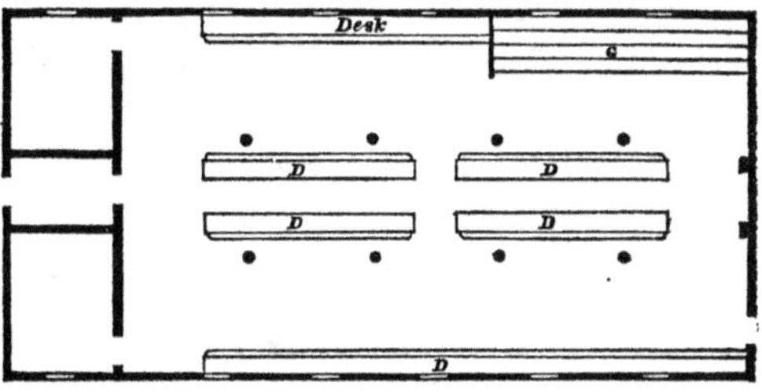

The annexed cut represents an infant school-room, modified in a few unimportant particulars, from the ground plan recommended by Mr. Wilderspin in his "*Early Education*," published in 1840. The original plan embraces a dwelling for the teacher's family, and two school-rooms, one for the boys and the other for the girls, each school having a gallery, class-room, and playground. The school-room is about 60 feet long by 38 wide, and the class-rooms each 13 ft. by 10. D. Desks and Seats. G. Gallery, capable of accommodating 100 children.

Plan of District School-House in Glocester, R. I.

The above cut represents the front elevation of a new school-house erected in District No. 13, in the town of Glocester, Rhode Island, which, for location, neatness, and proportion in the external appearance, mode of seating, warming and ventilation, can be consulted as a safe model for small agricultural districts. The cost of the building and furniture was $600. The style and arrangement of the seats and desks is indicated in Figures 3 and 4. The end pieces are of cast iron, and so shaped, as to facilitate the sweeping of the room, and the pupils getting in and out of their seats, and at the same time are firmly attached to the floor by screws. This building is 30 feet by 20 feet.

The room is heated by *Mott's Ventilating School Stove*, designed both for wood and hard coal. Fresh air is introduced from outside of the building by a flue beneath the floor, and is warmed by passing along the heated surfaces of the stove as indicated in the following section.

Fig. 2.

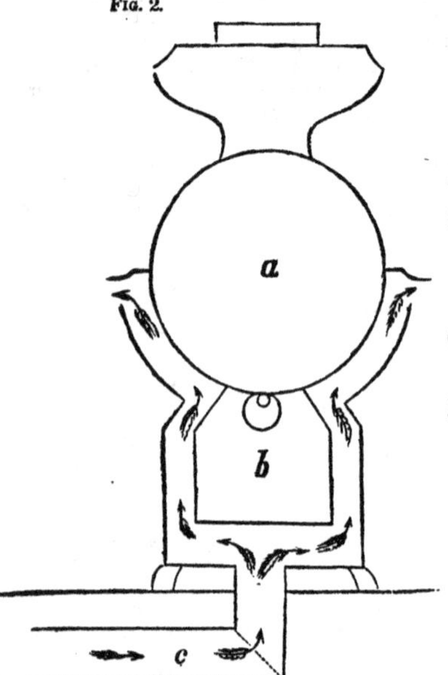

A. A chamber, for coal or wood.
B. A revolving grate with a cam motion, by which the ashes are easily detached and made to drop into the ash-pit below.
C. Ash-pit, by which also the draught can be regulated, and the stove made an air-tight.
D. Duct, or flue under the floor, by which fresh air from without is admitted under and around the stove, and circulates in the direction indicated by the arrows.

The smoke-pipe is carried in the usual way, high enough to prevent any injurious radiation of heat upon the heads of the pupils below, to the centre of the opposite end of the room, where, after passing through the ceiling, it enters the ventilating flue, which, commencing at the floor, is carried up through the attic and out above the roof, as shown in Figures 3 and 4. The heat of the smoke-pipe produces a lively upward current of the air in the upper portion of the ventilating flue, sufficient to draw off the lower stratum of air near the floor, and at the same time draw down, and diffuse equally through the room, the fresh air which is introduced and warmed by the stove at the opposite end.

A—Front entrance.
B—Girls' Entrance and lobby.
C—Boys' do. do.
D—Teachers' platform.
E—Seat and desk, for the pupils.
S—Mott's ventilating school stove.
V—Flue for ventilation.
F—Seats for classes at recitation.
d—Teacher's desk.
e—Library of reference in front of teacher's desk.
c—Closets for school library and apparatus.
f—Fence dividing back yard.

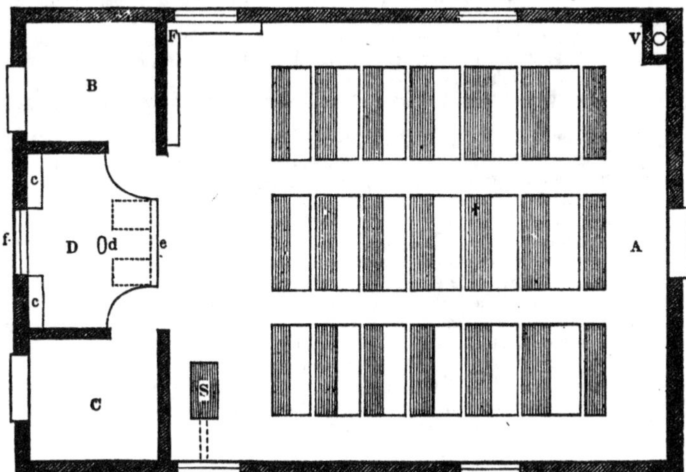

Plan and Description of School-House in Windsor, Ct.

The building stands 60 ft. from the highway, near the center of an elevated lot which slopes a little to the south and east. Much the larger portion of the lot is in front, affording a pleasant play ground, while in the rear there is a woodshed, and other appropriate buildings, with a separate yard for boys and girls. The walls are of brick, and are hollow, so as to save expense in securing the antaes or pilasters, and to prevent dampness. This building is 33 ft. 6 inches long, 21 ft. 8 inches wide, and 18 ft. 9 inches high from the ground to the eaves, including 2 ft. base or underpinning.

The entries A A, one for boys and the other for girls, are in the rear of the building, through the woodshed, which, with the yard, is also divided by a partition. Each entry is 7 ft. 3 inches, by 9 ft. 3 inches, and is supplied with a scraper and mat for the feet, and shelves and hooks for outer garments.

The school-room is 24 ft. 5 inches long, by 19 ft. 4 inches wide, and 15 ft. 6 inches high in the clear, allowing an area of 472 ft. including the recess for the teacher's platform, and an allowance of 200 cubic feet of air to a school of 36.

The teacher's platform B, is 5 ft. 2 inches wide, by 6 ft. deep, including 3 ft. of recess, and 9 inches high. On it stands a table, the legs of which are set into the floor, so as to be firm, and at the same time movable, in case the platform is needed for declamation, or other exercises of the scholars. Back of the teacher is a range of shelves *b*, already supplied with a library of near 400 volumes, and a globe, outline maps, and other apparatus. On the top of the case is a clock. A blackboard 5 ft. by 4, is suspended on weights, and steadied by a groove on each end, so as to admit of being raised and lowered by the teacher, directly in front of the book case, and in full view of the whole school. At the bottom of the blackboard is a trough to receive the chalk and the sponge, or soft cloth.

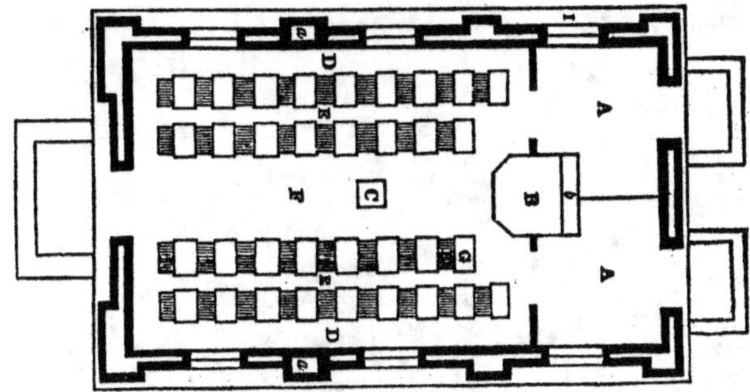

The passages D D, are 2 ft. wide, and extend round the room; E E are 15 inches, and allow of easy access to the seats and desks on either hand. F is 5 ft. 8 inches, and in the center stands an open stove C, the pipe of which goes into one of the flues, *a*. The temperature is regulated by a thermometer.

Each pupil is provided with a desk G, and seat H, the front of the former, constituting the back or support of the latter, which slopes 2½ inches in 16. The seat also inclines a little from the edge. The seats vary in height, from 9½ inches to 17, the youngest children occupying those nearest the platform. The desks are 2 ft. long by 18 inches wide, with a shelf beneath for books, and a groove on the back side *b*, (Fig. 4) to receive a slate, with which each desk is furnished by the district. The upper surface of the desk, except 3 inches of the most distant portion, slopes 1 inch in a foot, and the edge is in the same perpendicular line with the front of the seat. The level portion of the desk has a groove running along the line of the

Top of Desk.

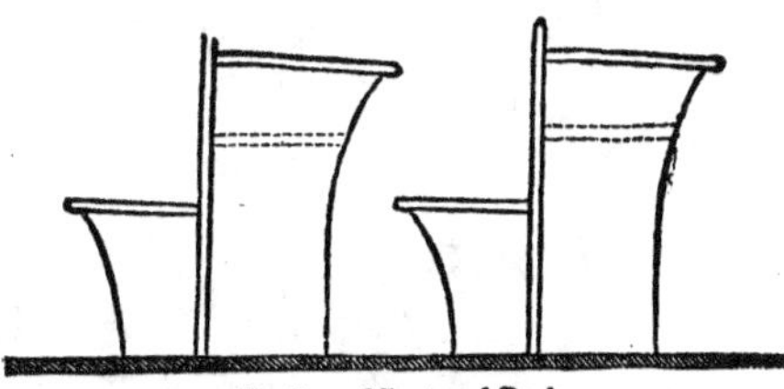
Section of Seat and Desk.

slope *a*, (Fig. 4) so as to prevent pencils and pens from rolling off, and an opening *c*, (Fig 8) to receive an inkstand, which is covered by a metallic lid.

The windows, I, three on the north and three on the south side, contain each 40 panes of 8 by 10 glass, are hung (both upper and lower sash) with weights so as to admit of being raised or lowered conveniently. The sills are three feet from the floor. Those on the south side are provided with curtains and blinds.

The proper ventilation of the room is provided for by the lowering of the upper sash, and by an opening 14 inches by 18, near the ceiling, into a flue, (Fig. 2.) *a*, which leads into the open air. This opening can be enlarged, diminished, or entirely closed by a shutter controlled by a cord.

PLAN OF DISTRICT SCHOOL-HOUSE IN BARRINGTON, R. I.

The above cut represents in perspective the new school-house in District No. 2, in the town of Barrington, Rhode Island—the most attractive, convenient, and complete structure of the kind in any agricultural district in the State—and, it is believed, in New England.

The house stands back from the highway in a lot, of an acre in extent, and commands an extensive view up and down Narraganset Bay, and of the rich cultivated fields for miles in every other direction.

The building is 40 feet long by 25 wide, and 12 feet high in the clear, and is built after working plans drawn by Mr. Teft, of Providence.

The school-room is calculated to accommodate 64 pupils, with seats and desks each for two pupils, similar to the folowing cut, and arranged as in Figure 3.

The end-piece, or supports, both of the desk and seat, are of cast-iron, and the wood-work is attached by screws. They are made of eight sizes, giving a seat from ten inches to seventeen, and a desk at the edge next to the scholar from seventeen to twenty-six inches from the floor.

Each pupil, when properly seated, can rest his feet on the floor without the muscle of the thigh pressing hard upon the front edge of the seat, and with a support for the muscles of the back.

The yards and entrance for the boys and girls are entirely separate, and each is appropriately fitted up with scraper, mats, broom, water-pails, sink, hooks and shelves.

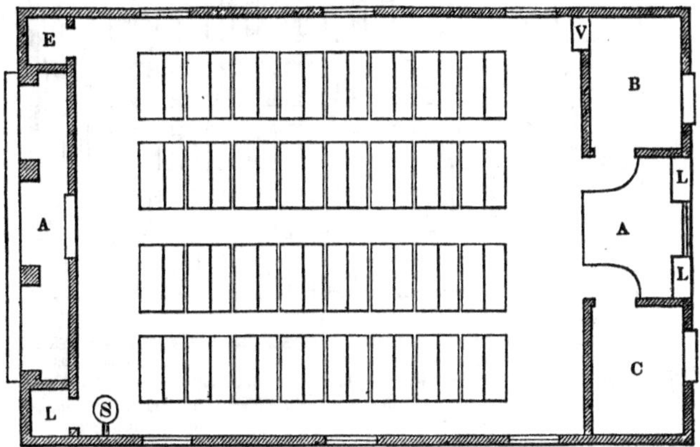

A—Front entrance.
B—Girls' entrance and lobby, fitted up with mats, scrapers, hooks, shelves.
C—Boys' entrance.
D—Teacher's platform.
S—Boston Ventilating Stove.
V—Flue for ventilation surmounted, by Emerson's Ejector.
L—Cases for library.
E—Closets for apparatus, &c.

The school is well supplied with blackboards, maps, globes, and diagrams, and such other instrumentalities as are necessary and useful in the studies usually taught in a district school.

There is abundance of unoccupied space around the sides of the room and between the ranges of desks to allow of the free movements of the teacher and of the pupils, in passing to and from their seats.

There is also a district library of about 600 volumes, containing a large number of books of reference, such as Dictionaries, Encyclopedia, and a variety of the best text books in the several studies of the school, to enable the teacher to extend his knowledge, and illustrate his recitations by additional information.

There are about one hundred volumes selected with reference to the youngest class of children, and about 400 volumes in the different departments of useful knowledge, calculated for circulation among the older pupils, in the families of the district generally.

The maps, apparatus and library were purchased by the Commissioner of Public Schools at an expense of $250, which was contributed by five or six individuals. The building, furniture and land, cost about $1200.

The school-room is warmed and ventilated under the direction of Mr. Gardner Chilson, Boston, by one of the *Boston Ventilating Stoves*, and by a flue constructed similar to those recently introduced into the Boston Public School houses by Dr. Henry G. Clark, and surmounted by Emerson's Ejector.

A cut and description of this stove, and of *Mott's Ventilating Stove* for burning wood as well as coal, is given on the next page.

The flue for ventilation is carried up in the partition wall, and is constructed of well seasoned boards, planed smooth on the inside.

SCHOOL FOR ONE HUNDRED AND TWENTY PUPILS.

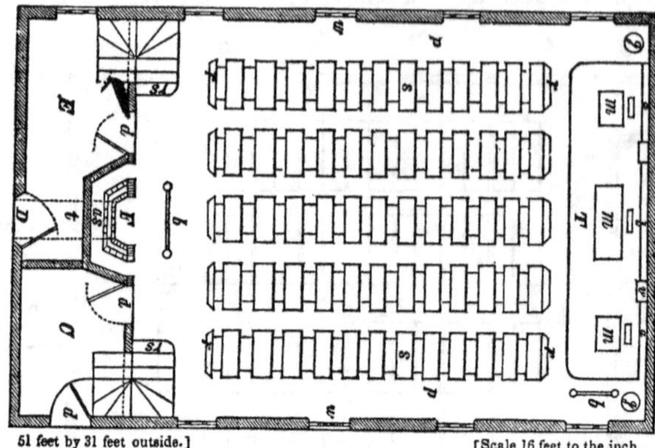

51 feet by 31 feet outside.] [Scale 16 feet to the inch.

D. Entrance door. E. Entry. F. Fireplace. C. Wood closet. T. Teacher's platform. *a.* Apparatus shelves. *t.* Air tube beneath the floor. *d.* Doors. *g.* Globes. *l.* Library shelves. *m.* Master's table and seat. *p.* Passages. *r.* Recitation seats. *s.* Scholars' desks and seats. *r s.* Stairs to recitation rooms in the attic. *v.* Ventilator. *w.* Windows. *b.* Movable blackboard. *a s.* Air space behind the fireplace.

SCHOOL FOR FORTY-EIGHT PUPILS.

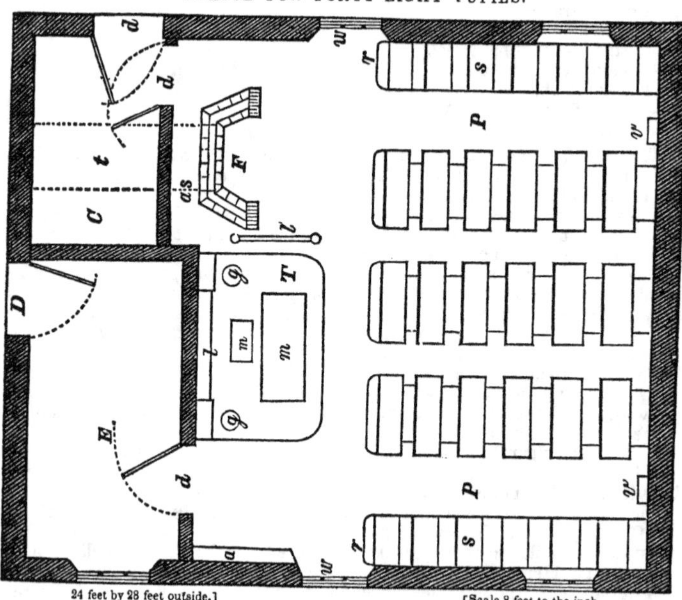

24 feet by 28 feet outside.] [Scale 8 feet to the inch.

D. Entrance door. E. Entry. F. Fireplace. C. Wood closet, or recitation room T. Teacher's platform. *a.* Apparatus shelves. *t.* Air tube beneath the floor. *d.* Doors *g.* Globes. *l.* Library shelves. *m.* Master's table and seat. *p.* Passages. *r.* Recitation seats. *s.* Scholars' desks and seats. *v.* Ventilator. *w.* Windows. *b.* Movable blackboard. *a. s.* Air space behind the fireplace.

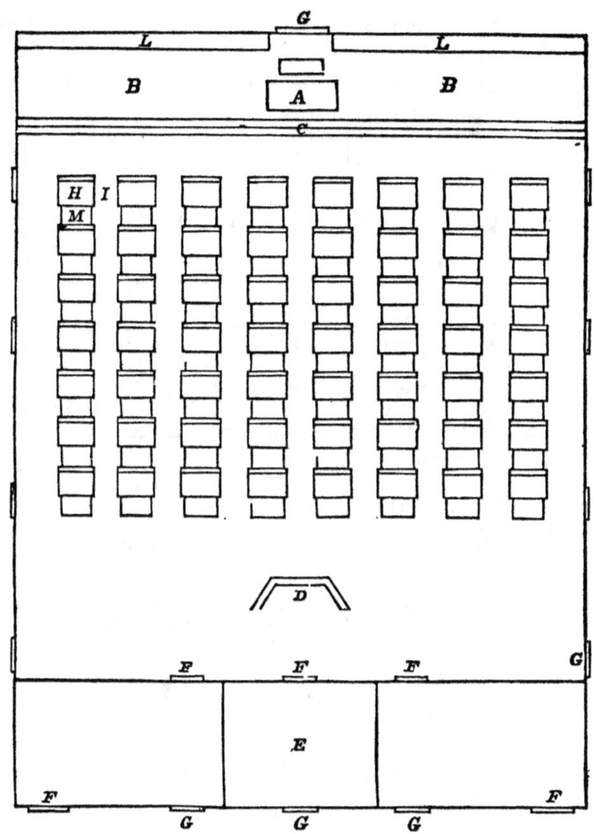

A. Represents the teacher's desk. *B B.* Teacher's platform, from 1 to 2 ft. in height. *C.* Step for ascending the platform. *L L.* Cases for books, apparatus, cabinet, &c. *H.* Pupils' single desks, 2 ft. by 18 inches. *M.* Pupils' seat, 1 ft. by 20 inches. *I.* Aisles, 1 ft. 6 inches in width. *D.* Place for stove, if one be used. *E.* Room for recitation, for retiring in case of sudden indisposition, for interview with parents, when necessary, &c. It may also be used for the library, &c. *F F F F F.* Doors into the boys' and girls' entries—from the entries into the school-room, and from the school-room into the recitation room. *G G G G.* Windows. The windows on the sides are not lettered.

For section of seat and desk constructed after Mr. Mann's plan, see p. 47. To avoid the necessity of fitting up the same school-room for old and young, and the inefficiency of such country schools as we now have, Mr. Mann proposed in this Report a union, for instance of four districts which did not cover more than four miles square, and the erection of four primary school-houses, (a a a a) for the younger children of each district, to be taught by female teachers, and one central or high school, (A) for the older children of the four districts, taught by a well qualified male teacher. This plan is recommended for its wise use of the means of the districts, and the efficiency of the instruction given.

2 m
a
2 m
a
A
a
a

Plan of School-House in Centreville, Warwick, R. I.

The following plan presents a mode of seating a District School-House similar to that adopted in several public school-houses in the city of New York.

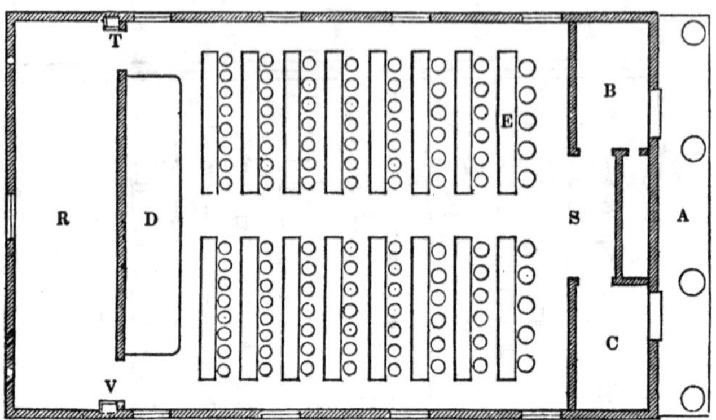

The building is 50 feet long (beside the porch 5½ feet in front) by 30 feet wide.

A—Porch.
B—Girls' entrance and lobby.
C—Boys' do.
D—Teacher's platform.
E—Mott's school desk and chair.
R—Recitation-room for assistant.
S—Stove.
T—Smoke flue.
V—Flue for ventilator.

The above mode of seating has been adopted in other districts, and in one instance, with the desks attached at one end to the wall, as in the following plan recommended by Hon. Ira Mayhew. There are serious objections to this arrangement of the seats and desk.

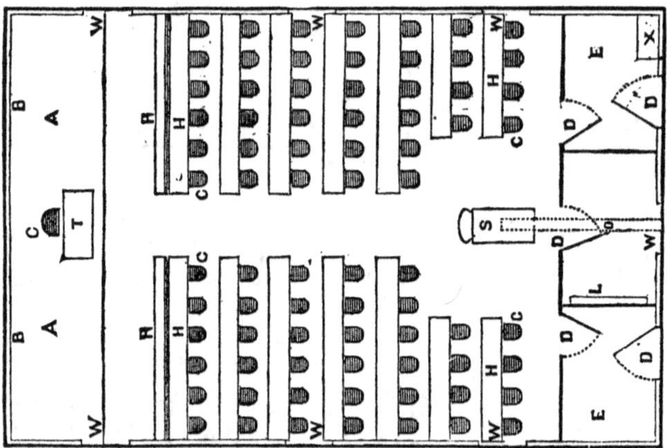

D, entrance and inner doors. W, windows. E, entries, lighted over doors, one for boys and the other for girls. A, teacher's platform. B, blackboard, reaching entirely across the end of the house. T, teacher's desk. H, desks 11 feet long, except the two next the entrance doors. C, Mott's patent cast-iron chairs. S stove. O, an air tube under the floor, through which pure air from without is introduced beneath the stove. L, shelves for library, apparatus, etc.

The following plan, although not followed throughout in any school-house in Rhode Island, presents substantially the internal arrangement which has been adopted in several instances, as in the school-house at Peacedale, in South Kingston, at Carolina Mills in Richmond, and in the lower room of the academy in Kingston.

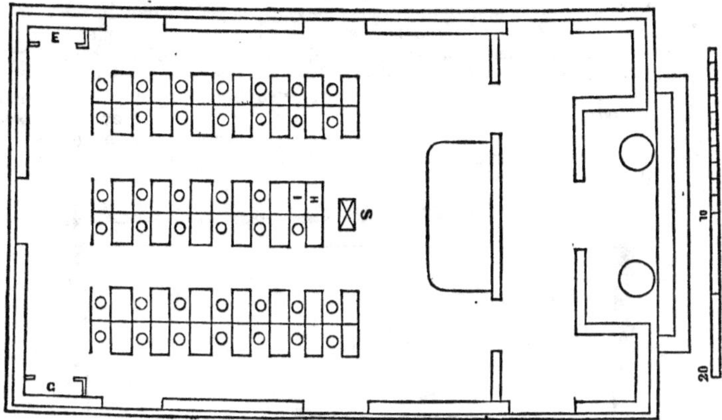

The following cut, which is copied from a plan of a district school-house recommended by Dr. Lord, Superintendent of the common schools of Columbus, Ohio, presents the plan of several district and village school-houses erected in Rhode Island. The house is 26 feet by 36 feet on the ground.

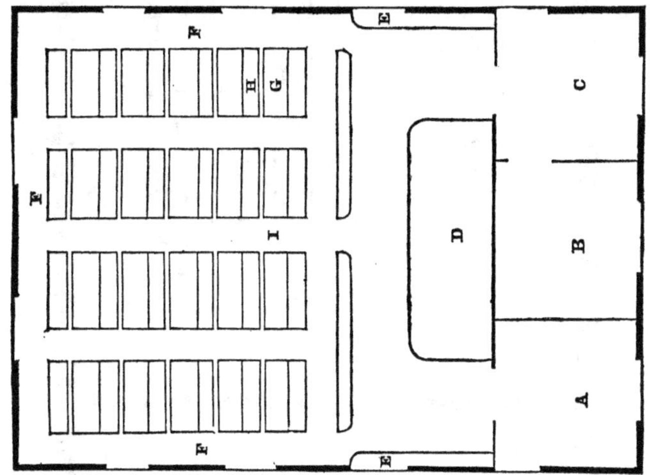

A—Entry for girls, 8 feet square.
C— do. for boys, do. do.
B—Library and apparatus room.
E—Recitation seats.
D—Teacher's platform.

H G—Seat and desk for two pupils, 4 feet long.
F—Aisles, 2 feet wide.
I— do. 18 inches wide.

PLAN OF DISTRICT SCHOOL-HOUSE IN GREENLAND, N. H.

The building is 50 feet long by 30 feet wide, and 12 feet high in the clear. It is built of brick. A large entry (E), is partitioned off from the school-room, and fitted up not only to receive the hats, bonnets, &c., of the pupils, but to accommodate all the pupils in rainy weather during recess, as well as those who reside at a distance, when they arrive at the school-house before the school-room is opened, and those who may be obliged to stay during recess. The entry and the school-room is heated by a large stove (S) placed in the partition. The teacher's platform (P) is placed at the end of the school-room, and is raised one step above the floor. Back of the teacher, along the wall, are cases (B) for apparatus, and a well-selected library of 200 vols. There are 48 separate desks of different heights, framed on posts permanently fixed to the timbers of the floor, and fitted with seats of corresponding heights set in cast iron frames secured to the floor; both seats and desks are stained and varnished.

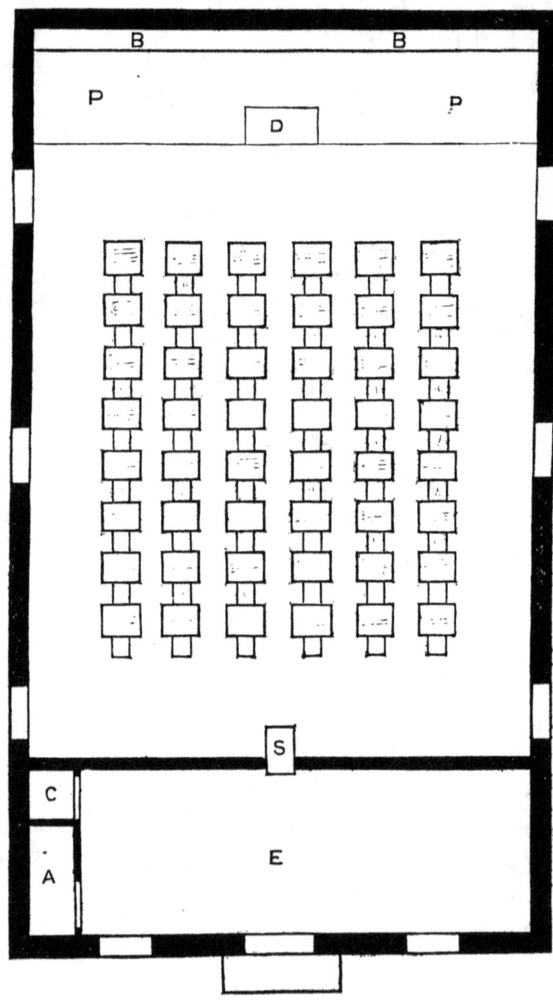

Plans of School-Houses for two or more Schools.

Before describing a few of the best school-houses which have been recently erected in cities and large villages, for two or more schools of different grades in the same building, a brief consideration of the importance of classification, or gradation, as applied to the schools of a district, or town, cannot be deemed irrelevant.

To enable children to derive the highest degree of benefit from their attendance at school, they should go through a regular course of training in a succession of classes, and schools arranged according to similarity of age, standing, and attainments, under teachers possessing the qualifications best adapted to each grade of school. The practice has been almost universal in New England, and in other states where the organization of the schools is based upon the division of the territory into school districts, to provide but one school for as many children of both sexes, and of all ages from four to sixteen years, as can be gathered in from certain territorial limits, into one apartment, under one teacher; a female teacher in summer, and a male teacher in winter. The disadvantages of this practice, both to pupils and teachers, are great and manifold.

There is a large amount of physical suffering and discomfort, as well as great hinderances in the proper arrangement of scholars and classes, caused by crowding the older and younger pupils into the same school-room, without seats and furniture appropriate to either; and the greatest amount of suffering and discomfort falls upon the young, who are least able to bear it, and who, in consequence, acquire a distaste to study and the school-room.

The work of education going on in such schools, cannot be appropriate and progressive. There cannot be a regular course of discipline and instruction, adapted to the age and proficiency of pupils—a series of processes, each adapted to certain periods in the development of the mind and character, the first intended to be followed by a second, and the second by a third,—the latter always depending on the earlier, and all intended to be conducted on the same general principles, and by methods varying with the work to be done, and the progress already made.

With the older and younger pupils in the same room, there cannot be a system of discipline which shall be equally well adapted to both classes. If it secures the cheerful obedience and subordination of the older, it will press with unwise severity upon the younger pupils. If it be adapted to the physical wants, and peculiar temperaments of the young, it will endanger the good order and habits of study of the more advanced pupils, by the frequent change of posture and position, and other indulgences which it permits and requires of the former.

With studies ranging from the alphabet and the simplest rudiments of knowledge, to the higher branches of an English education, a variety of methods of instruction and illustration are called for, which are seldom found together, or in an equal degree, in the same teacher, and which can never be pursued with equal success in the same school-room. The elementary principles of knowledge, to be made intelligible and interesting to the young, must be presented by a large use of the oral and simultaneous methods. The higher branches, especially all mathematical subjects, require patient application and habits of abstraction, on the part of the older pupils, which can with difficulty, if at all, be attained by many pupils, amid a multiplicity of distracting exercises, movements and sounds. The recitations of this class of pupils, to be profitable and satisfactory, must be conducted in a manner which requires time, discussion and explanation, and the undivided attention both of pupils and teachers.

From the number of class and individual recitations, to be attended to during each half day, these exercises are brief, hurried, and of little practical value. They consist, for the most part, of senseless repetitions of the words of a book. Instead of being the time and place where the real business of teaching is done, where the ploughshare of interrogation is driven down into the acquirements of each pupil, and his ability to comprehend clearly, remember accurately, discriminate wisely, and reason closely, is cultivated and tested,—where the difficult principles of each lesson are developed and illustrated, and additional information imparted, and the mind of the teacher brought in direct contact with the mind of each pupil, to arouse, interest, and direct its opening powers—instead of all this and more, the brief period passed in recitation, consists, on the part of the teacher, of hearing each individual and class in regular order, and quick succession, repeat words from a book; and on the part of the pupils, of *saying their lessons*, as the operation is significantly described by most teachers, when they summon the class to the stand. In the mean time the order of the school must be maintained, and the general business must be going forward. Little children without any authorized employment for their eyes and hands, and ever active curiosity, must be made to sit still, while every muscle is aching from suppressed activity; pens must be mended, copies set, arithmetical difficulties solved, excuses for tardiness or absence received, questions answered, whisperings allowed or suppressed, and more or less of extempore discipline administered. Were it not a most ruinous waste of precious time,—did it not involve the deadening, crushing, distorting, dwarfing of immortal faculties and noble sensibilities,—were it not an utter perversion of the noble objects for which schools are instituted, it would be difficult to conceive of a more diverting farce than an ordinary session of a large public school, whose chaotic and discordant elements have not been reduced to system by a proper classification. The teacher, at least the conscientious teacher, thinks it any thing but a farce to him. Compelled to hurry from one study to another, the most diverse,—from one class to another, requiring a knowledge of methods altogether distinct,—from one recitation to another, equally brief and unsatisfactory, one requiring a liveliness of manner, which he does not feel and cannot assume, and the other closeness of attention and abstraction of thought, which he cannot give amid the multiplicity and variety of cares,—from one case of discipline to another, pressing on him at the same time,—he goes through the same circuit day after day, with a dizzy brain and aching heart, and brings his school to a close with a feeling, that with all his diligence and fidelity, he has accomplished but little good.

But great as are the evils of a want of proper classification of schools, arising from the causes already specified, these evils are aggravated by the almost universal practice of employing one teacher in summer, and another in winter, and different teachers each successive summer and winter. Whatever progress one teacher may make in bringing order out of the chaotic elements of a large public school, is arrested by the termination of his school term. His experience is not available to his successor, who does not come into the school until after an interval of weeks or months, and in the mean time the former teacher has left the town or state. The new teacher is a stranger to the children and their parents, is unacquainted with the system pursued by his predecessor, and has himself but little or no experience in the business; in consequence, chaos comes back again, and the confusion is still worse confounded by the introduction of new books, for every teacher prefers to teach from the books in which he studied, or which he has been accustomed to teach, and many teachers cannot teach profitably from any other. Weeks are thus passed, in which the school is going through the process of organization, and the pupils are becoming accustomed to the methods and requirements of a new teacher—some of them are put back, or made to retrace their studies in new books, while others are pushed forward into studies for which they are not prepared; and at the end of three or four months, the school relapses into chaos. There is constant change, but no progress.

This want of system, and this succession of new teachers, goes on from term to term, and year to year—a process which would involve any other interest in speedy and utter ruin, where there was not provision made for fresh material to be experimented upon, and counteracting influences at work to restore, or at least obviate the injury done. What other business of society could escape utter wreck, if conducted with such want of system,—with such constant disregard of the fundamental principle of the division of labor, and with a succession of new agents every three months, none of them trained to the details of the business, each new agent acting without any knowledge of the plan of his predecessor, or any well settled plan of his own! The public school is not an anomaly, an exception, among the great interests of society. Its success or failure depends on the existence or absence of certain conditions; and if complete failure does not follow the utter neglect of these conditions, it is because every term brings into the schools a fresh supply of children to be experimented upon, and sweeps away others beyond the reach of bad school instruction and discipline; and because the minds of some of these children are, for a portion of each day, left to the action of their own inherent forces, and the more kindly influences of nature, the family and society.

Among these conditions of success in the operation of a system of public schools, is such a classification of the scholars as shall bring a larger number of similar age and attainments, at all times, and in every stage of their advancement, under teachers of the right qualifications, and shall enable these teachers to act upon numbers at once, for years in succession, and carry them all forward effectually together, in a regular course of instruction.

The great principle to be regarded in the classification, either of the schools of a town or district, or of scholars in the same school, is equality of attainments, which will generally include those of the same age. Those who have gone over substantially the same ground, or reached, or nearly reached the same point of attainment in several studies, should be put together, and constitute, whenever their numbers will authorize it, one school. These again should be arranged in different classes, for it is seldom practicable, even if it were ever desirable, to have but one class in every study in the same grade of school. Even in very large districts, where the scholars are promoted from a school of a lower grade to one of a higher, after being found qualified in certain studies, it is seldom that any considerable number will have reached a common standard of scholarship in all their studies. The same pupil will have made very different progress in different branches. He will stand higher in one and lower in another. By arranging scholars of the same general division in different classes, no pupil need be detained by companions who have made, or can make less progress, or be hurried over lessons and subjects in a superficial manner, to accommodate the more rapid advancement of others. Although equality of attainment should be regarded as the general principle, some regard should be paid to age, and other circumstances. A large boy of sixteen, from the deficiency of his early education, which may be his misfortune and not his fault, ought not to be put into a school or class of little children, although their attainments may be in advance of his. This step would mortify and discourage him. In such extreme cases, that arrangement will be best which will give the individual the greatest chance of improvement, with the least discomfort to himself, and hindrance to others. Great disparity of age in the same class, or the same school, is unfavorable to uniform and efficient discipline, and the adaptation of methods of teaching, and of motives to application and obedience. Some regard, too, should be had to the preferences of individuals, especially among the older pupils, and their probable destination in life. The mind comes into the requisitions of study more readily, and works with higher results, when led onward by the heart; and the utility of any branch of study, its relations to future success in life, once clearly apprehended, becomes a powerful motive to effort.

Each class in a school should be as large as is consistent with thoroughness and minuteness of individual examination, and practicable, without bringing together individuals of diverse capacity, knowledge, and habits of study. A good teacher can teach a class of forty with as much ease as a class of ten, and with far more profit to each individual, than if the same amount of time was divided up among four classes, each containing one-fourth of the whole number. When the class is large, there is a spirit, a glow, a struggle which can never be infused or called forth in a small class. Whatever time is spent upon a few, which could have been as profitably spent on a larger number, is a loss of power and time to the extent of the number who were not thus benefited. The recitations of a large class must be more varied, both as to order and methods, so as to reach those whose attention would wander if not under the pressure of constant excitement, or might become slothful from inaction or a sense of security. Some studies will admit of a larger number in a class than others.

The number of classes for recitation in the same apartment, by one teacher, should be small. This will facilitate the proper division of labor in instruction, and allow more time for each class. The teacher intrusted with the care of but few studies, and few recitations, can have no excuse but indolence, or the want of capacity, if he does not master these branches thoroughly, and soon acquire the most skillful and varied methods of teaching them. His attention will not be distracted by a multiplicity and variety of cares, pressing upon him at the same time. This principle does not require that every school should be small, but that each teacher should have a small number of studies and classes to superintend.

In a large school, properly classified, a division of labor can be introduced in the department of government, as well as in that of instruction. By assigning the different studies to a sufficient number of assistants, in separate class-rooms, each well qualified to teach the branches assigned, the principal teacher may be selected with special reference to his ability in arranging the studies, and order of exercises of the school, in administering its discipline, in adapting moral instruction to individual scholars, and superintending the operations of each class-room, so as to secure the harmonious action and progress of every department. The talents and tact required for these and similar duties, are more rarely found than the skill and attainments required to teach successfully a particular study. When found, the influence of such a principal, possessing in a high degree, the executive talent spoken of, will be felt through every class, and by every subordinate teacher, giving tone and efficiency to the whole school.

To facilitate the introduction of these, and similar principles of classification, into the organization and arrangements of the schools of a town or district, as fast and as far as the circumstances of the population will admit, the following provisions should be engrafted into the school system of every state.

1. Every town should be clothed with all the powers requisite to establish and maintain a sufficient number of schools of different grades, at convenient locations, to accommodate all the children re-

siding within their respective limits—irrespective of any territorial division of the town into school districts.

2. Should provision be made for the creation of territorial school districts, a gradation of districts should be recognized, and every district having over sixty children of an age to attend school, should be obliged to maintain a primary school under a female teacher for the young pupils, and provide a secondary school for the older and more advanced pupils.

3. No village, or populous district, in which two or more schools of different grades for the younger and older children respectively, can be conveniently established, should be sub-divided into two or more independent districts.

4. Any two or more adjoining districts, in the same, or adjoining towns, should be authorized to establish and maintain a secondary school for the older and more advanced pupils of such districts, for the whole, or any portion of the year.

5. Any district, not having children enough to require the permanent establishment of two grades of schools, should be authorized to determine the periods of the year in which the public school shall be kept, and to determine the age and studies of the children who shall attend at any particular period of the year, and also to send the older pupils to the secondary school of an adjoining district.

The extent to which the gradation of schools can be carried, in any town or district, and the limit to which the number of classes in any school can be reduced, will depend on the compactness, number, and other circumstances of the population, in that town or district, and the number and age of the pupils, and the studies and methods of instruction in that school. A regular gradation of schools might embrace Primary, Secondary and High Schools, with Intermediate Schools, or departments, between each grade, and Supplementary Schools, to meet the wants of a class of pupils not provided for in either of the above grades.

1. Primary Schools, as a general rule, should be designed for children between the ages of three and eight years, with a further classification of the very youngest children, when their number will admit of it. These schools can be accommodated, in compact villages, in the same building with the Secondary or High School; but in most large districts, it will be necessary and desirable to locate them in different neighborhoods, to meet the peculiarities of the population, and facilitate the regular attendance of very young children, and relieve the anxiety of parents for their safety on their way to and from school. The school-room should be light, cheerful, and large enough for the evolutions of large classes—furnished with appropriate seats, furniture, apparatus and means of visible illustration, and having a retired, dry and airy play-ground, with a shelter to resort to in inclement weather, and with flower borders, shrubbery and shade trees, which they should be taught to love and respect. The play-ground is as essential as the school-room, for a Primary School, and is indeed the uncovered school-room of physical and moral educa-

tion, and the place where the manners and personal habits of children can be better trained than elsewhere. With them, the hours of play and study, of confinement and recreation, must alternate more frequently than with older pupils. To teach these schools properly,—to regulate the hours of play and study so as to give variety, vivacity, and interest to all of the exercises, without over-exciting the nervous system, or over-tasking any faculty of mind or body,—to train boys and girls to mild dispositions, graceful and respectful manners, and unquestioning obedience,—to cultivate the senses to habits of quick and accurate observation and discrimination,—to prevent the formation of artificial and sing-song tones,—to teach the use of the voice, and of simple, ready and correct language, and to begin in this way and by appropriate exercises in drawing, calculation, and lessons on the properties and classification of objects, the cultivation of the intellectual faculties,—to do all these things and more, require in the teacher a rare union of qualities, seldom found in one in a hundred of the male sex, and to be looked for with the greatest chance of success among females, "in whose own hearts, love, hope and patience, have first kept school."

The earlier we can establish, in every populous district, primary schools, under female teachers, whose hearts are made strong by deep religious principle,—who have faith in the power of Christian love steadily exerted to fashion anew the bad manners, and soften the harsh and self-willed perverseness of neglected children,—with patience to begin every morning, with but little if any perceptible advance beyond where they began the previous morning,—with prompt and kind sympathies, and ready skill in music, drawing, and oral methods, the better it will be for the cause of education, and for every other good cause.

2. Secondary Schools should receive scholars at the age of eight years, or about that age, and carry them forward in those branches of instruction which lie at the foundation of all useful attainments in knowledge, and are indispensable to the proper exercise and development of all the faculties of the mind, and to the formation of good intellectual tastes and habits of application. If the primary schools have done their work properly, in forming habits of attention, and teaching practically the first uses of language,—in giving clear ideas of the elementary principles of arithmetic, geography, and the simplest lessons in drawing, the scholars of a well conducted secondary school, who will attend regularly for eight or ten months in the year, until they are twelve years of age, can acquire as thorough knowledge of reading, arithmetic, penmanship, drawing, geography, history, and the use of the language in composition and speech, as is ever given in common or public schools, as ordinarily conducted, to children at the age of sixteen. For this class of schools, well qualified female teachers, with good health, self-command, and firmness, are as well fitted as male teachers. But if the school is large, both a male and female teacher should be employed, as the influence of both are needed in the training of the moral character and manners.

Schools of this grade should be furnished with class-rooms for recitations, and if large, with a female assistant for every thirty pupils.

3. High Schools should receive pupils from schools of the grade below, and carry them forward in a more comprehensive course of instruction, embracing a continuation of their former studies, and especially of the English language, and drawing, and a knowledge of algebra, geometry and trigonometry, with their applications, the elements of mechanics and natural philosophy and chemistry, natural history, including natural theology, mental and moral science, political economy, physiology, and the constitution of the United States. These and other studies should form the course of instruction, modified according to the sex, age, and advancement, and to some extent, future destination of the pupils, and the standard fixed by the intelligence and intellectual wants of the district—a course which should give to every young man a thorough English education, preparatory to the pursuits of agriculture, commerce, trade, manufactures, and the mechanical arts, and if desired, for college; and to every young woman, a well disciplined mind, high moral aims, and practical views of her own duties, and those resources of health, thought, manners and conversation, which bless alike the highest and lowest stations in life. All which is now done in private schools of the highest grade, and where the wants of any considerable portion of the community create such private schools, should be provided for in the system of public schools, so that the same advantages, without being abridged or denied to the children of the rich and the educated, should be open at the same time to worthy and talented children of the poorest parent. In some districts a part of the studies of this grade of schools might be embraced in the Secondary Schools, which would thus take the place of the High School; in others, the High School could be open for only portions of the year; and in others, two departments, or two schools, one for either sex, would be required. However constituted, whether as one department, or two, as a distinct school, or as part of a secondary school, or an ordinary district school, and for the whole year, or part of the year, something of the kind is required to meet the wants of the whole community, and relieve the public schools from impotency. Unless it can be engrafted upon the public school system, or rather unless it can grow up and out of the system, as a provision made for the educational wants of the whole community, then the system will never gather about it the warmth and sustaining confidence and patronage of all classes, and especially of those who know best the value of a good education, and are willing to spend time and money to secure it for their own children.

4. Intermediate Schools or departments will be needed in large districts, to receive a class of pupils who are too old to be continued, without wounding their self-esteem, in the school below, or interfering with its methods of discipline and instruction, and are not prepared in attainments, and habits of study, or from irregular attendance, to be arranged in the regular classes of the school above.

Connected with this class of schools there might be opened a school or department for those who cannot attend school regularly, or for only a short period of the year, or who may wish to attend exclusively to a few studies. There is no place for this class of scholars, in a regularly constituted, permanent school, in a large village.

5. Supplementary Schools, and means of various kinds should be provided in every system of public instruction, for cities and large villages, to supply deficiencies in the education of individuals whose school attendance has been prematurely abridged, or from any cause interfered with, and to carry forward as far and as long as practicable into after life, the training and attainments commenced in childhood.

Evening Schools should be opened for apprentices, clerks, and other young persons, who have been hurried into active employment without a suitable elementary education. In these schools, those who have completed the ordinary course of school instruction, could devote themselves to such studies as are directly connected with their several trades or pursuits, while those whose early education was entirely neglected, can supply, to some extent, such deficiencics. It is not beyond the legitimate scope of a system of public instruction, to provide for the education of adults, who, from any cause, in early life were deprived of advantages of school instruction.

Libraries, and courses of familiar lectures, with practical illustrations, collections in natural history, and the natural sciences, a system of scientific exchanges between schools of the same, and of different towns,—these and other means of extending and improving the ordinary instruction of the school-room and of early life, ought to be provided, not only by individual enterprise and liberality, but by the public, and the authorities entrusted with the care and advancement of popular education.

One or more of that class of educational institutions known as "Reform Schools," "Schools of Industry," or "Schools for Juvenile Offenders," should receive such children, as defying the restraining influence of parental authority, and the discipline and regulations of the public schools, or such as are abandoned by orphanage, or worse than orphanage, by parental neglect or example, to idle, vicious and pilfering habits, are found hanging about places of public resort, polluting the atmosphere by their profane and vulgar speech, alluring, to their own bad practices, children of the same, and other conditions of life, and originating or participating in every street brawl and low-bred riot. Such children cannot be safely gathered into the public schools; and if they are, their vagrant habits are chafed by the restraints of school discipline. They soon become irregular, play truant, are punished and expelled, and from that time their course is almost uniformly downward, until on earth there is no lower point to reach.

Accustomed, as many such children have been from infancy, to sights and sounds of open and abandoned profligacy, trained to an utter want of self-respect, and the decencies and proprieties of life, as exhibited in dress, person, manners and language, strangers to those motives of self-improvement which spring from a sense of social, moral and religious obligation, their regeneration involves the harmonious co-operation of earnest philanthropy, missionary enterprise, and sanctified wisdom. The districts of all our large cities where this class of children are found, are the appropriate field of home missions, of unobtrusive personal effort and charity, and of systematized plans of local benevolence, embracing friendly intercourse with parents, an affectionate interest in the young, the gathering of the latter into week-day, infant, and primary schools, and schools where the use of the needle, and other forms of labor appropriate to the sex and age of the pupils can be given, the gathering of both old and young into Sabbath schools and worshipping assemblies, the circulation of books and tracts, of other than a strictly religious character, the encouragement of cheap, innocent and humanizing games, sports and festivities, the obtaining employment for adults who may need it, and procuring situations as apprentices, clerks, &c., for such young persons as may be qualified by age, capacity and character. By individual efforts and the combined efforts of many, working in these and other ways, from year to year, these moral jungles can be broken up,—these infected districts can be purified,—these waste places of society can be reclaimed, and many abodes of penury, ignorance and vice can be converted by education, economy and industry, into homes of comfort, peace and joy.

Plan and Description of District School-House in Centremill, North Providence, R. I.

This house was erected after designs by Mr. Teft, of Providence. It stands back from the highway, on an elevated site, in the midst of a grove, and for beauty of design and convenience of arrangement, is not surpassed by any similar structure in New England. It is 26 feet by 51, and 13 feet high in the clear, with two departments on the same floor.

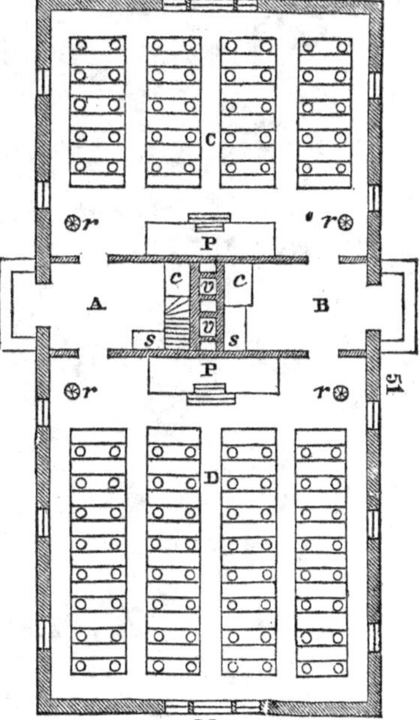

A, Boys' entry, 6 feet by 10.
B, Girls' ditto.
C, Primary department, 20 feet by 25, with desks and seats attached for 70 pupils.
D, Secondary, or Grammar department, 25 feet by 25, with desks and chairs for 64 pupils; *see p.* 120.
r, Register for hot air.
v, *v*, Flues for ventilation.
c, Closets for dinner pails of those who come from a distance.
s, Sink.

The smoke pipe is carried up between the ventilating flues, and the top of the chimney is finished so as to accommodate the bell.

Fig. 3. Side Elevation.

Side elevation of the new School-house in Arsenal District, Hartford, as originally designed for two departments. The flues for smoke and for ventilation are carried up in the belfry, which is of brick.

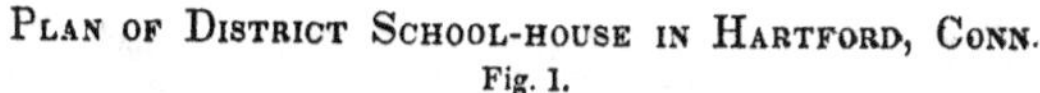
Plan of District School-house in Hartford, Conn.

Fig. 1.

The above cut represents the front elevation of a new school-house erected in Arsenal District, in Hartford, after designs by Octavius Jordan, Architect. As originally planned there were to be two rooms, as shown in side elevation, (Fig. 3.) The largest (Fig. 2) room is forty-five feet long by twenty-five wide, with a recitation-room (C) fourteen feet by twelve, and two entries, one for boys (A) and one for girls, (B), each twelve feet by six, furnished with sink, hooks, &c. There are thirty-two desks, each for two pupils, with sixty-four chairs, (page 143, Fig. 2), and thirty-two chairs for young children, (Fig. 3, page 129.) The room is warmed by Mott's School Stove, (page 146,) and ventilated by flues in the walls, opening at the top and bottom of the room, which is fifteen feet high in the clear. The material is brick, and the cost $1800.

Fig. 2. Ground Plan.

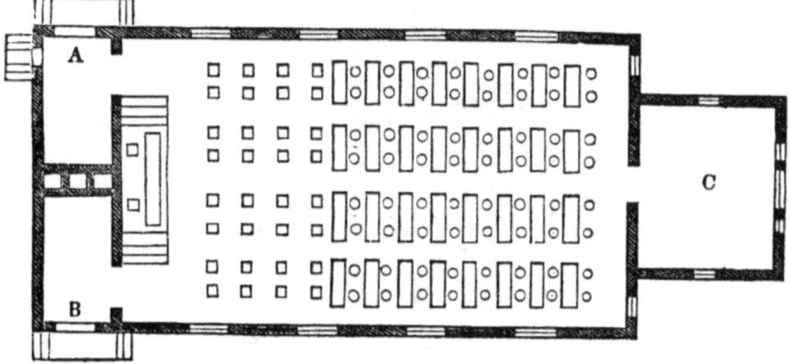

PLAN OF SCHOOL-HOUSE AT WASHINGTON VILLAGE IN COVENTRY, R. I.

The following cut presents the ground plan of the new school-house in the village of Washington, in the town of Coventry, R. I. The location is on the high ground in the rear of the village, and commands an extensive prospect in every direction. The site and yard, occupying one acre, was given to the district by Governor Whipple. The whole structure, without and within, is an ornament to the village, and ranks among the best school-houses in Rhode Island.

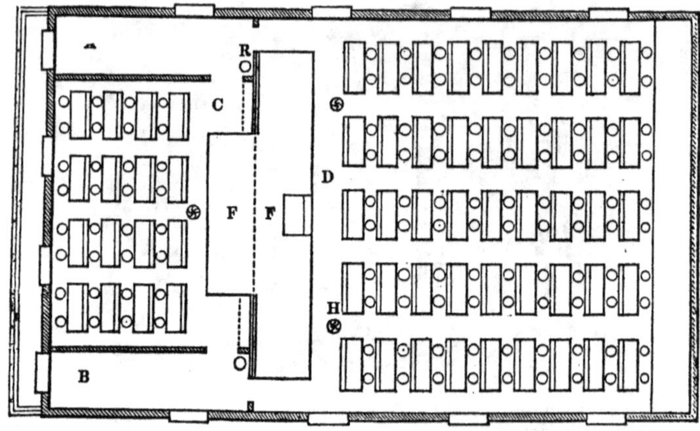

A—Boy's entrance.
B—Girl's entrance.
C—Primary school-room.
D—Secondary, or Grammar Department.
E—Teacher's platform.
F—Desks for two, with iron end-piece.
G—Chairs supported on iron pedestal.
H—Register for hot air.
R—Flue for ventilation, within which is carried up the smoke-pipe.

The two school-rooms can be thrown into one, for any general exercise of the two schools, by sliding doors.

The two rooms are uniformly heated by a furnace in the basement.

There is a well, sink, basin, mats, scrapers, bell, and all the necessary fixtures and appendages of a school-house of the first class.

The cost of the building and furuiture was $2,300.

The district possesses a library of upwards of four hundred volumes, the cost of which was raised by subscription in the District.

ALBANY NORMAL SCHOOL CHAIR AND DESK.

Plan of a Village School-house in England.

Fig. 4.

We are indebted to A. J. Downing, Esq. for the reduced cuts of a plan by J. Kendal, for a National School near Brentwood, in England. It affords accommodation for sixty children. The door is sheltered by a porch, and on the other side is a covered waiting-place for the children coming before school-hours. The cost, with the belfry, was $750. A house in this old English domestic character would give a pleasing variety to the everlasting sameness of our rural school architecture.

Fig. 5. Ground Plan.

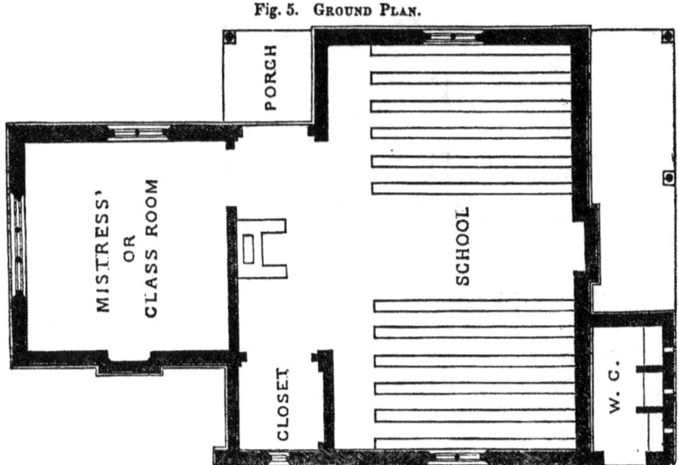

Union School-House, at Woonsocket and Chepachet, R. I.

By the school law of Rhode Island, two or more adjoining school districts in the same, or adjoining towns, may, by concurrent vote, agree to unite for the purpose of maintaining a secondary or grammar school, for the older and more advanced pupils of such associating districts. Under this provision the four school districts in the town of Cumberland, which comprise the village of Woonsocket, voted to unite and provide a school-house for the more advanced pupils, leaving the younger to be accommodated in their respective districts. The Union school-house is located on a beautiful site, the donation of Edward Harris, Esq., and is built substantially after the plan of the Warren Public school-house, already described, at a cost of $7,000. The following are the front and side elevations, as originally drawn by Mr. Teft, but not adopted by the committee.

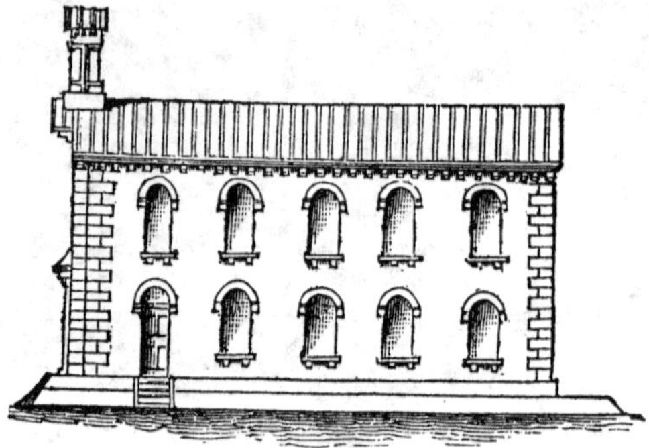

Side Elevation.

Front Elevation.

Under the provision above cited, the three districts into which the village of Chepachet, in the town of Glocester, is divided, voted to establish a Union School, and to provide a suitable house for the same. The building is 50 feet by 34, with two stories, and stands in the centre of a large lot, a little removed from the main street, and is the ornament and pride of the village. The lower floor is divided into two apartments; one for the Primary, and the other for an Intermediate School, for the younger pupils of the village, while the Union or Secondary School occupies the whole of the second floor.

Fig. 1.—PLAN OF FIRST FLOOR.

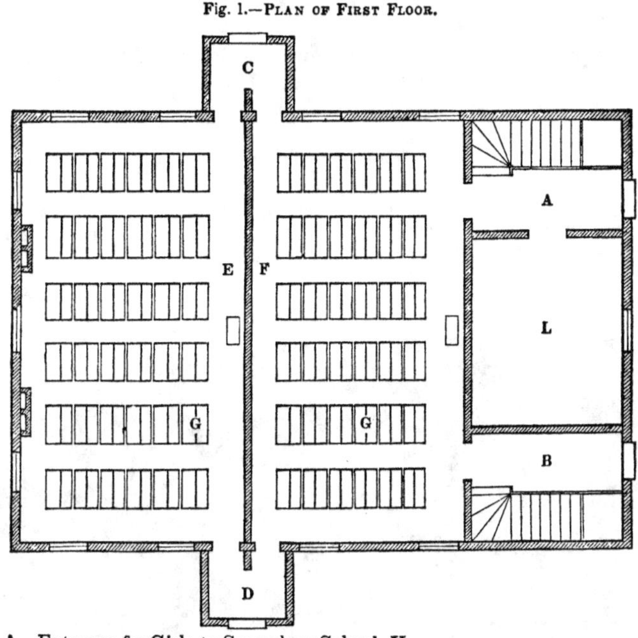

A—Entrance for Girls to Secondary School, U.
B— " " Boys " " "
C— " " Girls to Primary, E, and Intermediate School, F.
D— " " Boys " " " " "
E—Primary School-room.
F—Intermediate "
U—Secondary " L—Manton Glocester Library of 900 volumes.
R—Recitation room. S—Stove. V—Flue for ventilation.
G—Seat and desk attached, for two pupils, with iron ends.

Fig. 2.—PLAN OF SECOND FLOOR.

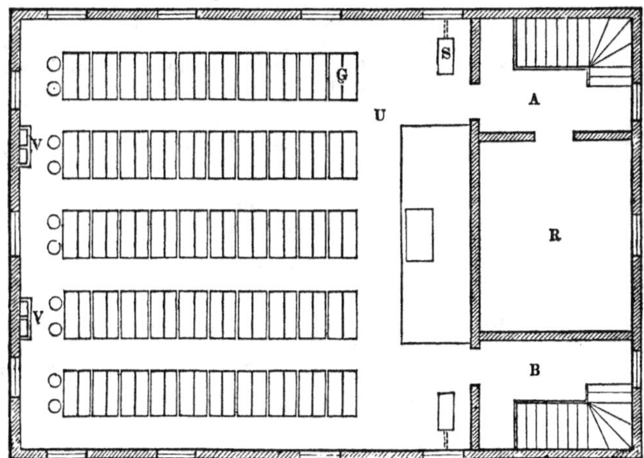

Report of Nathan Bishop, Esq., on the Public School-Houses of Providence, R. I.

Primary School-Houses.

These buildings are located in different parts of the city, and are designed for the accommodation of children from four to six or seven years of age, or until they are prepared to enter the intermediate schools.

No. 1.—View of a Primary School-House.

These school-houses stand back from thirty to sixty feet from the line of the street, and near the center of lots varying from eighty to one hundred feet in breadth, and from one hundred to one hundred and twenty feet in length. Each lot is inclosed by a neat and substantial fence, six feet high, and is divided into two yards—one for boys and the other for girls—with suitable out-buildings, shade trees, and shrubbery.

These houses are each forty feet long by thirty-three feet wide, with twelve-feet posts, built of wood, in a plain, substantial manner, and, with the fences, are painted white, presenting a neat and attractive exterior.

The entrance is into a lobby [A] and thence into an open area, where stands the stove [*a*]. A portion of the lobby is appropriated to bins for charcoal [*c*] and anthracite [*d*], which is the fuel used in all the schools; the remainder [B] is occupied by a sink, and as depositories for brooms, brushes, &c. Each room is arched, thereby securing an average height of thirteen feet, with an opening in the center of the arch, two feet in diameter, for ventilation. The ventilator is controlled by a cord passing over a pulley, and descending into the room near the teacher's desk [*b*]. In each end of the attic is a circular window, which, turning on an axis, can be opened and closed by cords, in the same manner as the ventilator.

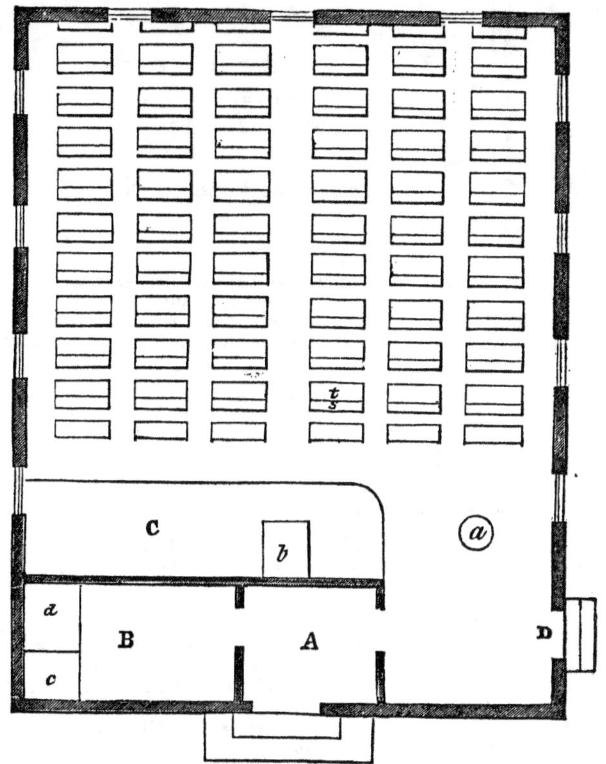

No. 2.—Interior of a Primary School-House.

The teacher's platform [C] is five feet wide, twenty feet long, and seven inches high, with a black-board ten feet long and three feet wide on the wall in the rear.

The floor is of inch and a half plank, tongued and grooved; and, for the purpose of securing warmth and firmness, and avoiding noise, is laid on cement.

The windows, eleven in number, of twenty-four lights, of seven by nine glass, are hung with weights, and furnished with inside blinds. The sides of the room and entries are ceiled all round with wood as high as the window-sills, which are four feet from the floor. The rest of the walls are plastered, and covered with white hard finish. Each room is provided with sixty seats [s] and desks [t], placed in six ranges; each range containing ten seats and desks, of three different sizes, and each seat and desk accommodating two scholars, or one hundred and twenty in all.

The center aisle is three feet and a half wide, and each of the others about two feet.

The desks are over three feet long, by sixteen inches wide, with a shelf beneath for books. The upper surface of the desk [a], except about two inches at the top [b], slopes one inch and a half in a foot.

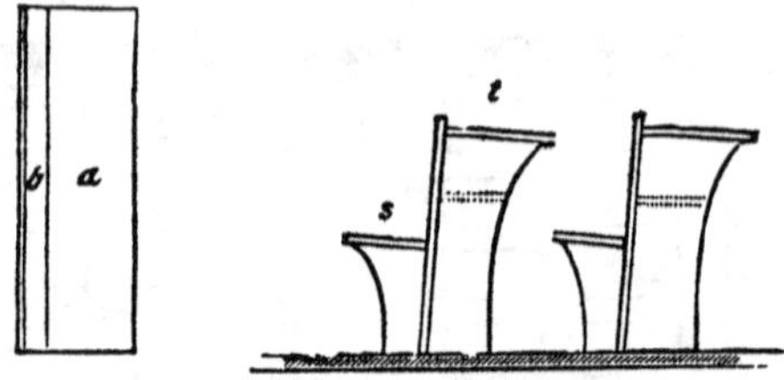

No. 3.—View of Top of a Desk, and Sectional View of Primary Seats and Desks.

The front of the desk, constituting the back of the next seat, slopes one inch in a foot. The seat also inclines a very little from the edge. The seats are of four different sizes, varying from seven to ten inches wide, and from nine to fourteen inches in height, the lowest being nearest the teacher's platform.

Intermediate School-Houses.

All the buildings of this class are two stories high, affording accommodations for two schools, a primary and an intermediate. These houses are generally in pleasant situations, on large lots, varying in size from one hundred feet wide by one hundred and twenty feet long, to one hundred and fifty by two hundred feet.

Rows of shade trees, consisting of elms, lindens, and maples, are planted along the side-walks and the fences inclosing the yards; and evergreens, the mountain ash, and other ornamental trees, are placed within the inclosures.

These houses are forty-four feet long, by thirty-three feet wide. Some of them are built of wood, the remainder of brick, and all in a tasteful and substantial style.

The rooms are large, and easily ventilated, being twelve feet in the clear, with large openings in the ceiling of the upper room, and on the sides in the lower room, leading into flues in the walls, which conduct the foul air into the attic, from which it escapes at circular windows in the gables of the buildings. These flues and windows can be opened and closed by cords passing over pulleys, and descending into the rooms below, where the teachers can control them with ease.

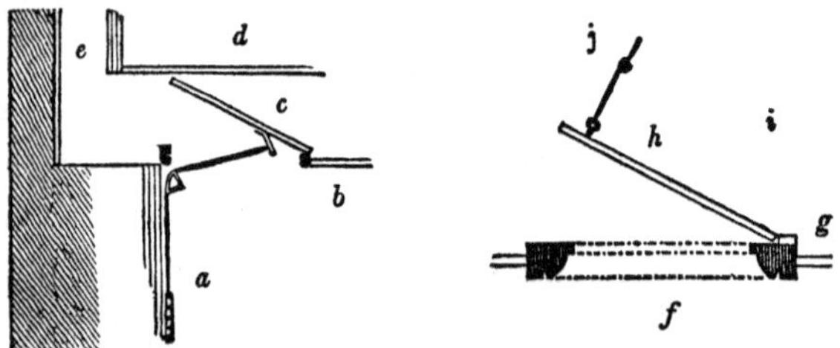

No. 5.—Sections of Ventilators.

In this cut, the cord [*i*], passing over the pulley [*j*], raising [*h*], hung on hinges at [*g*], opens wholly or partially the ventilator [*f*], a circular aperture three feet in diameter. The plan of ventilating the lower rooms is shown on

No. 4.—View of an Intermediate School-House.

the other part of the diagram, in which [a] represents a cord running over a pulley, and attached to [c], a board three feet long by one foot wide, opening the space between [b], the top of the lower room, and [d], the floor of the upper, leading into the flue [e], ascending to the attic.

The windows, nine in number in each school-room, of twelve lights, of ten by sixteen glass, are hung with weights, so as to be easily opened at top and bottom, and furnished with Venetian blinds inside, to regulate the amount of light admitted.

The floors are of hard pine boards, an inch and a half thick, and about six inches wide, tongued and grooved, and laid on mortar, as a protection against fire, for the prevention of noise, and to secure warmth and firmness. All the rooms, entries, and stairways are ceiled up with matched boards about four feet, as high as the window-sills. The remaining portions of the walls are plastered, and coated with white hard finish.

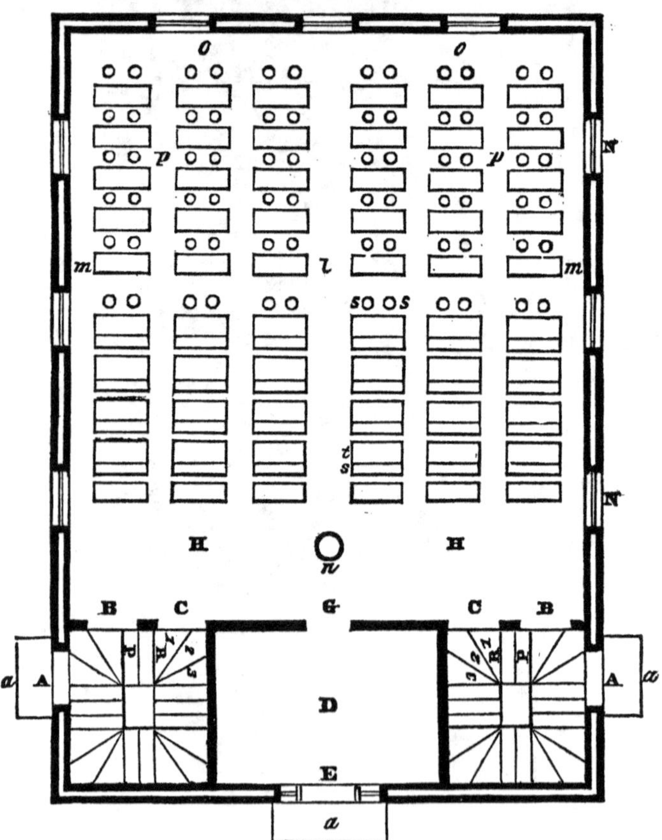

No. 6.—Interior of an Intermediate School-House.

The walls of some of these buildings are solid stone-work, faced with brick; others are built with double brick walls, as above shown, connected by ties of iron or brick.

As the rooms in the lower stories of this class of buildings are appropriated to primary schools, and are furnished in the same manner as those already described, the preceding cut is intended to serve the double purpose of exhibiting on the *first* floor only the improvements on the former plan, and, on the *second*, the whole view of a room for an intermediate school.

The steps [*a, a, a*] are broad, granite blocks, with scrapers on each end. The side doors [A, A], one for boys, the other for girls, lead into entries, eight feet by ten, from which the pupils of the primary schools pass through the doors [B, B] into the main rooms, which differ from those above described, in having a space [*o, o*], two feet wide, on the back part of the rooms, for reading and other class exercises; and the recitation-room, [D], another valuable improvement, as it avoids the confusion arising from having two recitations in one room at the same time.

The flight of stairs in each entry, commencing at the points [R, R], and ascending in the direction of [1, 2, 3], lands on the open space [P] in the upper entry, from which the pupils pass through the doors [C, C] into the school-room.

Coal-bins and convenient closets, for brooms, brushes, &c., are built under the stairs, in the lower entries; and similar closets, for the same purposes, are provided in the upper entries.

The large area [H, H], thirty feet long by seven wide, is the same in both the rooms, and is occupied by the principal teacher in each school, for such class exercises as may be more conveniently managed there than in the other place [*o, o*], left for the same purpose. The position of the stove [*n*] is such as not to render it uncomfortably warm on the front seats, and, at the same time, not to interfere with the passage of classes through the door [G] into the recitation-room [D], which is fourteen feet by ten, and, like all the school-rooms, furnished with black-boards. The lower room is lighted by a window over the front door, and by the side-lights; and the upper one by a double or mullion window, of sixteen lights, of ten by sixteen glass.

The side aisles [*m, m*] are two feet and a half wide; the others [P, P, &c.] are only eighteen inches wide, except the middle one [C], which is three and a half feet. The passage across the center of the room is about a foot and a half wide, and is very convenient for teachers in passing to the different parts of the room, and also for scholars in going to and from their recitations.

The seats and desks, in the front part of this room, are made and arranged on the same plan as those in the primary school-rooms above described, differing from them only in being one size larger. The lower end, or foot of each perpendicular support, or end-piece, is strongly fastened into a groove in a "shoe," or piece of plank, which, being screwed to the floor, secures the desks in a durable manner, and in a firm position.

The others are constructed upon a different plan, designed especially for the accommodation of pupils while writing. These desks and seats are of three different sizes.

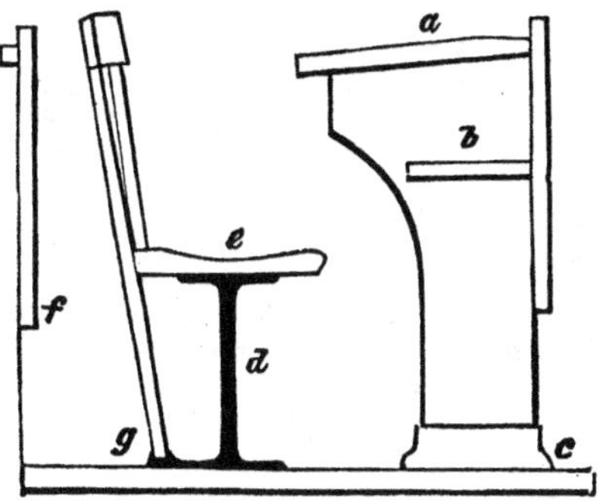

No. 7.—Section of a Writing-Desk and Seat.

The top of the desk [*a*] is of pine, one inch and a half thick, fifteen inches wide, and three feet and a half long. These desks are twenty-seven inches high on the front, and twenty-four on the side next to the seats. A space about three inches wide, on the front edge of the top, is planed down to a level, and an inkstand is let into the center of this, even with the surface, and covered with a small lid. The ends of these desks are an inch and a half thick, and fastened by a strong tenon to the shoe [*c*], which is screwed to the floor. The front of the desk, and the shelf [*b*], for books, &c., are inch boards; the whole desk, made in the strongest manner, is painted a pleasant green, and varnished. In the next smaller size, the same proportion is observed, but all the dimensions are one inch *less;* and in the third, or smallest size, the dimensions are all one inch less than in the second. For each desk there are two chairs, resting on cast-iron supporters [*d*], an inch and a quarter in diameter, with a wide *flange* at each end; the upper one, screwed to the under side of the seat [*e*], is a little smaller than the lower, which is fastened to the floor by five strong screws, rendering the chair almost immovable. The largest size seats [*e*] in these rooms are fourteen inches in diameter and fifteen inches high, with backs, twenty-eight inches from [*g*] to the top, slanting an inch and a quarter to a foot. These backs are made with three slats, fastened by strong tenons into a top-piece, like some styles of common chairs, and screwed to the seat, while the middle one extends down into a socket on the foot of the iron standard. The seats, like the desks, are diminished one inch for the middle size, and two for the smallest, preserving the proportions in the different sizes, which adapts them to the sizes of the desks.

Grammar School-Houses.

There are six buildings of this class, constructed on the same plan, and of the same size. They are seventy feet long by forty wide, with a front projection, twenty-eight feet long by fourteen feet wide. They are located on very large lots, varying from one hundred and fifty to two hundred feet long—from a hundred and twenty to a hundred and fifty feet wide. All of them, except one, are on corner lots, and all have large open spaces around them. These, and all the other public school-houses in the city, are protected with Quimby's lightning-rods, and each is furnished with a bell, which can be heard in the remotest parts of its district.

In the accompanying view, No. 9, the engraver has represented a *few* trees, a little *larger* than any at present around these buildings, because he could not crowd all the trees and shrubbery into the picture, without obscuring the lower part of the house.

The cut on p. 91, No. 10, is a ground plan, on a reduced scale, of a Grammar School-House, including a general view of the cellar, yards, fences, gates, sidewalks, &c.

The yards around each of the grammar school-houses contain from 18,000 to 20,000 square feet, or between a third and half an acre. These grounds are inclosed, and divided into three separate yards, by substantial close board fences [*f, f, f, f*], six feet high, neatly made, and painted white. The boys' play-ground [B], and that of the girls [G], are large; but the front yard [E] is small, and, not being occupied by pupils, is planted with trees and shrubbery. The graveled sidewalks [*s, s, s*], running on two sides of all the grammar school lots, and on three of some of them, are shaded by rows of elms, maples, and lindens, set near the curb-stones. The gates [A, C, D] and the graveled walks [*d, d, d*] lead to the front and the two side doors of the school-house; and [*f*] is a large gate for carting in coal, &c. The out-buildings [*i, i*] are arranged with a large number of separate apartments on both sides, all well ventilated, each furnished with a door, and the whole surrounded with evergreens.

In the plan of the projection [H] the stairway [*r*] leads to the cellar, which is seven feet in the clear, and extends under the whole of the main building. These cellars are well lighted, having eight windows [W, W], with ten lights of seven by nine glass. The windows, being hung with hinges on the upper

No. 9.—View of a Grammar School-House.

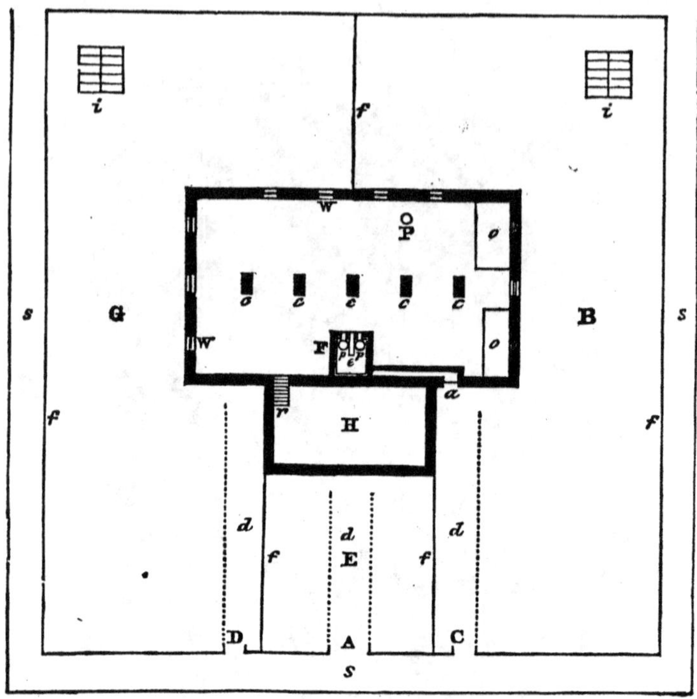

No.10.—Ground Plan, &c., of a Grammar School-House.

side, and fastened with hooks and staples at the lower edge, may be opened by raising them intc a horizontal position, where they are fastened with hooks as when closed. With this arrangement, it is easy to keep the cellars well ventilated at all seasons. The openings for the admission of coal into the bins [*o, o*], one for anthracite, and the other for charcoal, are furnished with sheet-iron shutters, fastening on the inside. Every school-house has, in the cellar, an abundant supply of good water, obtained from a fountain, or from a well, which is generally outside of the building, the water being brought in by a pump [P]. A supply of good water for a school-house should not be considered merely as a convenience, but as absolutely necessary.

The horizontal section of a furnace [F] shows merely the ground plan. The cold air passes through [*a*] to the air-chamber, where it is warmed by the fires in [*p, p*], two cast-iron cylinders, fourteen inches in diameter. The evaporator [*e*] holds about fifteen gallons of water, which is kept in a state of rapid evaporation, thus supplying the air-chamber with an abundance of moisture.

In the plan and construction of the various parts of these furnaces, special pains have been taken to remove all danger of fire—an important consideration, which should never be overlooked. The furnace is covered with stone, thickly coated with mortar, and the under side of the floor above is lathed and plastered, not only above the furnace, but at least ten feet from it in every direction.

A full description of the construction and operation of the furnaces used in the public school-houses will be given under another diagram. The cellar walls and the stone piers [*c, c, c, c, c*] are well pointed, and the whole inside, including the wood-work overhead, is neatly whitewashed, giving this apartment a neat and pleasant appearance.

The walls of all these buildings are of stone, about two feet thick, faced with common brick, and painted a tasteful color.

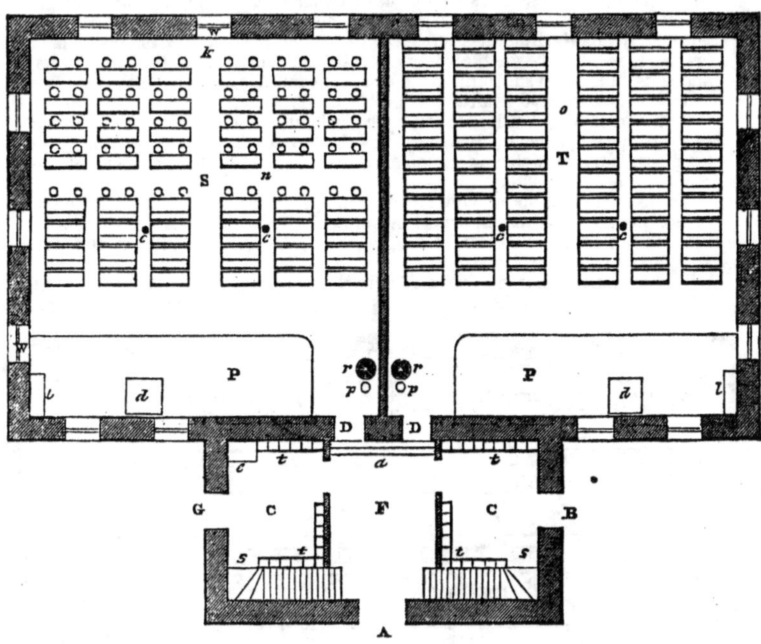

No. 11.—Plan of the First Floor of a Grammar School-House.

There are three entrances to these houses; the front [A], and the two side doors [B], for boys, and [G], for girls, leading into the entries [F, C, C]. The front is a large double door, with a beautiful frontice of fine hammered Quincy granite. At all the outside doors are two or three hewn granite steps, furnished with four or six scrapers at each door.

Pupils belonging to the schools in the lower story pass from the side entries into the middle one, and, ascending two steps at [*a*], enter their respective rooms [T, S], which are rather larger than those in the primary and intermediate school-houses, previously described, being thirty-six feet by thirty-two inside, and eleven feet high in the clear.

In each of the entries [C, C] there is a provision [*t*, *t*, *t*, *t*] for setting up umbrellas. It resembles a ladder placed in a horizontal position, and is fastened to the ceiling on one side, and supported on the other by substantial posts of oak or other strong wood, turned in a tasteful style, and set into the floor.

The seats and desks in the rooms [T and S] are of the same dimensions, and arranged in the same manner as those in the primary and the intermediate school-rooms before described. The small iron posts [*c*, *c*, *c*, *c*], about two and a half inches in diameter, supporting the floor above, are placed against the ends of the seats, so close as not to obstruct the passages at all. Besides the platforms [P, P], twenty feet by six—the tables, three feet by four, for the teachers, and the closets [*l*, *l*], for brushes, &c., there are black-boards, painted upon the walls, extending from the doors [D, D] to the windows, fourteen feet long by four wide, with the lines of a stave painted on one end, to aid in giving instruction in vocal music.

The plan of ventilating these rooms on the first floor is represented by cut No. 5, page 85. Every room is provided with two ventilators, each three feet long by about twelve inches wide, opening into flues of the same dimensions, leading into the attic, from which the impure air escapes at circular windows in the gables. These flues should have extended down to the bottom of the rooms, with openings on a level with the floors, so that, when the rooms are warmed with air from the furnaces above the temperature of the human breath, they might be ventilated by removing the foul air from the lower parts, and thus causing fresh, warm air to be slowly settling down upon the scholars —a very pleasant and healthful mode of ventilation.

These rooms are well warmed by heated air, admitted through registers [*r*, *r*], eighteen inches in diameter, from the furnace below, from which [*p*, *p*] tin pipes, fourteen inches in diameter, convey the air to the grammar school-rooms in the second story.

These rooms are large, with arched ceilings, measuring twelve feet to the foot of the arch, and seventeen to its crown. They are each provided with two ventilators, three feet and a half in diameter, placed in the crown of the arch, about twenty feet apart.

The entrances to the Grammar School-rooms are by two short flights of stairs on a side; from the lower entries to [*s*, *s*], spaces about three feet square,

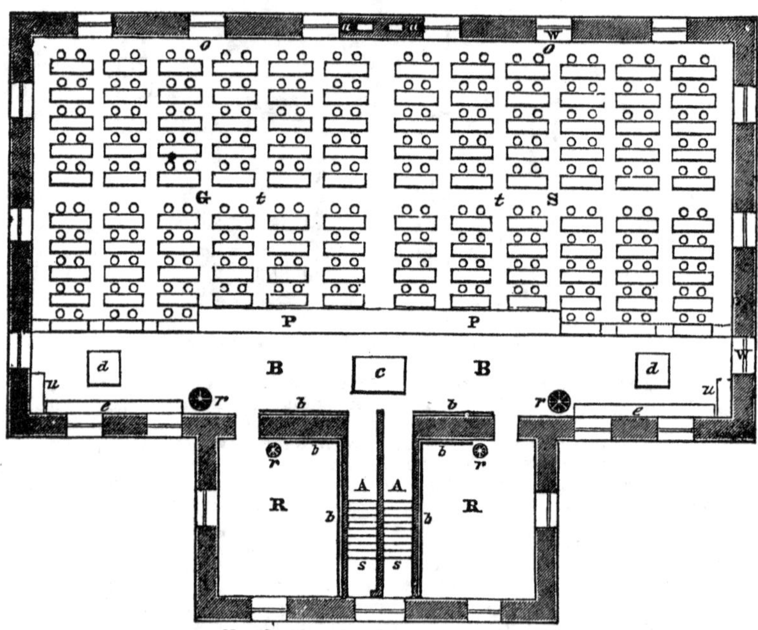

No. 12.—Plan of a Grammar School-Room.

and thence to [A, A], spaces three by five feet, extending from the top of the stairs to the doors opening into the school-room.

The master's table [*c*], as well as tables [*d*, *d*], for the assistants, are movable. The large area [B, B], being fourteen inches above the floor of the room, is eight feet wide by sixty-four long, with large closets [*u*, *u*] at the ends, fitted up with shelves, &c., for the use of the teachers.

The school-room is warmed by heated air, admitted at the registers, [*r*, *r*] and the recitation-rooms [R, R] in the same manner, by the small registers, [*r*, *r*] all of which are connected with the furnace in the cellar by large tin pipes or conductors.

The black-boards, four feet wide, painted upon the hard-finished walls, are indicated by the lines [*b*, *b*, *b*, &c.] in the recitation-rooms, and along the walls behind the master's table, extending on each side to the windows beyond, [*e*, *e*] making, in each Grammar School, about three hundred square feet of black-board.

The long benches [*e*, *e*] are used for seating *temporarily* new pupils on their entering school, until the master can assign them regular seats; also for seating visitors at the quarterly examinations. The space [P, P], a broad step, eighteen feet long and two feet wide, is used for some class exercises on the black-boards. The passage [*t*, *t*], about eighteen inches wide, running the whole length of the room, affords great facility in the movements of pupils to and from the recitations and other class exercises. The master's classes generally recite in the space [*o*, *o*] on the back side of the room, four feet wide and sixty-four feet long, where seats are placed for scholars to sit during recitation, when it is necessary; and the same accommodations are provided in the recitation-rooms.

The windows [W, W, &c.], which are hung with weights, and furnished with inside blinds, in the manner before described, contain twelve lights each, of ten by sixteen glass, of the strongest kind, the Saranac or Redford glass.

The quantity of air furnished for each scholar in the public school-rooms is a matter of no small importance. The rooms for the primary and the intermediate schools—the former designed to accommodate one hundred and twenty, and the latter only ninety-six pupils—contain between fifteen and sixteen thousand cubic feet of atmospheric air. The rooms for the grammar schools, intended to accommodate two hundred pupils, contain over thirty-five thousand cubic feet, after a suitable deduction for the furniture is made.

This estimate allows every child, when the rooms are not crowded, about one hundred and fifty cubic feet of air for every hour and a half, on the supposition that no change takes place, except at the times of recess, and at the close of each session. But the rate at which warm air is constantly coming into the rooms from the furnaces, increases the allowance for every child to about three hundred cubic feet for every hour and a half.

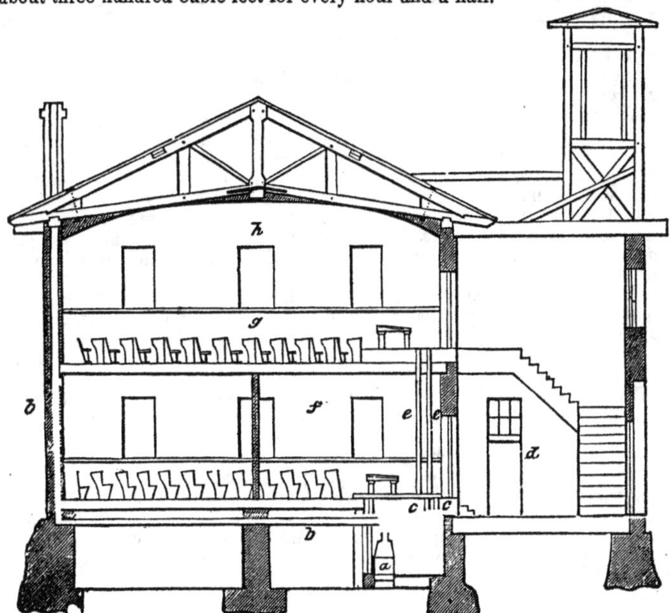

No. 13.—Transverse Section of a Grammar School-House.

The preceding cut is given in order to show an *end view*, the projection, belfry, rooms, seats, desks, and cellar. An imperfect section of the warming apparatus is presented, giving an outline of the plan of its construction. The smoke-pipe, connected with [*a*], the heater, coiled twice around in the air-chamber, passes off in the direction of [*b*, *b*] to the chimney. The short tin pipes [*c*, *c*] conduct the warm air into the lower rooms; and the long ones [*e*, *e*] convey it to the rooms in the second story. On each side of the projection over the door [*d*] is a window, lighting the outside entry, and also the middle entry by another window over the inside door. The end views of seats and desks do not represent the different sizes very accurately, but sufficiently so to give a correct idea of the general plan.

The High School-House.

This building occupies an elevated and beautiful situation, at the head of President street, near the central part of the city. It is a specimen of plain, but tasteful architecture, on which the eye reposes with pleasure. The lot, somewhat irregular in its form, is equivalent to one a hundred feet by a hundred and fifteen, and lies on a gentle hill-side, rendering it easy to construct a basement almost entirely above ground, except on the back side. The extensive grounds in front, and on either side, all planted with trees, and separated from the High School only by the width of the streets, add much to the beauty and pleasantness of its situation. The yards around it are inclosed by a handsome baluster fence, resting in front on heavy blocks of rough granite. The steps are of hewn granite, twelve feet long, making a very convenient entrance.

The High School being designed for both boys and girls, an entirely separate entrance is provided for each department. The front door, at which the girls enter, has a very beautiful frontispiece, with double columns (thus providing for large side-lights), and a heavy ornamented cap, all cut from Quincy granite in the best style.

The door in the circular projection, fronting on another street, has also a fine frontispiece, cut from Quincy granite.

The size of this building is fifty feet by seventy-six, with a projection of seven feet. The walls of the basement are of stone, three feet thick, and faced with rough-hewn granite, laid in courses twenty inches wide. Each stone has a "chiseled draft, fine cut," an inch wide around the face, and all the joints as close and true as if the whole were fine hammered. The remaining portions of the walls, diminishing in thickness as they rise, are faced with the best quality of Danvers pressed brick, giving the building a beautiful appearance. The roof is covered with tin, every joint soldered, and the whole surface kept well painted.

The rooms in the basement story, which is twelve feet high in the clear, are separated from each other by solid brick walls. The pupils in the girls' department, entering the house at [A], pass into the large lobby [C], twelve feet by twenty-eight, from which they can go to all parts of the building appropriated to their use.

The furnace-room [H] has a brick floor, and is kept in as good order as the other parts of the house. The coal-bins [*n*, *n*] and the furnace [F] are so constructed, that, with an ordinary degree of care, the room may be kept as clean as any of the school-rooms. The arrangements [*m*, *m*] for setting up umbrellas have been described. The pump [*p*], accessible to all in the girls' department, connected with a nice sink, lined with lead, affords an abundant supply of excellent water. The rooms [E, G, I], each not far from sixteen by twenty-four feet, are appropriated as the Superintendent's Office, and for such meetings of the School Committee, and of its sub-committees, as may be appointed there.

The large lecture-room, on the opposite side of the lobby, is furnished with settees, which will accommodate about two hundred and fifty pupils. On the

No. 14.—View of the High School-House.

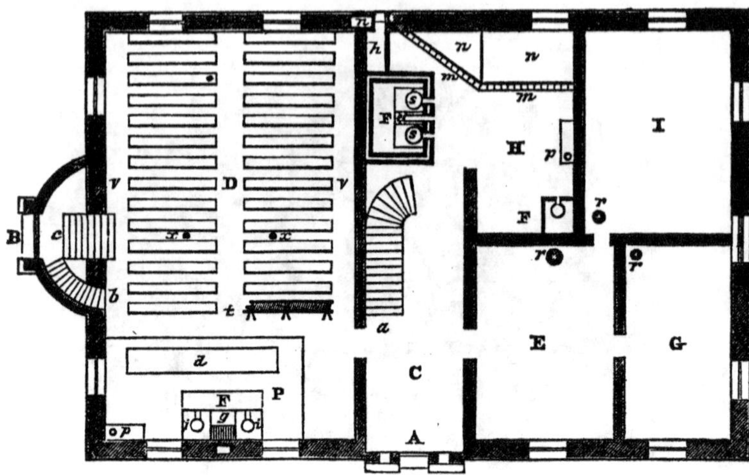

No. 15.—Plan of the Basement of High School.

platform [P], raised seven inches from the floor, a long table or counter [*d*], made convenient for experimental lectures in Chemistry, Natural Philosophy, &c., having pneumatic cisterns for holding gasses. At [F, &c.] are suitable provisions for the fires used in the preparations of chemical experiments. The pump [*p*], with a sink like the other, is used exclusively by the pupils in the boys' department.

In all lectures, and other exercises in this room, the girls, entering at [*a*], occupy the seats on the right of [D], the middle aisle. The boys, entering by descending the short flight of stairs [*b*], are seated on the opposite side of the room. This may seem like descending to useless particulars, but it is done to show that there are no grounds for the objections sometimes made against having a school for boys and for girls in the same building, where the departments are kept entirely separate, except in exercises in vocal music and occasional lectures. The boys enter the house at the end door [B], which is six feet above the basement floor, and, by a short flight of stairs, they reach the first story at [*e*].

The three rooms [C, D, F] are appropriated to the department for girls. They are easy of access to the pupils, who, ascending the broad flight of stairs, terminating at [B], can pass readily into their respective rooms.

The course of instruction in the school occupying three years, the room [D] is appropriated to the studies for the first, [E] to those of the second, and [F] to the course for the third year. In each room there are three sizes of seats and desks, and their arrangement in all is uniform. The largest are on the back side of the room. The largest desks are four feet eight inches long, and twenty-two inches wide on the top; the middle size is two inches smaller, and the other is reduced in the same proportions. The largest seats are as high as common chairs, about seventeen inches, and the remaining sizes are reduced to correspond with the desks. The passages around the sides of the rooms vary from two to four feet wide, and those between the rows of desks, from eighteen to twenty-four inches.

On the raised platforms [P, P, P, P] are the teachers' tables [*d, d, d, d*], covered with dark woolen cloth, and furnished with four drawers each. The registers [*f, f, f, f*] admit the warm air from the furnace, and the pipes [*p, p, p*] conduct it into the rooms in the upper story. The passage [*b*] leads into the back yard, which is ornamented with a variety of shrubbery.

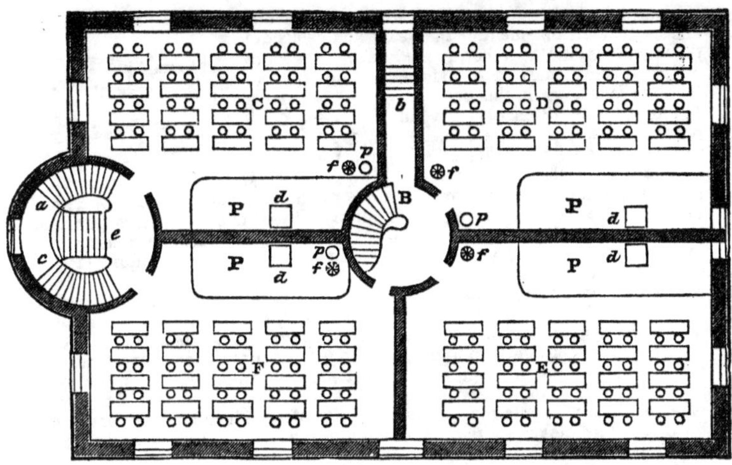

No. 16.—Plan of the First Story of the High School.

The door leading from the room [F] is used only for teachers and visitors, except when the two departments assemble in the hall.

In the room [C] the boys pursue the studies prescribed for the first year; the other rooms in this department are in the next story.

Pupils ascending from the area [e], by two circular stairways, land on the broad space [a, c], from which, by a short flight of stairs, they reach [A], in the following cut, the floor of the upper story, which is sixteen feet in the clear.

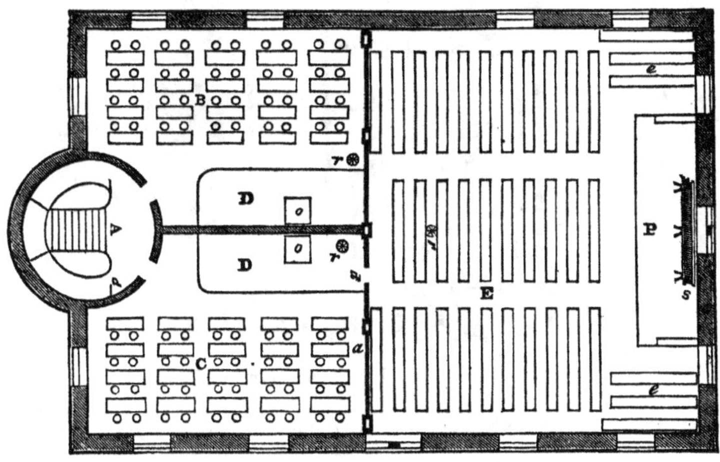

No. 17.—Plan of the Second Story of the High School-House.

The room [B] is appropriated to the middle class, and [C] to the senior class. The arrangement of the seats and desks are the same as in the other rooms, except they are *movable*—being screwed to a frame not fastened to the floor, as shown in this cut.

The cross partition [*a*]—see cut No. 17—is composed of four very large doors, about fourteen feet square, hung with weights in such a manner that they may be raised into the attic, thus throwing the whole upper story into one large hall—an arrangement by which one room can be changed into *three*, and three into *one*, as the occasion may require. On all public occasions, such as Quarterly Examinations, and Annual Exhibitions, the rooms are thus thrown together, and the seats and desks turned so as to face the platform [P], in [E], the principal hall.

Observation and experiment, relative to the modes of warming the public school-rooms, have proved that very *large* stoves, eighteen inches in diameter, render the temperature of the rooms *more uniform and pleasant*, and that they are also *more economical*, both in regard to the amount of fuel consumed, and the amount of repairs required. It is a general principle, that a warming apparatus, containing a *large* quantity of fuel, undergoing a *slow* combustion, is better than one containing a *small* quantity of fuel, in a state of *rapid* combustion. The stoves in the small buildings, and the furnaces in the large ones, are constructed on this principle.

In regard to the construction of furnaces for warming public buildings or private dwellings, so much depends upon circumstances, that no specific plan can be given which would be successful in all cases. One familiar with the principles which regulate the motions of currents of air at different temperatures, can, with an ordinary degree of good judgment and mechanical skill, make a furnace in any place, where one can be made at all, that will accomplish all which the laws of nature will permit.

The following cut is intended to illustrate *two* plans for a furnace.

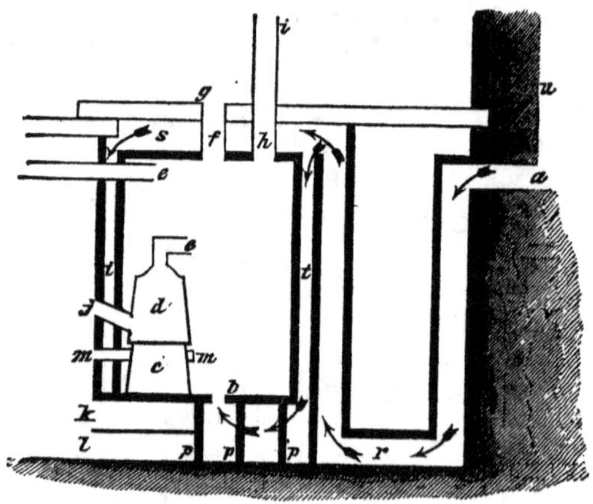

No. 18.—A Vertical Section of a Furnace

In the first, the cold air is admitted at [*a*], through the outside walls of the building, and descends in the direction described by the arrows, to [*r*], and thence rises to the top of the furnace, as shown by the arrows. At this place, the cold air diffuses itself over the whole upper surface, about eight feet by ten, and passes down between the double walls of the furnace, in the spaces [*t*, *t*], which extend all around the furnace, and rises from beneath, through a large opening [*b*], into the air-chamber, where it is heated and conducted to the rooms by large pipes, [*f*, *h*]. The object of this mode of taking in air is two-fold. In the first place, the constant currents of cold air, passing over the top of the furnace, keep that surface comparatively cool, and also keep the floors above the furnace cool, thus removing all danger of setting fire to the wood-work over the furnace.

In the second place, as the inside walls are constantly becoming heated, and the currents of cold air, passing down on all sides of the walls, become rarified by their radiation, and thus, as it were, take the heat from the outside of the inner walls, and bring it round into the air-chamber again, at [*b*]. This is not mere theory, but has been found to work well in practice. On this plan, the outside walls are kept so cool, that very little heat is wasted by radiation.

In the second plan, the cold air is admitted as before; but, instead of ascending from [*r*] to the top of the furnace, it passes through a large opening, directly from [*r*], to [*p*, *p*, *p*], representing small piers, supporting the inside walls, and thence into the air-chamber at [*b*], and also *up* the spaces [*t*, *t*], to the top [*s*], from which the air warmed by coming up between the walls is taken into the rooms by separate registers, or is let into the sides of the pipes [*f*, *h*].

By this plan, the air passes more rapidly through the air-chamber, and enters the rooms in *larger* quantities, but at a *lower* temperature. This is the better mode, if the furnace be properly constructed with large inlets and outlets for air, so that no parts become highly heated; otherwise, the wood-work over the furnace will be in some danger of taking fire. The general defects in the construction of furnaces are:—*too small* openings for the admission of cold air—*too small* pipes for conveying the warm air in all horizontal and inclined directions—and defective dampers in the perpendicular pipes. A frequent cause of failure in warming public buildings and private dwellings may be found in the ignorance and negligence of attendants.

A single remark will close this report, which has been extended, perhaps, too far by specific details—a want of which is often complained of by mechanics who are engaged in building school-houses.

It is believed to be *best*, and, all things considered, *cheapest*, in the end, to build *very good* school-houses—to make their external appearance pleasant and attractive, and their internal arrangements comfortable and convenient—to keep them in *first-rate* order, well repaired, and *always clean*.

The amount of damage done to school property in this city has uniformly been *least* in those houses in which the teachers have done *most* to keep every thing in very good order. The very appearance of school property well taken care of rebukes the spirit of mischief, and thus elevates the taste and character of the pupils.

Respectfully submitted.

N. BISHOP,
Superintendent of Public Schools.

PROVIDENCE, August, 1846.

Since the foregoing Report was published, important alterations have been made in several of the Grammar and Primary School-houses of Providence. In the Grammar School-houses, a projection of the same size and in the same relative position as that in front of the building, is carried up in the rear so as to secure two additional rooms for recitation on the second floor, and one for each school-room on the first. A second story has been added to the Primary School-houses, so as to accommodate a large number of pupils, and secure a better classification of the same. The Superintendent, than whom no one in the country has a better scientific and practical knowledge of the subject, has devised a plan of ventilation, at once cheap and thorough, which will be carried out as soon as means for this purpose are placed at the disposal of the School Committee by the City Council.

The following cut presents a front elevation of one of the new Intermediate School-houses in Providence, designed by Mr. Teft.

The only private school edifice in Providence which can be compared with the Public School-houses, is a beautiful structure erected by Mr. John Kingsbury, at his own expense, after plans of Mr. Teft, for the accommodation of a school of forty girls. This house is a perfect gem in school architecture, and no young lady can be educated within its walls without receiving not only the benefit of its every appliance for health, comfort and neatness, but at the same time, some advancement in esthetical culture from the exhibition of taste all around her.

The improvements in education, introduced by Mr. Kingsbury in his private school from 1826 to 1838, prepared the way for improvements in the organization and instruction of the public schools, and the improvement of the latter since 1840, have made it necessary for Mr. Kingsbury to take and maintain still higher ground. Mr. Kingsbury has always given his best efforts to improve the public schools.

Public School-House in Warren, R. I.

Fig. 1.

Perspective of Mr. John Kingsbury's Female Seminary, Providence, R. I.

The lot is 225 deep and 100 feet wide for a depth of 125 feet, and 161 feet wide for the remaining 64 feet. It is divided into three yards, as exhibited in the ground plan, (Fig. 2,) each substantially inclosed, and planted with trees and shrubbery.

The dimensions of the building are 62 feet by 44 on the ground. It is built of brick in the most workmanlike manner.

Most of the details of construction, and of the arrangement in the interior, are similar to those described on page 214.

Each room is ventilated by openings controlled by registers, both at the floor and the ceiling, into four flues carried up in the wall, and by a large flue constructed of thoroughly seasoned boards, smooth on the inside, in the partition wall, (Fig. 3, x.)

The whole building is uniformly warmed by two of Culver's furnaces placed in the cellar.

Every means of cleanliness are provided, such as scrapers, mats, sink with pump, wash basin, towels, hooks for outer garments, umbrella stands, &c.

The tops of the desks are covered with cloth, and the aisles are to be cheaply carpeted, so as to diminish, if not entirely prevent, the noise which the moving of slates and books, and the passing to and fro, occasion in a school-room.

Fig. 2.

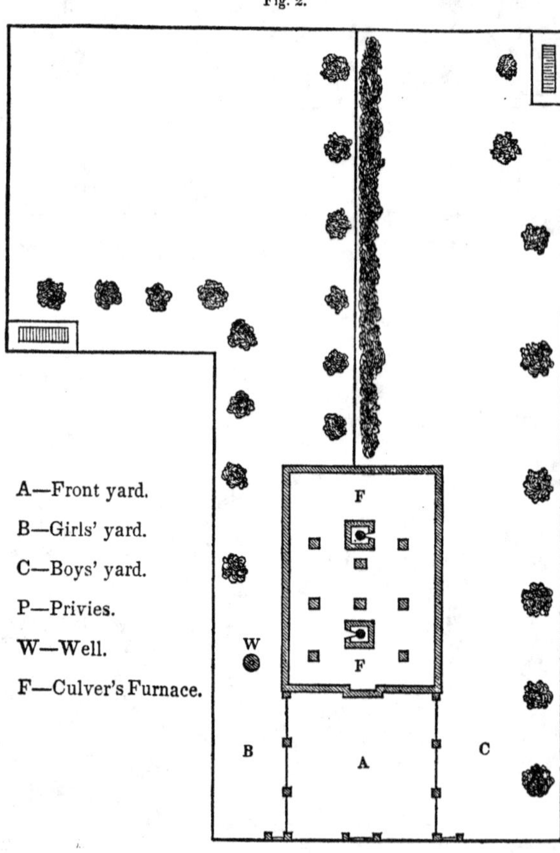

Fig. 3.—FIRST FLOOR.

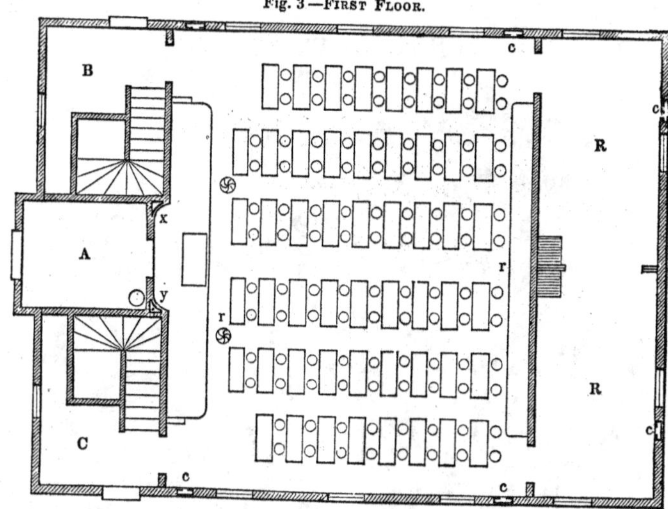

A—Front entrance.
B—Girls' entrance, with mats, scrapers, hooks for clothes, a sink, pump, basin, &c.
C—Boys' entrance do.
R—Recitation rooms, connected by sliding doors.
R, P—Platform for recitation, with a blackboard in the rear.
T—Teacher's platform.
S—Seats and desks; see page 205.

Q—Library and apparatus.
w—Windows, with inside Venetian blinds.
c—Flues for ventilation in the outer wall.
x—Flue for ventilation, lined with smooth, well seasoned boards.
y—Bell-rope, accessible to the teacher by an opening in the wall.
r—Hot air registers.

Fig. 4.—SECOND FLOOR.

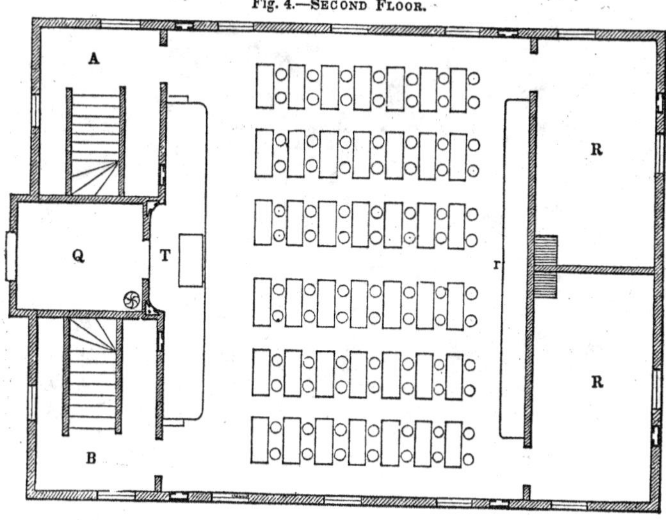

PRIMARY SCHOOL IN WESTERLY, R. I.

VILLAGE SCHOOL-HOUSE IN ALLENDALE, N. PROVIDENCE, R. I.

Ingraham Primary School-House, Boston.

The Schoolhouse, to which the following description and plans more particularly refer, is situated in Sheafe street, at the north part of the City, and on the slope of Copp's Hill, famed in our Revolutionary history. It occupies a space of twenty-six by fifty-three feet, exclusive of the play-ground in front, between it and the street, which is sixteen by fifty-three feet. This front is hardly long enough. Sixty feet would have been much better. The main building is twenty-six by forty-four feet; and there are projections at each end,—one on the west, four and a half by sixteen and a half feet, containing the privies, and one at the east end, three and a half by twenty-one and a half feet, in which is the passage from the lower schoolroom to the play-ground.

The building is three stories in height. Each story contains a Schoolroom, Recitation-rooms, Closets, Entries, and Privies, and is finished twelve feet high, in the clear. Each Schoolroom is lighted by four windows, which are all on one side. The first floor is set eighteen inches above the ground at the front of the building. The Cellar is finished seven and a half feet high, in the clear; and its floor is on a level with the surface of the ground at the back of the building, where is the entrance-door to the first story.

The Schoolrooms in the first and second stories are thirty feet in length, by twenty-two feet and four inches in width, and contain six hundred and seventy square feet of floor. That in the third story is thirty-two feet in length, by twenty-two feet and nine inches in breadth, and contains seven hundred and thirty square feet of floor. Thus allowing from ten to twelve or thirteen square feet of floor, and one hundred and fifty cubic feet of air, to each scholar.

The following diagram will show the arrangement of the ground-floor, with the Play-ground in front.

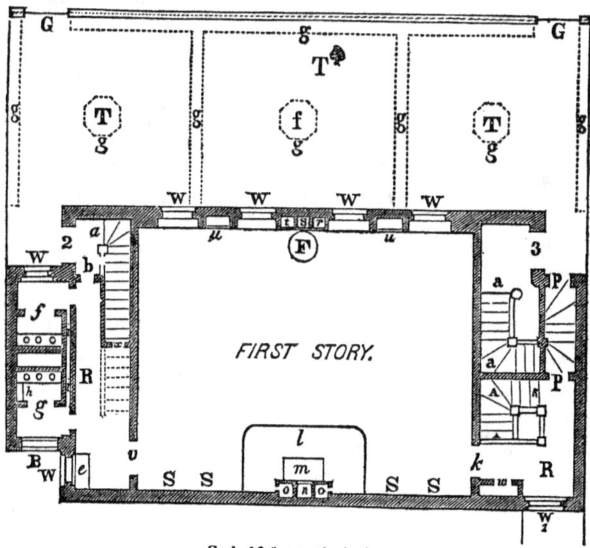

Scale 16 feet to the inch.

The following references will apply to the ground-plan of each of the three stories.

1, Entrance to First Story, by a door under the window W, the back part of the building being eight feet lower than the front.

2, 3, Entrance-doors to the Second and Third Stories.

A, A, A, Stairs to First Story, from the Entrance-door 1.

B, Blinds in Boys' Privies.

F, Fireplace or Furnace-flue, or Stove, when one is used instead of a Furnace.

G, G, Entrance-gates to Second and Third Stories. The Iron Fence extends the whole length of the front on the street, broken only by these two gates.

R, R, Recitation-rooms, or spaces used for that purpose. In the *first story*, that on the right being the entrance-passage to the schoolroom, and that on the left, the passage to the Second Story.

S, S, S, S, Large Slates, measuring four by two and a half feet, affixed to the walls, instead of Blackboards.

T, T, T, Trees in Play-ground. That near the fence, is an old horse-chestnut tree.

U, Umbrella stands. The place of those of the *second story* only are shown. In the other stories, they are also in the entrance-passages.

W, W, Windows.

a, Stairs to Second Story.

b, *b*, *b*, In *second story*, Entry, and place for Boys' Clothes-hooks, also used as a Recitation-room. In *third story*, place for Clothes-hooks.

c, In *second story*, Door into the Recitation-room where are the Sink and Girls' Clothes-hooks. In *third story*, Door into Recitation-room where is the Brush Closet and entrance to Girls' Privy.

d, *d*, *d*, In *second story*, Girls' Clothes-hooks.

e, Sinks.

f, Privy for Girls. *g*, Privy for Boys. *h*, Trough in ditto.

i, *i*, Space between the walls of the Privies and main building, for more perfect ventilation, and cutting off of any unpleasant odor. [This space is here too much contracted, on account of the want of room. It would be much better, if greatly increased.]

k, Entrance-door to Schoolroom, through which, only, scholars are allowed to enter. In *third story*, the passage from the stairs to the Entrance-door is through the Recitation-room.

l, Teachers' Platforms, six feet wide and twelve feet long, raised seven inches from the floors.

m, Teachers' Tables.

n, Ventiduct. That for each room is in the centre of that room. These are better shown in the diagram representing the Ventilating arrangement, (p. 183.)

o, *o*, Closets, in the vacant spaces on the sides of the Ventiducts, in the First and Second Stories. In *first story*, they are on each side of the Ventiduct; in *second story* only on one side. In the *third story*, there are of course none. See the diagram of the Ventilating arrangement, (p. 183.)

p, *p*, Ventiducts for other rooms. In plan of *second story*, *p* shows the position of the Ventiduct for first story. In *third story* plan, *p p* show the positions of those for both the lower stories.

q, *q*, *q*, Childrens' chairs, arranged in the *second story*. Their form is represented in another diagram, (p. 181.)

r, *s*, *t*, Hot-air Flues from the Furnace, Cold-air Flues if Stoves are used, and Smoke Flues. These will be better understood by a reference to the diagram explanatory of the Chimney Pier, (p. 182.)

u, *u*, Cabinets for Minerals, Shells, and other objects of Natural History or Curiosity.

v, Door of Recitation-room. In *first story*, this door leads to the entry in which are the Sink, Brush-Closet, entrance to the Privies, and passage to Second Story. In *second story*, it leads to the Recitation-room where is the Teacher's Press-closet; and in the *third story*, to that in which are the Sink, entrance to the Privies, and Stairs to the Attic.

w, Teacher's Press-closet, fitted with shelves and brass clothes-hooks.

x, Closet for Brooms, Brushes, Coalhods, &c. That for the *first story* is under the Second-Story stairs.

a, a, a, Stairs to the Third Story.

b, b, Doors connecting First and Second, and Second and Third Stories.

f, Place for Fountain, in the centre of the Play-ground.

g, g, g, Grass-plats, or Flower-beds.

p, Passage from the First-Story Schoolroom to the Play-ground.

The Plan of the *second story*, on the next page, is drawn on a larger scale, for greater convenience in showing all the arrangements. The references on this diagram are more copious and minute than on either of the others.

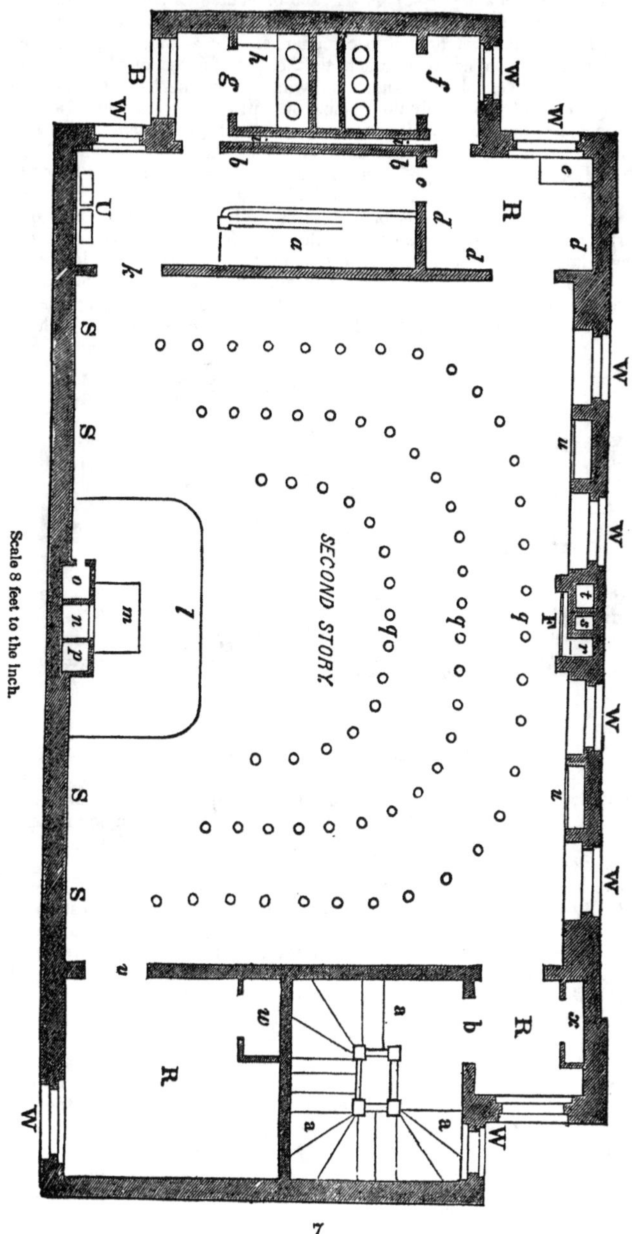

Scale 8 feet to the Inch.

The building fronts nearly N. N. E., and of course all the light comes into the Schoolrooms from the North. At the same time, in order to secure the benefit of the winds that prevail in Summer, and the admission of "a streak of sunshine," which adds so much to the cheerfulness of any room, and particularly of a schoolroom, there are windows in the back or southerly wall, opening into the recitation-rooms or entries, through which, and the entrance-doors, the sunlight finds its way into each schoolroom. The Neapolitan proverb, "Where the sun does not come, the physician must," has not been lost sight of; though it must be confessed that we have not been able to pay so much attention to it as would be desirable.

The next diagram, which is on the same scale with the first, will show the arrangement of the *third story*, which differs from the first and second in having a larger schoolroom, and more space for recitation-rooms; less space being occupied for stairways than in the other stories. The partitions at the ends are set one foot each way nearer to the ends of the building, making the Schoolroom thirty-two feet in length, while the others are only thirty.

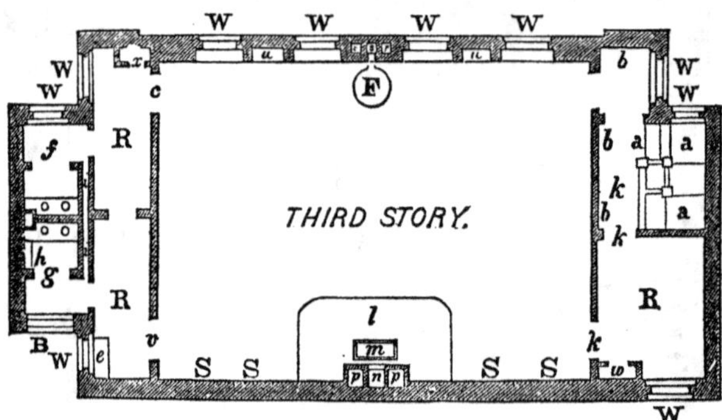

Scale 16 feet to the inch.

It will be seen, that the ends of the building are cut off from the schoolrooms, by entries, stairways, recitation-rooms, &c., and the back and end walls are left blank, for convenience in displaying Maps, Charts, Pictures, &c., and for the large Slates, used instead of Blackboards. As ample provision, as was practicable, has been made for recitation-rooms, closets, and other necessary conveniences.

It will be seen, from the Plans of the different Stories, that the Entrance-door (*k*) to each Schoolroom is in that part of the partition nearest to the back walls; so that, on entering the room, the Teacher's Platform is directly before the scholar or visiter. This Platform is six feet wide and twelve feet long, and is raised seven inches above the floor, that being a sufficient height to give the Teacher a full view of the whole school. In the transverse-sectional elevation, (p. 184,) the raised Platform is shown at P.

On this Platform, is a Table, (*m*,) instead of a Desk, that being the more convenient article for the Teacher's use. On it, are constantly kept, in full view of the scholars, THE LAWS OF THE SCHOOL,—the *Holy Bible*, the Rule and Guide of Life, the Moral and Religious Law; the *Dictionary*, the Law of Language, the Authority for Orthography and Orthoepy; and the *Rules and Regulations of the Committee*. These should be always on every Teacher's table or desk, and should be frequently appealed to. On this Table, also, are the Record Book of the School, Ink-standish, Table Bell, and other necessary articles.

In front of the Teacher's Platform, and facing it, arranged in a semi-circular form, as shown at *q q q*, in the Plan of the Second Story, are the Seats for the scholars. These are comfortable and convenient Arm-chairs, of which the annexed diagram shows the form. Each has a rack at the side (A) for convenience in holding the books or slates of the scholars. These chairs were the contrivance of Mr. Ingraham, and were introduced by him into the Primary Schools, in 1842, since which time, the Primary School Board have recommended their introduction into all their schools, in preference to any other seats, and about one hundred and thirty of the one hundred and sixty schools are now supplied with them. They are *not* fastened to the floor, but can be moved whenever necessary; and this is found to be a great convenience, and productive of no disadvantage. They have been strongly recommended by the Committees on School and Philosophical Apparatus, at the Exhibitions of the Massachusetts Charitable Mechanics' Association, in 1844 and 1847, and premiums were awarded for them in both those years.

The following diagram is an elevation of the Front wall of the Schoolroom, as seen from the Teacher's Platform. It is on the same scale with the preceding Plan of the Second Story,—eight feet to the inch.

Each Schoolroom is lighted by four windows; and in the central pier, between the windows, are the Cold-air and Chimney Flues, or the Furnace Flues. The Fire-place, or Furnace Flue, is represented at F, as in the preceding Plans of the different Stories. The arrangement of the Flues, in this pier, will be seen in the next diagram.

On the mantel-piece, over the Furnace Flue, is, in one room, a Vase of Native Grasses, or Flowers, and in the others, ornamental Statues, or Statuettes, furnished by the Teachers. Above this, suspended on the pier, is the Clock.

Between the other windows, are Cabinets, for the reception of Minerals, Shells, and other objects of Natural History or Curiosity. Their location is seen at *u u*, in the Plans of the respective Stories. There are two of these Cabinets in each Schoolroom, between the windows, above the skirting, and as high as the windows, with double sash-doors, of cherry-wood, hung with brass hinges, fastened with thumb-slides and locks, and fitted with rosewood knobs. There are twelve shelves in each, six of them being inclined, with narrow ledges on each, to prevent the specimens from rolling off. Immediately below them are small Closets, with four shelves in each, and double doors, hung and fastened in the same manner as the sash doors.

The Blinds of the Second Story, represented in this diagram, are framed, two parts to each window, and are hung with weights and pulleys, in the same manner as the window sashes. They run up above the tops of the windows, and behind the skirting of the next story above, in close boxes, and have rings on the bottom rails, to draw them down. In this elevation, they are shown in different positions. The windows in the First Story are fitted with Venetian Blinds, and those in the Third Story with Inside Shutter-Blinds.

All the window-stools are wide, and contain Vases of Native Grasses, or Flowers.

Particular attention has been given to the mode of Heating and Ventilating these buildings; and provision has been made for a copious and constant supply of fresh air, from out-of-doors, which is so introduced, that it is sufficiently warmed before it enters the Schoolrooms.

The Sheafe-street building is heated by one of Chilson's largest-sized Furnaces; though it was originally constructed with a view to using Dr. Clark's excellent Ventilating Stoves, as in the other two buildings.*

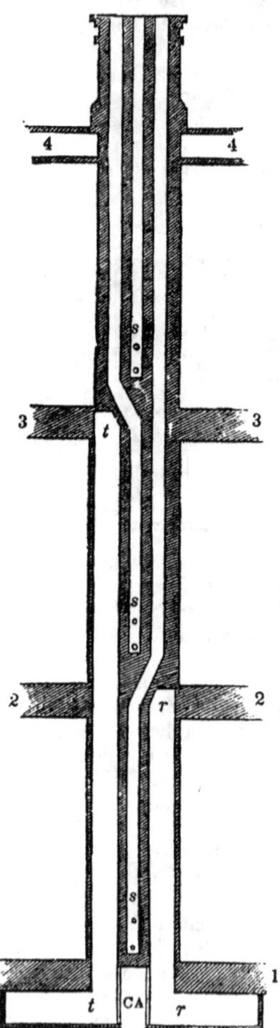

Scale 10 feet to the inch.

The accompanying diagram shows the arrangement of the Cold-air and Smoke Flues, as arranged for the Stoves. It will be well to examine it in connection with the transverse-sectional elevation, (p. 184,) and the Floor Plans of the different Stories, (pp. 177, 179, 180.)

1, 2, 3, Floorings of the First, Second, and Third Stories. 4, Roof.

CA, Cold-air Flue for First Story, which delivers the air from without, under the Stove, as shown at C A, in the transverse-section, (p. 184,) and at F, in the floor-plans.

r, *r*, Cold-air Flue for Second Story, which empties into the box under the Stove, at CA, in the Second Story of the transverse-sectional elevation. It corresponds to *r*, in the Floor Plans of the *first* and *second stories*.

t, *t*, Cold-air Flue for Third Story, which empties into the box CA, under the Stove of that Story, as seen in the transverse-sectional elevation, and at F, in the Floor Plan. It corresponds to *t*, in the Floor Plans.

These Cold-air Ducts are twelve by eighteen inches, *inside*, and are *smoothly* plastered, throughout. This is hardly large enough, however.

s, *s*, Smoke Flues. That of First Story corresponds to *s*, in the floor plan of *first story*, and to *r*, in those of the *second* and *third*. That of Second Story corresponds to *s*, in *second-story* Plan, and to *t*, in *third-story* Plan. That of Third Story corresponds to *s*, on the Plan of that Story.

These Smoke Flues are eight inches square, *inside*, and are *smoothly* plastered, throughout. That of each Story commences in the centre of the pier in the room to which it belongs.

[The pier in which these Cold-air Ducts and Smoke Flues are placed, is wider than the piers between the other windows, in order to allow sufficient width to the Ducts. It must be at least six feet.]

It will be seen, from the transverse-sectional elevation, (p. 184,) (the Smoke Flue in which is represented as continuous, it not being practicable to show the bends,) as well as from the Plans of each Story, that the arrangements for Ventilation are directly opposite the Chimney Flues. The Ventiducts are contained in the projecting pier back of the Teachers' Platforms and Tables shown at *l*, *m*, in the Floor Plans.

It has already been stated, that particular attention has been paid to the

* Descriptions and Plans of this Furnace and Stove will be found on page 148.

mode of Ventilation; and it is believed that the system, if not perfect, is better adapted to its purpose than any other. The Ventiduct for each room is of sufficient size for the room; and the three are arranged as shown in the next diagram. It will be seen, that the Ventiduct for each room is in the centre of the pier, thus avoiding any unsymmetrical or one-sided (and of course unsightly) appearance.

1, 2, 3, 4, Floorings of the First, Second, and Third Stories, and Attic. 5, Roof.

c, c, c, Ventiduct of First Story, commencing in the centre of the pier. Between the ceiling of this room and the floor of the Second Story, this flue is turned to the left, and then continues in a straight line to the Attic, where it contracts and empties into the Ventilator *V*, on the Roof.

d, d, d, Ventiduct of Second Story, also commencing in the centre of the pier, and turning to the right, between the ceiling of the Second and floor of the Third Story, whence it is continued to the Attic, and empties into the Ventilator *V*.

e, e, Ventiduct of Third Story, also emptying into *V*.

These Ventiducts are made of thoroughly seasoned pine boards, smooth on the inside, and put together with two-inch screws. Each, as will be seen, is placed in the centre of the room to which it belongs. They are *kept entirely separate from each other*, through their whole length, from their bases to the point where they are discharged into the Ventilators on the Roof. Each is sixteen inches square *inside*, through its whole length to the Attic. where, as will be seen by the diagram, each is made narrower as it approaches its termination, till it is only eight inches in width, on the front, the three together measuring twenty-five inches, the diameter of the base of the Ventilator on the roof. As they are contracted, however, in this direction, they are gradually enlarged from back to front, so that each is increased from sixteen to twenty-four inches, the three together then forming a square of twenty-five inches, and fitting the base of the Ventilator into which they are discharged. The increase in this direction will be better seen in the Elevation on p. 184, where V V represents one Ventiduct, continued from the lower floor to the Ventilator.

V, Ventilator, on the Roof, into which the three Ventiducts from the schoolrooms are discharged. This is twenty-five inches in diameter.*

v, v, Registers, to regulate the draught of air through the Ventiducts. There are two of these in each Ventiduct,—one at the bottom, to carry off the lower and heavier stratum of foul air, which always settles near the floor; and the other near the ceiling of the room, for the escape of the lighter impure air, which ascends with the heat to the top of the room. Each of these Registers has a swivel-blind, fitted with a stay-rod, and may be easily opened or closed by the Teacher.

o, o, Closets. The Ventiduct of each Story being in the centre of the projecting pier, affords room for Closets, on each side in the First Story, and on one side in the Second Story, as shown at *o o*. There are four in the First Story, two above and two below the wainscot. In the Second Story, there are two only, one above and the other below the wainscot; the other side of the pier being occupied by the Ventiduct of the First Story. In the Third Story there are of course none.

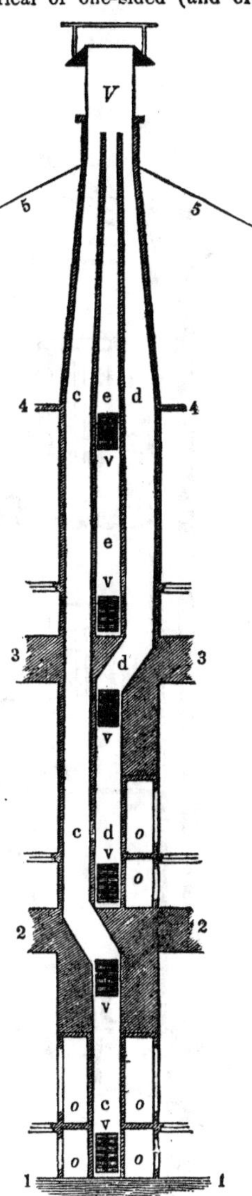

Scale 10 feet to the inch.

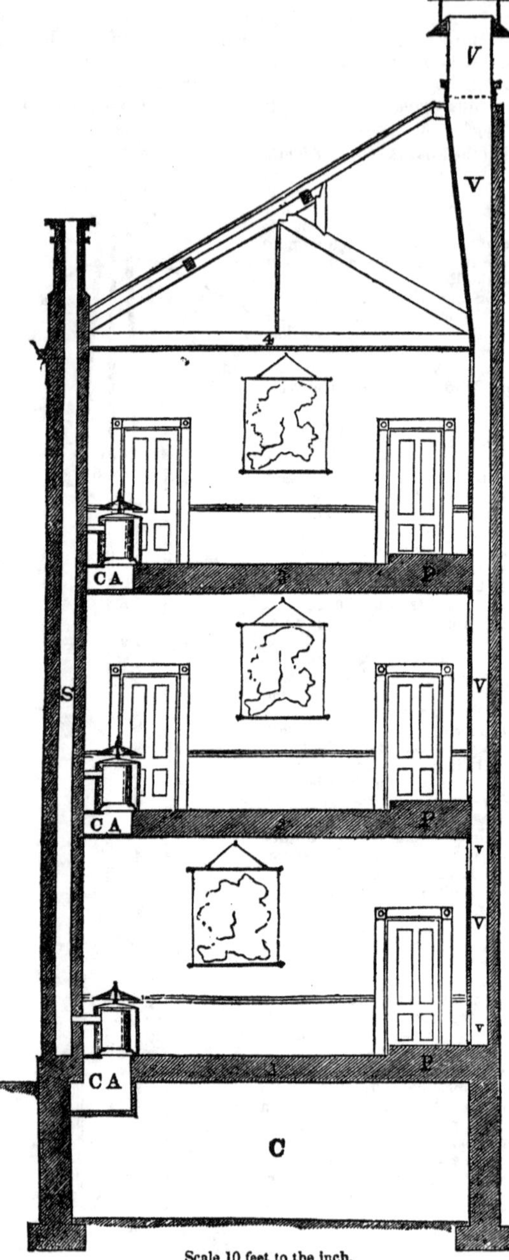

Scale 10 feet to the inch.

1, 2, 3, 4, Floorings of the First Second, and Third, Stories, and the Attic.

C, The Cellar.

C A, Cold-air Boxes, opening under the Stoves.

S, Smoke Flue.

P, Teachers' Platforms.

V, Ventiduct, emptying into the Ventilator on the Roof.

v, v, Ventiduct Registers.

V, Ventilator.

This plan of arranging the Heating and Ventilating apparatus has been adopted by the Committee on Ventilation of the Grammar School Board;* but as their plans and diagrams were taken from Mr. Ingraham's first draughts, before his final arrangement was decided upon, they are not so complete as these.

The preceding diagram gives a transverse-sectional elevation of the building.

It has already been stated, that the children are seated with their backs to the light, and their faces towards the Teacher's Table and the wall above and on either side of it. On this wall, and also on the two end walls, (as shown in the transverse-section,) are suspended Maps, Charts, and Pictures, not only for ornament, but for the communication of instruction. Vases of Flowers and Native Grasses ornament the window-stools and the Teachers' Tables; and Statuettes and other useful ornaments and decorations are placed in various parts of the rooms: so that whatever meets the eyes of the children is intended to convey useful and pleasing impressions, encouraging and gratifying the love of the beautiful, and combining the useful with the agreeable. The Cabinets of Minerals, Shells, and other objects of Natural History and Curiosity, add much to the interest and beauty of the rooms.

On the back wall, on either side of the Teacher's Platform, at S S S S, are four large Slates, in cherry-wood frames, each two and a half by four feet, used instead of Blackboards. These Slates are far preferable to the *best* Blackboards, and cost about the same as common ones. The Teachers greatly prefer them to Blackboards. In using them, slate pencils are of course employed, instead of chalk or crayons, and thus the dust and dirt of the chalk or crayons,—which is not only disagreeable to the senses, but deleterious to health, by being drawn into the lungs,—are avoided. These Slates may be procured in Boston, of A. Wilbur.

Each School has convenient Recitation-rooms; though, in consequence of the space occupied by the stairs to the Second and Third Stories, the lower Story is not so conveniently accommodated, in this respect, as could be desired. It has, however, two good Entries, which are used for this purpose. In the Second and Third Stories, there are three of these rooms, of which much use is made. Their location is shown in the Floor Plans.

In these ante-rooms, are Closets for Brooms, Brushes, and other necessary articles of that description, and also Press-closets, furnished with shelves and brass clothes-hooks, for the Teachers' private use. In these, also, are Sinks, furnished with drawers and cupboards, pails, basins and ewers, mugs, &c. Pipes leading from the Sinks, convey the waste water into the Vaults; and in a short time, the waters of Lake Cochituate will be led into each Story.

Each School has its own separate entrance; so that they will not interfere with each other. And each is provided with sufficient conveniences in its entry, for hanging the clothing of the pupils, thus avoiding the necessity of its ever being brought into the Schoolroom. Each has also two Umbrella-stands in its entry.

In the Cellar, are placed the Furnace, and necessary conveniences attached to it, with Bins for coal and wood. Also two Rain-water Butts, one at each end, which receive all the water from the Roofs. Being connected with each other, by leaden pipes, under ground, the water in both stands at the same level; and a pipe, leading from the top of one of them into the Vault, prevents their ever running over.

The Cellar is paved with brick, and is convenient for a play-room, when the weather is too stormy for the children to go out of doors at recess-time

Instead of having the usual out-door conveniences in the yard, they are here connected with the entries of the respective schoolrooms, so that no child has to go into the open air, except for play in recess-time, or to go

home. This is considered a very great convenience, and a matter of the highest importance.

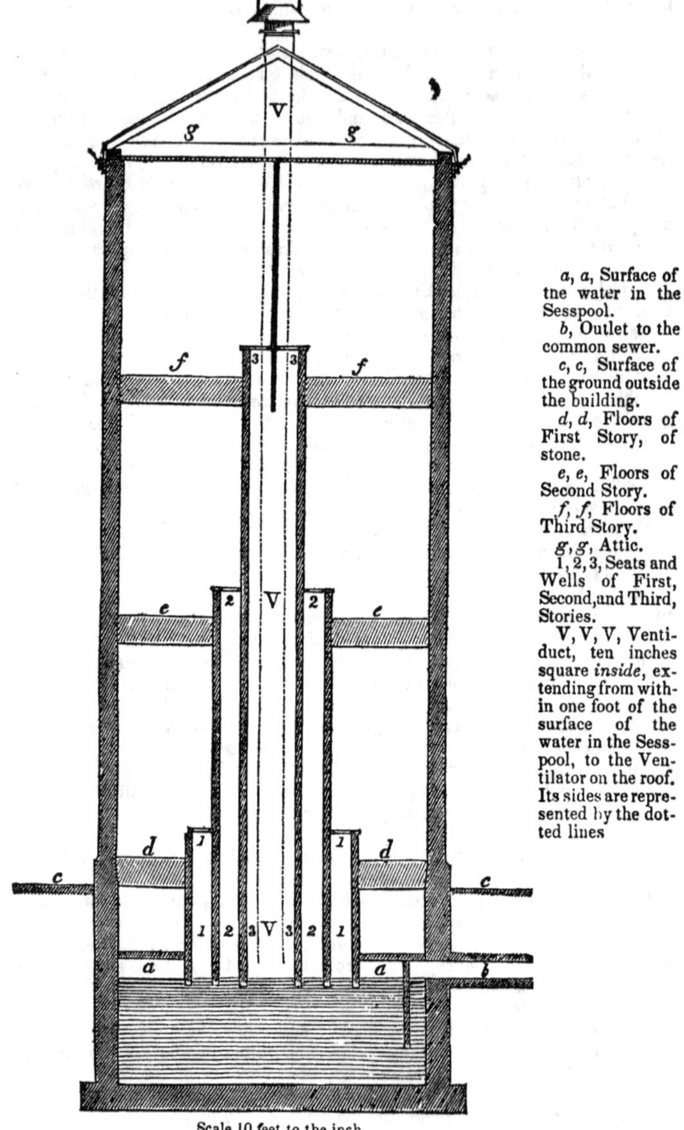

Scale 10 feet to the inch.

The preceding transverse-section will show the peculiar arrangement of the Privies to the different stories, and the manner in which all unpleasant consequences or inconveniences are, it is believed, effectually guarded against.

By the Plans of the different Stories, it will be seen, that the Privies are in a Projection on the western end of the building, the wall of which is separated from that of the main building, by the space *i i*, this space being four inches between the walls, and extending from the floor of the First Story to the Attic. The doors leading from the entries are kept closed, by strong springs; and at B, in the southern wall, is a Blind, through which the air constantly passes into this space, and up to the Attic, whence it is conveyed in a tight box to the Ventilator on the Roof. Except in very cold or stormy weather, the window in the northern side is kept open, (the outer blinds being closed,) and thus the whole of the Projection is cut off from the main building by external air. The space between the Projection and the main building is not, however, so great as it would have been made, had there been more room.

It will be seen, that there is a distinct Well to each Privy, separated from the others by a brick wall ending *below* the surface of the water in the sesspool. Of course, the only odor that can possibly come into either of the apartments, must come from the well of *that* apartment, there being no communication with any other, except through the water. And as every time it rains, or water is thrown in from the sinks, the water in the sesspool will be changed, and washed into the common sewer, it would seem that no danger of unpleasant odor need be feared. When the City water is carried to every floor of the building, the conveniences for frequently washing out the sesspool will be greatly increased.

There are two apartments on each floor; one for the girls, at *f*, and another for the boys, at *g*. In the latter, is a trough, (*h*,) with a sesspool, and pipe leading into the well, under the seat. There is no window in the boys' apartment, but merely the blind, B, which extends from the floor to the ceiling. The girls' apartment, being in the front part of the Projection, is provided with a window similar to the others, and outside blinds.

Each apartment is fitted with pine risers, seats, and covers. The covers are hung with stout duck or India-rubber cloth, instead of metal hinges, which would be liable to corrode, and are so arranged that they will fall of themselves, when left. The edges of the cloth are covered with narrow slats. There is a box for paper in each apartment. The whole finish is equal to that of any other part of the building.

The interior plastering of all the walls of the building is hard-finished, suitably for being painted.

All the Rooms, Entries, Stairways, and Privies, are skirted up as high as the window-stools, with narrow matched beaded lining, gauged to a width not exceeding seven inches, and *set perpendicularly*.

The interior wood-work of the lower Schoolroom, as well as the interior of all the Closets and Cabinets, is painted white. The skirting of the Secono Story is of maple, unpainted, but varnished. All the rest of the inside wood-work is painted and grained in imitation of maple, and varnished. The outside doors are painted bronze. The blinds are painted with four coats of Paris green, and varnished.

In some other schoolrooms in the City, the interior wood-work,—even of common white pine,—has been left unpainted, but varnished, with a very good effect; and it is contemplated to have some of the new Schoolhouses soon to be erected, finished in the same way. White pine, stained with asphaltum, and varnished, presents a beautiful finish, and is cheaper than painting or graining.

In the angles formed by the meeting of the walls with the ceiling of each room, and entirely around the room, are placed rods, fitted with moveable rings, for convenience in suspending maps, charts, and pictures, and to avoid the necessity of driving nails into the walls.

Plan and Description of Bowdoin Grammar School-House.

The new Bowdoin School-house, completed in 1848, is situated on Myrtle street, and with the yard occupies an area of about 75 feet by 68 feet, bounded on each of the four sides by a street. It is built of brick with a basement story of hammered granite, and measures 75 feet 9 inches extreme length by 54 feet 6 inches extreme breadth—having three stories, the first and second being 13 feet, and the third, 15 feet high in the clear. The ground descends rapidly from Myrtle street, thereby securing a basement of 15 feet in the rear. One third of which is finished into entries, or occupied by three furnaces, coal bins, pumps, &c., and the remaining two thirds is open to the yard, thereby affording a covered play-ground for the pupils.

The third story is finished into one hall 72 feet long by 38 feet wide, with seats and desks for 180 pupils. On the south side of this hall there are two recitation rooms, each 16 feet by 12 feet, and a room for a library, &c. There are three rooms of the same size on the two floors below.

The second story is divided into two rooms by a partition wall, each of which is 35 feet by 38, and accommodates 90 pupils, and so connected by sliding doors that all the pupils of both schools can be brought under the eye and voice of the teacher.

The first story corresponds to the second, except there are no sliding doors in the partition, and no connection between the room except through the front entry. The two rooms on this floor have each seats and desks for 100 pupils.

Each story is thoroughly ventilated, and warmed by one of Chilson's Furnaces. In each furnace the air chambers, the apertures for conducting the cold air into them, and the flues for constructing the heated air into the rooms in each story, being all large, a great quantity of warm air is constantly rushing into the rooms, and the ventilating flues or ventiducts being so constructed and arranged that the air of the rooms will be frequently changed, and that a pure and healthy atmosphere will at all times be found in each of these rooms, provided the furnaces are properly and judiciously managed. On the top of the building there are two of Emerson's large ventilators, connected with the attic and ventilating flues, through which the impure air passes out into the atmosphere above.

To accommodate pupils who come to school with wet feet or clothes, there is an open fire in a grate in one of the recitation rooms.

Each room is furnished with Wales' American School Chair, and Ross's Desk, and both desk and chair are in material, form and style, as described on page 202 and 205.

This is a school for girls only, and consists of two departments, one of which is called the Grammar department, and the other the Writing department; the master of each department being independent of the other.

The number of assistant female teachers in each department of this school, when full, will be four, the teachers in each department being independent of the master and teacher in the other.

The master of the Grammar department and two of his assistants will occupy the large hall in the third story, and his other two assistants will occupy one of the rooms in the first story.

The master of the writing department and two of his assistants will occupy the rooms in the second story, and his other two assistants will occupy the other room in the first story, each master being the superintendence of his own department.

The school, when full, will be divided into five classes, and each class into two divisions, nearly equal in numbers. The first week after the vacation in August, the first division of each class will attend in the grammar department in the morning, and the second division of each class will attend in the writing department; and in the afternoon, the second division of each class will attend in the grammar department, and the first, in the writing department. The next week, this order of attendance is to be reversed, and this alteration is to continue through the year, the weeks of vacation not being counted.

This house and the Quincy Grammar School-house are built after designs by Mr. Bryant.

PLAN OF FIRST AND SECOND FLOOR.

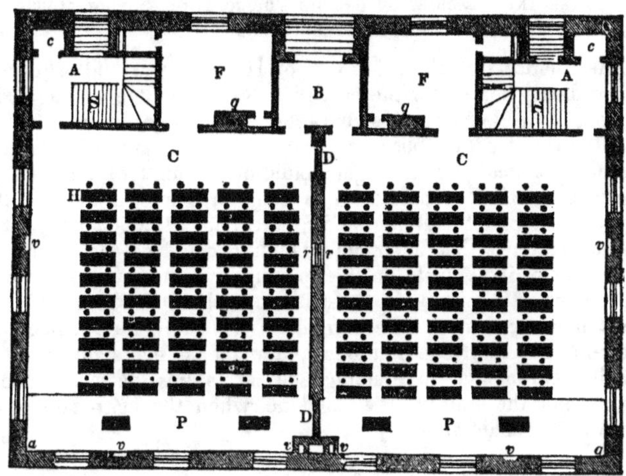

A, A, Entrance for Pupils.
B, Ditto for Teacher.
C, C, Study halls, each 35 by 38 feet; with seats and desks for 100 pupils.
D, Sliding door, by which the two rooms on the second floor are thrown into one.
E, Study hall, 72 feet by 38.
F, F, Two recitation rooms on each floor, 16 feet by 12.
G, Room 10 feet by 12, for library, apparatus, &c.
H, Ross' desk, and Wales' chair.
P, Teacher's platform with desk for teacher and assistants.
S, S, Staircase leading to second and third floors.
a, Case with glass doors for apparatus.
c, Closet for Teacher.
q, Grate.
r, Hot air register.
v, Flues for ventilation.

PLAN OF THIRD FLOOR.

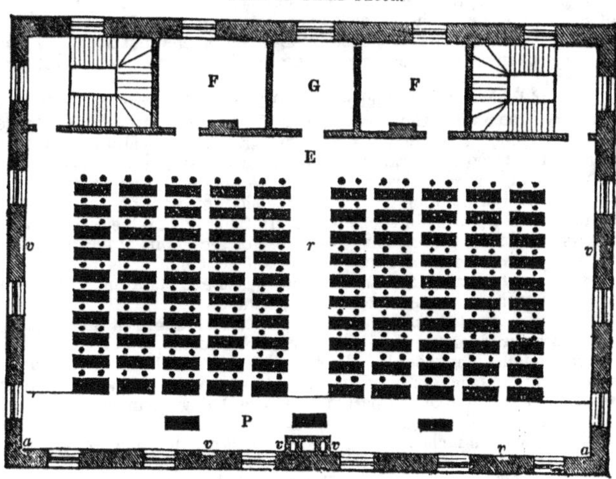

Plans and Description of the Public High School-House, Hartford, Conn.

The Public High School-House of Hartford was built after more than ordinary search for the best plan, (a committee having visited Boston, Lowell, Salem, Newburyport, Worcester, Providence, and Middletown, for this purpose,) under the constant oversight of a prudent, practical and intelligent building committee, and with due regard to a wise economy. The committee were limited in their expenditure for lot, building, and fixtures, to $12,000; and when it was ascertained that a suitable building could not be constructed for that sum, individuals on the committee immediately contributed $2,400 out of their own pockets to complete the house with the latest improvements. The committee have now the satisfaction of knowing that their contributions and personal oversight have been mainly instrumental in erecting and furnishing the most complete structure of the kind in New England, when the aggregate cost is taken into consideration.

The High School is designed for both males and females, and the arrangements of the buildings, and the grounds, are made with reference to the separation of the sexes, so far as this is desirable in the same school.

The lot on which the building stands is at the corner of Asylum and Ann streets, and is at once central, and large enough for the appropriate yards. The yards are separated by a close and substantial board fence, and the grounds are well laid out and properly inclosed; they will also soon be planted with trees and shrubbery. The building is of brick, three stories high, upon a firm stone basement. Its dimensions are 50 by 75 feet. The basement is 13 feet in the clear, six feet of which are above the level of the yard. This part of the building is occupied by furnaces, coal bins, sinks, pumps, entrance rooms, &c. At one end, and on two opposite sides of the building, a stair case eleven feet in width extends from each of the two entrance rooms, to the upper story, with spacious landings on the first and second floors. Two rooms, each 11 by 14 feet, are between the stair cases, the one on the first floor being used for a front entry to the building, and the one on the second floor being appropriated to the Library and Apparatus. Two closets, eleven by four feet on the first floor, and immediately beneath the stair cases, receive the outer garments, umbrellas, &c., of the teachers.

An aisle of four feet four inches in width extends between the desks and outer walls of the rooms, and between every two ranges of desks is an aisle of two feet four inches in width. An aisle of eight feet in width passes through the middle of the rooms, parallel to the narrower passages. A space of five feet in width is likewise reserved between the remote seats in the ranges and the partition wall of the rooms. Around the sides of the rooms, tastefully constructed settees are placed for occasional recitations, and for the accommodation of visiters, and in the upper room for the use of the pupils of the room below, during the opening and closing exercises of the school.

The pupils, when seated, face the teachers' desks and platforms, which occupy the space between the entrance doors of each room.

A blackboard, or black plaster surface, forty feet long, and five broad, extends between the doors leading to the recitation rooms, which are also lined with a continuous blackboard. There is also a blackboard extending the entire length of the teachers' platform in the lower room, and two of smaller dimensions in the room above, a part of the space being occupied by the folding doors leading to the library and apparatus room. Twenty chairs, of small dimensions and sixteen inches in height, are placed around each recitation room, thirteen inches apart and seven inches from the walls, and securely fastened to the floor. A clock, with a circular gilt frame and eighteen-inch dial plate, is placed over the teachers' platform in each school room, in full view of the pupils. A small bell is also placed above the teachers' platform in the lower room, with a wire attached, passing to the desk of the Principal, in the room above, by which the time of recesses, change of recitation classes, &c., are signified to the members of the lower rooms.

The school-rooms in the first and second stories are 50 feet square, and 13 feet in height—to each of which, two recitation rooms 12 by 23 feet are attached. The large rooms are furnished with "Kimball's improved School Chairs and Desks," placed in six ranges, extending back from the teachers' platforms, ten desks forming a range, and two chairs attached to each desk, furnishing accommodations in each room for 120 pupils—60 of either sex. Ample room yet remains in front of these ranges to increase the number of desks when the wants of the school demand them. The desks are four feet in length and one foot four inches in breadth, constructed of cherry, oiled and varnished. The moderately inclined tops are *fixed* to the end supporters, and the openings for books are in front of the pupils. Glass inkstands are inserted in the tops of the desks, and the ink protected from dust and the action of the atmosphere by mahogany covers turning on pivots. The chairs are constructed with seats of basswood, hollowed, and backs of cherry, moulded both to add beauty to the form of the chair, and to afford support and comfort to the occupants. All are neatly stained and varnished, and they, as well as the desks, rest on iron supporters, firmly screwed to the floor.

The entire upper story is converted into a hall, being twelve feet in height at the walls, rising thence in an arch to the height of seventeen feet. This is appropriated to reading, and declamation, and for the female department of the school, to daily recess, and calisthenic exercises. A moderately raised platform is located at one end, above which an extended blackboard is placed, and settees are ranged around the walls; these, properly arranged, together with the settees from the lower rooms, which are easily transported above, speedily convert the open *Hall* into a commodious Lecture room,—and also adapt it to the purposes of public examinations and exhibitions.

In each of the two entrance rooms are placed the means of cleanliness and comfort,—a pump of the most approved construction, an ample sink, two wash basins with towels, glass drinking tumblers, and a looking-glass. Ranges of hooks for hats, coats, bonnets, cloaks, &c., extend around the rooms, and are numbered to correspond with the number of pupils, of each sex, which the capacity of the house will accommodate. In the girls' room, pairs of small iron hooks are placed directly beneath the bonnet hooks, and twelve inches from the floor, for holding the over-shoes. In the boys' room, boot-jacks are provided to facilitate the exchange of boots for slippers when they enter the building—an important article, and of which no one in this department of the school is destitute. A thin plank, moderately inclined by hollowing the upper side, is placed upon the floor, and extends around the walls of the room, to receive the boots and convey the melted ice and snow from them, by a pipe, beneath the floor. A large umbrella stand is furnished in each of the two entrance rooms, also with pipes for conveying away the water. Stools are secured to the floors for convenience in exchanging boots, shoes, &c. Directly under the stairs is an OMNIUM GATHERUM—an appropriate vessel, in which are carefully deposited shreds of paper, and whatever comes under the denomination of *litter*, subject, of course, to frequent removal. These rooms, in common with the others, are carefully warmed. The wainscoting of the entrance rooms, and the stair case, is formed of narrow boards, grooved and tongued, placed perpendicularly, and crowned with a simple moulding. The railing of the stair case is of black walnut. A paneled wainscoting reaching from the floor to the base of the windows, extends around the walls of the remaining rooms. All the wood work, including the library and apparatus cases, is neatly painted, oak-grained, and varnished. The teachers' tables are made of cherry, eight feet in length, and two feet four inches in breadth, with three drawers in each, and are supported on eight legs. A movable writing desk of the same material is placed on each. Immediately in front of the teachers' desk in the upper room, a piano is to be placed, for use during the opening and closing exercises of the school, and for the use of the young ladies during the recesses. Venetian window blinds with rolling slats, are placed inside the windows, and being of a slight buff color, they modify the light without imparting a sombre hue to the room.

The ventilation of the school-rooms, or the rapid discharge of the air which has become impure by respiration, is most thoroughly secured in connection with a constant influx of pure warm air from the furnaces, by discharging ventiducts or flues, situated on each side of the building at the part of the rooms most distant from the registers of the furnaces. The ventiducts of each room are eighteen inches in diameter, and are carried from the floor entirely separate to the Stationary Top, or Ejector above the roof. The openings into the ventiducts, both at the top and bottom of the room, are two feet square, and are governed by a sliding door or blind.

Fig. 2—Ground Plan, Yard, Basement, &c.

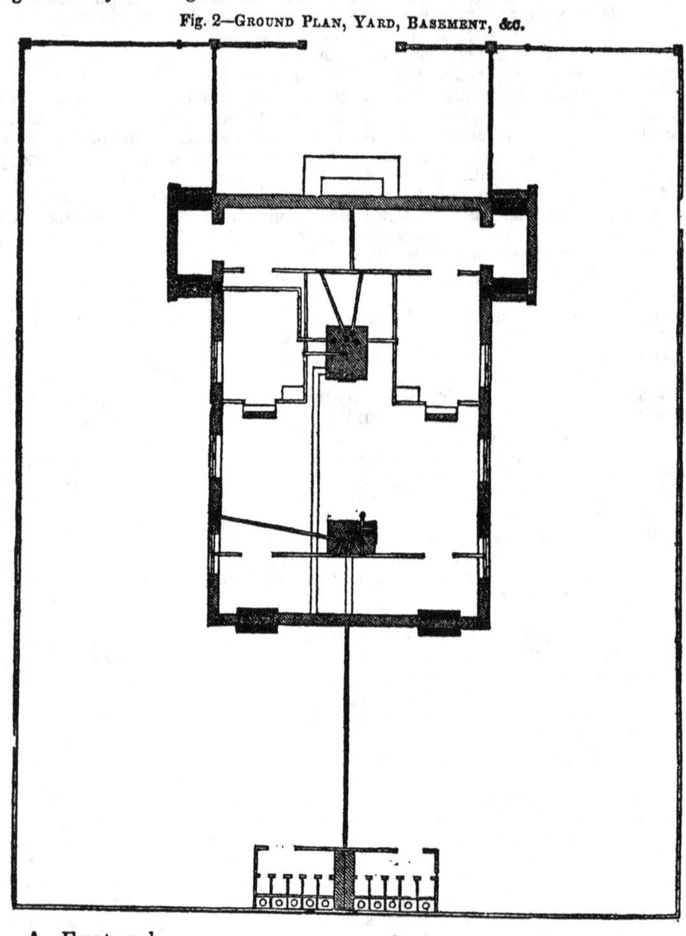

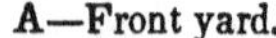

A—Front yard.
B—Girls' yard.
C—Boys' yard.
D—Door.
E—Boys' entrance rooms.
G—Girls' entrance rooms.
F—Furnace.
S—Stairs.
W—Windows.
P—Privies, with screen, doors, &c.
X—Gates.

a—Cold air ducts.
b—Warm air ducts.
c—Foul air ducts or ventilating flues.
d—Smoke pipe.
e—Pump, sink.
f—Umbrella stand.
g—Hollowed plank to receive wet boots, overshoes, &c.
o—Bins for hard coal, charcoal, &c.
j—Close board fence.

Figs. 5 and 6. PLANS EXHIBITING MODE OF VENTILATION.

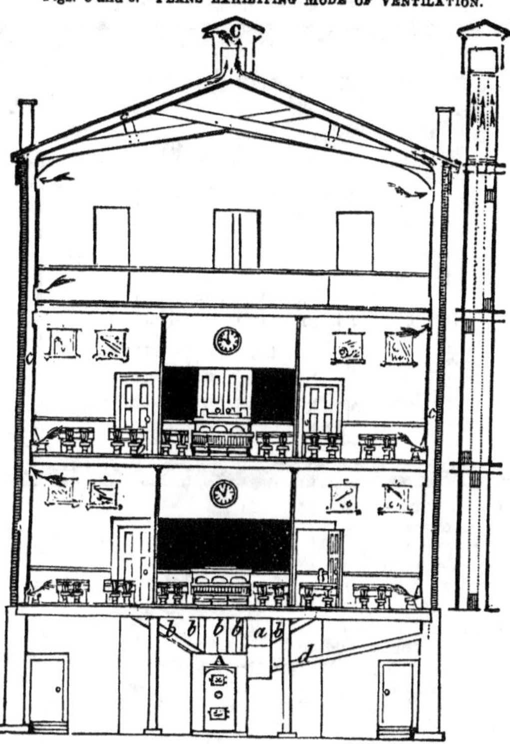

Fig. 5. Transverse section exhibiting the manner in which the ventiducts or hot air flues are carried up on the inside of the walls, under the roof, till they discharge into the Stationary Top or Ejector.

Fig. 6. Lateral section of the ventiducts or foul air flues, showing the manner in which the flues are packed together and carried up separately from the floor of each room until they discharge into the common Ejector. The cut does not represent properly the manner in which the flues are carried under and out of the roof.

Fig. 3.

Fig. 2.

Each desk is fitted up with a glass ink-well (Fig. 2,) set firmly into the desk, and covered with a lid. The ink-well may be set into a cast iron box (Fig. 3,) having a cover; the box being let in and screwed to the desk, and the ink-well being removable for convenience in filling, cleaning, and emptying in cold weather.

Fig. 3—Plan of First Floor.

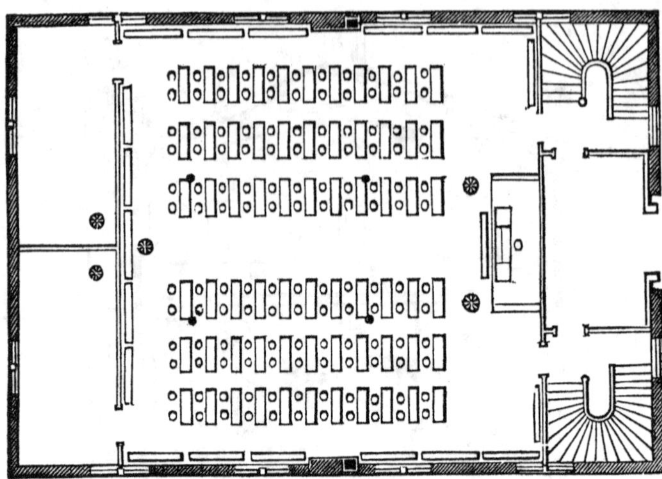

A—Front entrance.
B—Girls' entrance.
C—Boys' entrance.
I—Centre aisle, eight feet.
L—Aisle between each range of seats and desks, two feet four inches.
K—Side aisle, four feet four inches.
M—Space five feet wide.
T—Teachers' platform and desk.
R—Recitation rooms, each twenty-three feet by twelve, furnished with twenty chairs, seven inches from the wall and thirteen inches apart.
S—Library and apparatus, from eleven feet by fourteen feet.
N—Kimball's desk and two chairs.
O—Piano.
r—Hot air registers.
c—Ventilating flue or foul air duct.

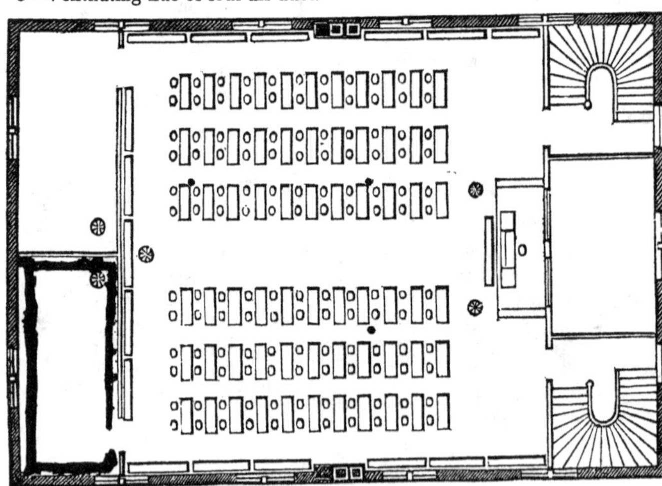

Fig. 4—Plan of Second Floor.

Plans and Description of the Putnam Free School-House, Newburyport, Mass.

We are indebted to W. H. Wells, Esq., the gentleman who has been selected as Principal of the Putnam Free School, and to whom the work of organizing this important institution has been committed, for the following plans and description.

The Putnam Free School was founded by Mr. Oliver Putnam, a native of Newbury. It has a permanent fund of fifty thousand dollars, besides the amount invested in the school-house and its appurtenances.

The number of pupils to be admitted at the opening of the school (April, 1848,) is limited by the Trustees to 80. No pupil can be received under twelve years of age, nor for less time than one year.

The object of the Institution is to lead pupils through an extended course of English study. It is open to students from any portion of the country, who are prepared to meet the requirements for admission. No charge is made for tuition.

This building is situated on High street, directly opposite the Common or Mall. It is constructed of brick, with corners, door-sills, underpinning, steps, etc., of freestone. It is two stories in height, exclusive of a basement story, 85½ feet in length, and 52½ in breadth.

The upper story is divided into two principal school-rooms, each 49½ feet by 40½. There is also a small room in this story for the use of the Principal. The lower story contains a hall for lectures and other general exercises, and four recitation rooms. The hall is 44 feet by 48½. Two of the recitation rooms are 14 feet by 17, and two are 11 by 20.

Each of the principal school-rooms is furnished with 64 single seats and desks, besides recitation chairs, settees, etc. The desks are made of cherry; and both the desks and the chairs are supported by iron castings, screwed firmly to the floor. In form and construction, they are similar to Kimball's "Improved School Chairs and Desks."

The central aisles are two feet and eight inches in width; the side aisles, four feet and four inches; and the remaining aisles, two feet.

The building is warmed by two furnaces. It is ventilated by six flues from the hall on the lower floor, six from each of the school-rooms on the second floor, and one from each of the recitation rooms. Each of these flues has two registers; one near the floor, and the other near the ceiling. The two principal school-rooms are furnished with double windows.

The institution is provided with ample play-grounds and garden plots, back of the building and at the ends. It has also a bell weighing 340 lbs.

The first appropriation of the Trustees for the purchase of apparatus, is one thousand dollars. Other appropriations will probably be made, as the wants of the school may require. In addition to the apparatus procured by the Trustees, the institution is to have the use of an achromatic telescope, which will cost between three and four hundred dollars.

The cost of the building and ground, with the various appurtenances, exclusive of apparatus, has amounted to twenty-six thousand dollars.

The accompanying plans give a correct representation of the arrangements on the two principal floors.

The building was erected after designs and specifications by Mr. Bryant, Architect, Boston.

PUTNAM FREE SCHOOL-HOUSE.—LOWER STORY.

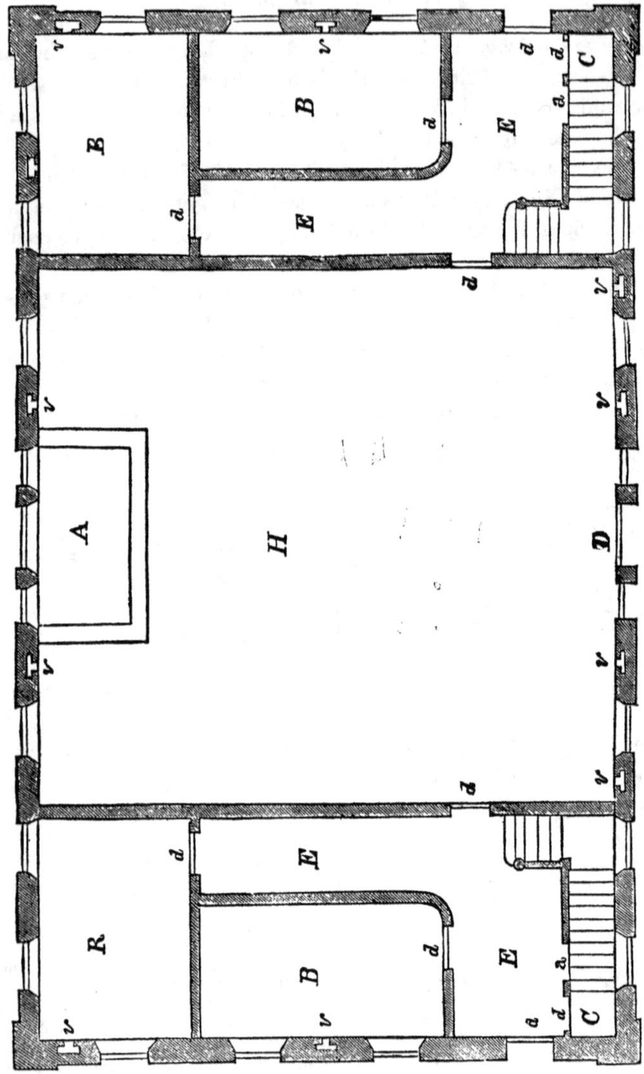

H—Hall for lectures and other general exercises, 44 feet by 48½. A—Raised platform for desk. D—Front door. (The portico in front does not appear in the plate.) B, B—Recitation rooms, 11 feet by 20. R, R—Recitation rooms, 14 feet by 17. E, E, E, E—Entries. C, C—Wash closets, under the stairs. a, a—Doors leading to the basement story. d, d, d, d, d, d, d, d, d, d—Doors. v, v, v, v, v, v, v, v, v, v.—Ventilating flues.

PUTNAM FREE SCHOOL-HOUSE.—UPPER STORY.

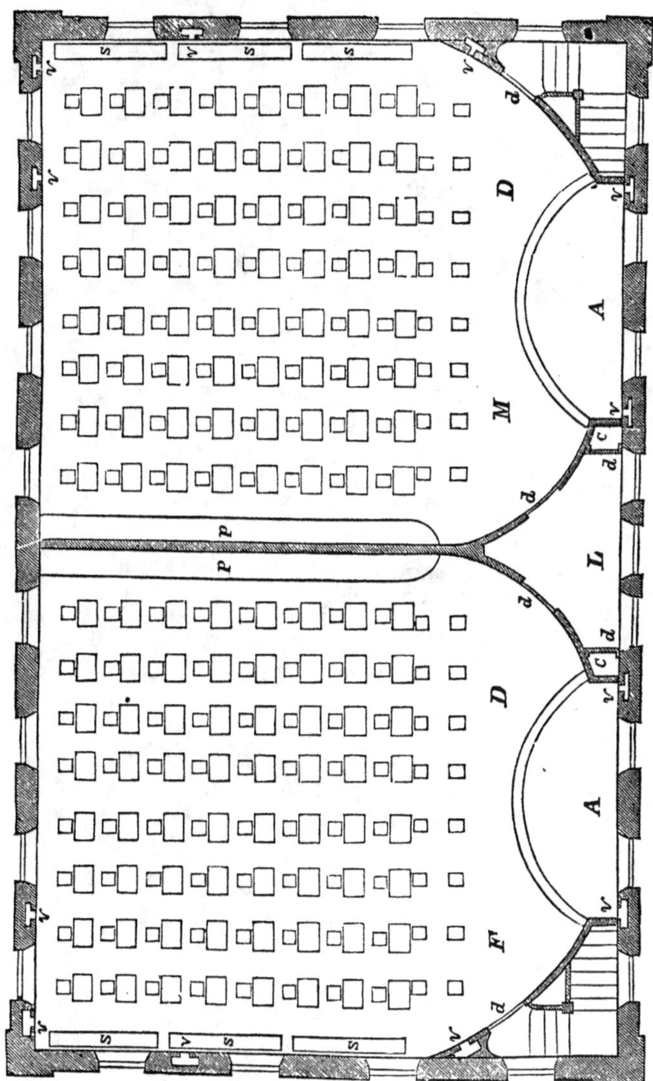

M. D—Room for Male Department. F, D—Room for Female Department. A, A—Raised platforms for teachers' desks. L—Principal's room. C, C—Closets. p, p—Raised platforms under the black-boards. s, s, s, s, s, s—Settees. d, d, d, d, d, d—Doors. v, v, v, v, v, v, v, v, v, v, v, v—Ventilating flues.

Plans and Description of the Academy Building, Rome, N. Y.

We are indebted to Edward Huntington, Esq., for the following plans and description of the new Academy building recently erected in Rome, N. Y., under his supervision. The building is 70 feet by 44 feet on the ground.

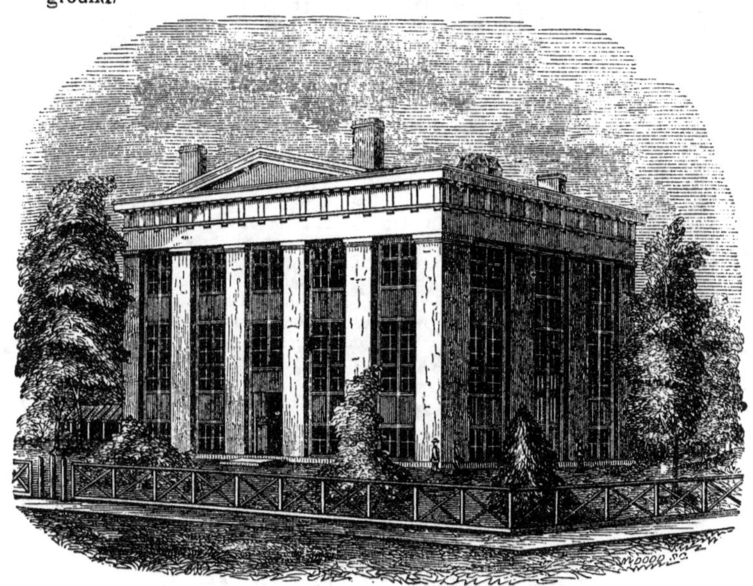

Fig. 2. Basement.

A—Lecture-room and Chapel. B—Laboratory. C, C—Furnaces. D, D, D—Janitor's rooms. E—Entry. F—Hall.

The building was erected in 1848, on a lot 198 by 170 feet, on the corner of Court and James streets, fronting the public square, and is of brick, 70 by 44 feet on the ground. The basement wall, up to the water table, is of stone, laid in hydraulic cement. The roof is covered with tin, laid in white lead.

The basement, 10 feet high in the clear, contains a lecture-room (which serves also as a chapel,) 26½ by 40 feet, with comfortable seats to accommodate conveniently 200 pupils. The floor descends 2 feet from the rear of the room to the platform, giving 12 feet height immediately in front of it. A laboratory, 12 by 15½ feet, adjoins the lecture-room, with which it communicates by a door at the end of a platform. The remainder of the basement floor is occupied by the furnaces for warming the building, and by the rooms of the Janitor.

The First Floor is occupied by the male department, and consists of a school-room about 30 by 54 feet, and nearly 15 feet in clear height, with two recitation-rooms, entries, &c. There are 62 desks, each four feet long and accommodating two pupils.

On the Second Floor are the girls' school-room, about 28 by 40 feet, with seats for 76 pupils, 2 recitation-rooms, library, hall, and room occupied by Primary department. There is a large skylight in the centre of the girls' school-room, and another in the library. The rooms are 15 feet in height.

The building is thoroughly and uniformly warmed by two furnaces in the basement, and a change of air is secured by ventilators at the top of the rooms, and also near the floor, opening into flues which are carried up in the chimneys. The warmth imparted by the smoke which passes up in the adjoining flues secures a good draft. In the upper story additional means of ventilation are furnished by the skylights, which can be partially opened.

The desks are of varnished cherry, similar in form to Ross's school desk.

Fig. 5.

The supports are of wood, however, instead of cast-iron, and the seats are easy Windsor chairs. Both seats and desks are firmly secured to the floor by small iron knees and screws.

The school and recitation rooms are all furnished with large slates set in the wall, in the room of blackboards.

The teachers' desks in the school-rooms are similar to Fig. 6.

Fig. 6.

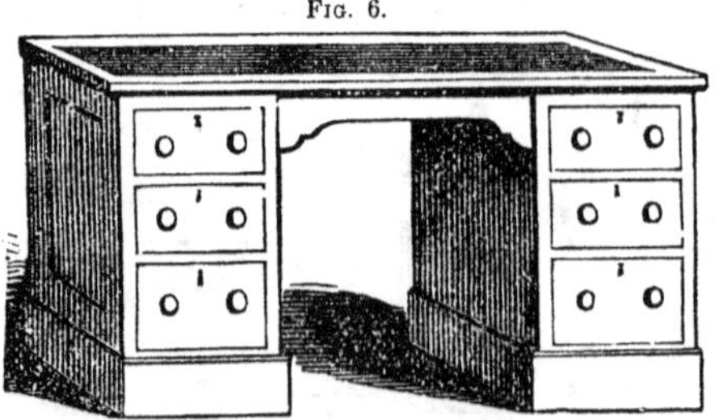

The whole cost of the building, including furnaces, scholars' desks and chairs, slates and inkstands, was about 6,000 dollars.

FIG. 3. PLAN OF FIRST FLOOR.

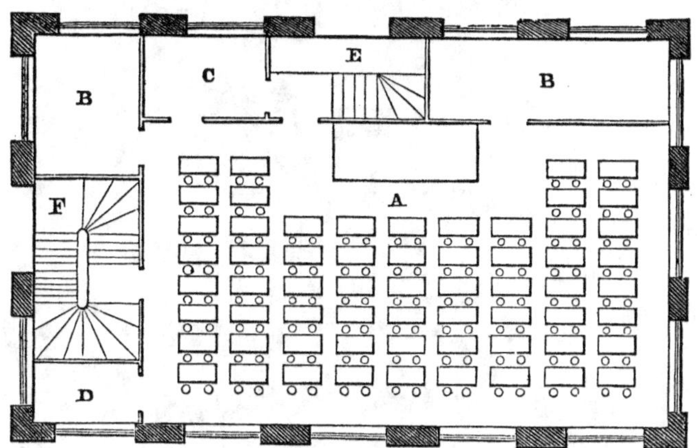

A—Boys' School-room, with 124 seats.
B, B—Recitation-rooms.
C—Dressing-room.
D—Closet for Apparatus.
E—Entrance for Boys.
F—Entrance for Girls.

FIG. 4. PLAN OF SECOND FLOOR.

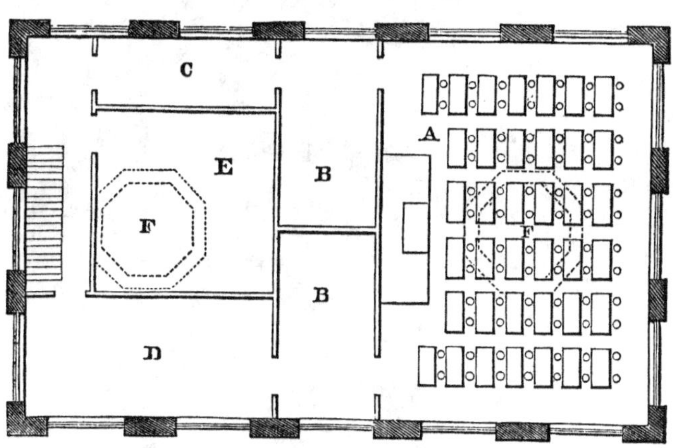

A—Girls' School-room, with 76 seats.
B, B—Recitation-rooms.
C—Dressing-room.
D—Primary Department.
E—Library, lighted by skylight.
F—Skylight in ceiling.

KNELLER HALL TRAINING SCHOOL, ENGLAND.

Public High School.

In the preceding pages we have presented a variety of plans for the construction and internal arrangements of buildings designed and erected for Public High Schools. Whenever and wherever the interest of the community can be sufficiently awakened to call for a public school of the grade generally understood by the term High School, there will be no difficulty in raising the funds necessary to erect and furnish a suitable edifice for the accommodation of the school. It may not, then, be amiss in this place to present a few considerations and facts bearing upon the establishment of a school of this grade in every large village and city in our country.

By a Public or Common High School, is intended a public or common school for the older and more advanced scholars of the community in which the same is located, in a course of instruction adapted to their age, and intellectual and moral wants, and, to some extent, to their future pursuits in life. It is common or public in the same sense in which the district school, or any lower grade of school established and supported under a general law and for the public benefit, is common or public. It is open to all the children of the community to which the school belongs, under such regulations as to age, attainments, &c., as the good of the institution may require, or the community may adopt. A Public High School is not necessarily a free school. It may be supported by a fund, a public tax, or an assessment or rate of tuition per scholar, or by a combination of all, or any two of these modes. Much less is it a public or common school in the sense of being cheap, inferior, ordinary. To be truly a public school, a High School must embrace in its course of instruction studies which can be more profitably pursued there than in public schools of a lower grade, or which gather their pupils from a more circumscribed territory, and as profitably as in any private school of the same pretensions. It must make a good education common in the highest and best sense of the word common—common because it is good enough for the best, and cheap enough for the poorest family in the community. It would be a mockery of the idea of such a school, to call it a Public High School, if the course of instruction pursued in it is not higher and better than can be got in public schools of a lower grade, or if it does not meet the wants of the wealthiest and best educated families, or, if the course of instruction is liberal and thorough, and at the same time the worthy and talented child of a poor family is shut out from its privileges by a high rate of tuition. The school, to be common practically, must be both cheap and good. To be cheap, its support must be provided for wholly or mainly out of a fund, or by public tax. And to justify the imposition of a public tax, the advantages of such a school must accrue to the whole community. It must be shown to be a common benefit, a common interest, which cannot be secured so well, or at all, except through the medium of taxation. What, then, are the advantages which may reasonably be anticipated from the establishment of a Public High School, properly organized, instructed, and supervised?

First. Every thing which is now done in the several district schools, and schools of lower grade, can be better done, and in a shorter time, because the teachers will be relieved from the necessity of devoting the time and attention now required by few of the older and more advanced pupils, and can bestow all their time and attention upon the preparatory studies and younger children. These studies will be taught in methods suited to the age and attainments of the pupils. A right beginning can thus be made in the lower schools, in giving a thorough practical knowledge of elementary principles, and in the formation of correct mental and moral habits, which are indispensable to all sound education. All this will be done under the additional stimulus of being early and thoroughly fitted for the High School.

Second. A High School will give completeness to the system of public instruction which may be in operation. It will make suitable provision for the older and more advanced pupils of both sexes, and will admit of the methods of instruction and discipline which cannot be profitably introduced into the schools below. The lower grade of schools—those which are established for young children,—require a large use of oral and simultaneous methods, and a frequent change of place and position on the part of the pupils. The higher branches, especially all mathematical subjects, require patient application and habits of abstraction on the part of the older pupils, which can with difficulty, if at all, be attained by many pupils amid a multiplicity of distracting exercises, movements, and sounds. The recitations of this class of pupils, to be profitable and satisfactory, must be conducted in a manner which requires time, discussion, and explanation, and the undivided attention both of pupils and teacher. The course of instruction provided in the High School will be equal in extent and value to that which may be given in any private school, academy, or female seminary in the place, and which is now virtually denied to the great mass of the children by the burdensome charge of tuition.

As has been already implied, the advantages of a High School should not be confined to the male sex. The great influence of the female sex, as daughters, sisters, wives, mothers, companions, and teachers, in determining the manners, morals, and intelligence of the whole community, leaves no room to question the necessity of providing for the girls the best means of intellectual and moral culture. The course of instruction should embrace the first principles of natural and mechanical philosophy, by which inventive genius and practical skill in the useful arts can be fostered; such studies as navigation, book-keeping, surveying, botany, chemistry, and kindred studies, which are directly connected with success in the varied departments of domestic and inland trade, with foreign commerce, with gardening, agriculture, the manufacturing and domestic arts;

such studies as astronomy, physiology, the history of our own state and nation, the principles of our state and national constitutions, political economy, and moral science; in fine, such a course of study as is now given in more than fifty towns and cities in New England, and which shall prepare every young man, whose parents may desire it, for business, or for college, and give to every young woman a well disciplined mind, high moral aims, refined tastes, gentle and graceful manners, practical views of her own duties, and those resources of health, thought, conversation, and occupation, which bless alike the highest and lowest station in life. When such a course is provided and carried out, the true idea of the High School will be realized.

Third. It will equalize the opportunities of a good education, and exert a happy, social influence throughout the whole community from which it gathers its scholars. From the want of a public school of this character, the children of such families as rely exclusively on the district school are isolated, and are condemned to an inferior education, both in quality and quantity; they are cut off from the stimulus and sympathy which the mingling of children of the same age from different parts of the same community would impart. The benefits, direct and indirect, which will result to the country districts, or poor families who live in the outskirts of the city, from the establishment of a school of this class, cannot easily be overestimated. The number of young men and young women who will receive a thorough education, qualifying them for business, and to be teachers, will increase from year to year; and the number who will press up to the front ranks of scholarship in the school, bearing away the palm of excellence by the vigor of sound minds in sound bodies, of minds and bodies made vigorous by long walks and muscular labor in the open air, will be greater in proportion to their number than from the city districts. It will do both classes good, the children of the city, and the children of the country districts, to measure themselves intellectually in the same fields of study, and to subject the peculiarities of their respective manners, the roughness and awkwardness sometimes characteristic of the one, and the artificiality and flippancy of the other, to the harmonizing influence of reciprocal action and reaction. The isolation and estrangement which now divide and subdivide the community into country and city clans, which, if not hostile, are strangers to each other, will give place to the frequent intercourse and esteem of individual and family friendship, commenced in the school-room, and on the play-ground of the school. The school will thus become a bond of union, a channel of sympathy, a spring-head of healthy influence, and stimulus to the whole commnnity.

Fourth. The privileges of a good school will be brought within the reach of all classes of the community, and will actually be enjoyed by children of the same age from families of the most diverse circumstances as to wealth, education, and occupation. Side by side in the same recitations, heart and hand in the same sports, pressing up together to the same high attainments in knowledge and character, will be found the children of the rich and poor, the more and the less favored in outward circumstances, without knowing or caring to know how far their families are separated by the arbitrary distinctions which divide and distract society. With nearly equal opportunities of education in childhood and youth, the prizes of life, its best fields of usefulness, and sources of happiness will be open to all, whatever may have been their accidents of birth and fortune. From many obscure and humble homes in the city and in the country, will be called forth and trained inventive talent, productive skill, intellectual taste, and God-like benevolence, which will add to the general wealth, multiply workshops, increase the value of farms, and carry forward every moral and religious enterprise which aims to bless, purify, and elevate society.

Fifth. The influence of the annual or semi-annual examination of candidates for admission into the High School, will operate as a powerful and abiding stimulus to exertion throughout all the lower schools. The privileges of the High School will be held forth as the reward of exertion in the lower grade of schools; and promotion to it, based on the result of an impartial examination, will form an unobjectional standard by which the relative standing of the different schools can be ascertained, and will also indicate the studies and departments of education to which the teachers in particular schools should devote special attention. This influence upon the lower schools, upon scholars and teachers, upon those who reach, and those who do not reach the High School, will be worth more than all it costs, independent of the advantages received by its pupils.

Sixth. While the expenses of public or common schools will necessarily be increased by the establishment of a school of this class, in addition to those already supported, the aggregate expenditures for education, including public and private schools, will be diminished. Private schools of the same relative standing will be discontinued for want of patronage, while those of a higher grade, if really called for by the educational wants of the community, will be improved. A healthy competition will necessarily exist between the public and private schools of the highest grade, and the school or schools which do not come up to the highest mark, must go down in public estimation. Other things being equal, viz., school-houses, teachers, classification, and the means and appliances of instruction, the public school is always better than the private. From the uniform experience of those places where a High School has been established, it may be safely stated, that there will be an annual saving in the expenses of education to any community, equal to one half the amount paid for tuition in private schools, and, with this saving of expense, there will be a better state of education.

Seventh. The successful establishment of a High School, by improving the whole system of common schools, and interesting a larger number of families in the prosperity of the schools, will create a better public sentiment on the subject than has heretofore existed, and the schools will be regarded as the common property, the common glory, the common security of the whole community. The wealthy will feel that the small additional tax required to establish and sustain this school, if not saved to them in the diminished tuition for the education of their own children in private schools, at home and abroad, is returned to them a hundred fold in the enterprise which it will quicken, in the increased value given to property, and in the number of families which will resort to the place where it is located, as a desirable residence, because of the facilities enjoyed for a good education. The poor will feel that, whatever may betide them, their children are born to an inheritance more valuable than lands or shops, in the free access to institutions where as good an education can be had as money can buy at home or abroad. The stranger will be invited to visit not only the institutions which public or individual benevolence has provided for the poor, the orphan, the deaf mute, and the criminal, but schools where the children and youth of the community are trained to inventive and creative habits of mind, to a practical knowledge of the fundamental principles of business, to sound moral habits, refined tastes, and respectful manners. And in what balance, it has well been asked in reference to the cost of good public schools, as compared with these advantages, shall we weigh the value of cultivated, intelligent, energetic, polished, and virtuous citizens? How much would a community be justified in paying for a physician who should discover or practice some mode of treatment through which many lives should be preserved? How much for a judge, who, in the able administration of the laws, should secure many fortunes, or rights more precious than fortunes, that might else be lost? How much for a minister of religion who should be the instrument of saving hundreds from vice and crime, and persuading them to the exertion of their best powers for the common good? How much for the ingenious inventor, who, proceeding from the first principles of science onward, should produce some improvement that should enlarge all the comforts of society, not to say a steam-engine or a magnetic telegraph? How much for the patriotic statesman, who, in difficult times, becomes the savior of his country? How much for the well-instructed and enterprising merchant who should suggest and commence the branches of business that should bring in a vast accession of wealth and strength? One such person as any of these might repay what a High School would cost for centuries. Whether, in the course of centuries, every High School would produce one such person, it would be useless to prophesy. But it is certain that it would produce many intelligent citizens, intelligent men of business, intelligent servants of the state, intelligent teachers, intelligent wives and daughters, who, in their several spheres, would repay to any community much more than they and all their associates had received. The very taxes of a town, in twenty years, will be lessened by the existence of a school which will continually have sent forth those who were so educated as to become not burdens but benefactors.

These results have been realized wherever a Public High School has been opened under circumstances favorable to the success of a private school of the same grade,—wherever a good school-house, good regulations, (for admission, attendance, studies, and books,) good teachers, and good supervision have been provided.

The Principal of the Latin High School of Boston, in a letter written 1846, says,—

"There is no institution so truly republican as such a school as this. While we, the present teachers, were undergraduates of the school, the rich sent their sons to the school because it was the best that could be found. They ascertained that it was not a source of contamination, but that their boys learned here to compare themselves with others, and to feel the necessity of something more that mere *wealth* to gain consideration. At that time, poor men sent their sons hither because they knew that they here would get that education which they could afford to give them in no other way. They gained too by intercourse with their wealthier mates a polish of exterior manners, and an intellectual turn of mind which their friends could appreciate and perceive, although they could not tell what it was that had been acquired. Oftentimes also the poor boy would take the lead of his more pampered classmate, and take the honors of the school.

In a class lately belonging to the school were two boys, one the son of a man of extreme wealth, whose property cannot be less than $500,000; and the other the son of an Irish laborer employed by the city at a dollar a day to sweep the streets. The latter boy was the better scholar."

The Principal of the English High School in a letter writes,—

"The school under my charge is pricipally composed of what are called the middling classes of our city. At present, about one third of my pupils are sons of merchants; the remaining two thirds are sons of professional men, mechanics and others. Some of our best scholars are sons of coopers, lamplighters, and day laborers. A few years ago, he who ranked, the last year of his course, as our third scholar, was the son of a lamplighter, and worked three nights per week, during his whole course, to save his father the expense of books, &c., while at school. This year my second (if not the first,) scholar, is a cooper's son. We have several sons of clergymen of distinction and lawyers of eminence. Indeed, the school is a perfect example of the poor and the rich, meeting on common ground and on terms quite democratic.

The Principal of the High School for girls in Newburyport, writes,

"The Female High School was established by the town of Newburyport nearly three years since, under great opposition. It was the desire of its principal advocates to make it such a school, in respect to the course of instruction, and facilities for acquiring knowledge, and laying the foundation for usefulness, as should so successfully compete with our best private schools, as to supersede their necessity."

"A few days after we were organized, a gentleman came into the school-room to make some inquiries respecting the classes of society most fully represented amongst us. I was totally unable to give him the desired information, and judging from the appearance of the individuals of my charge, I could form no idea as to who were the children of poor parents, or of those in better circumstances. I mentioned the names of the parents of several, which I had just taken, and, amongst others, of two young ladies of seventeen or eighteen years of age, who, at that moment, it being recess, were walking down the room, with their arms closely entwined about each other's necks. 'The first of the two,' said the gentleman, 'is a daughter of one of our first merchants, the other has a father worse than none, who obtains a livelihood from one of the lowest and most questionable occupations, and is himself most degraded.' These two young ladies were classmates for more than two years, and very nearly equal in scholarship. The friendship they have formed, I am confident no circumstances of station in life can ever impair.

"We have had in our number many from the best families, in all respects, in the place. They sit side by side, they recite, and they associate most freely with those of the humblest parentage, whose widowed mothers, perhaps, toil day after day, at a wash-tub, without fear of contamination, or, as I honestly believe, a thought of the differences which exist. I have, at present, both extremes under my charge—the child of affluence and the child of low parentage and deep poverty. As my arrangements of pupils in divisions, &c. are, most of them, alphabetical, it often happens that the two extremes are brought together. This never causes a murmur, or look of dislike.

A member of the School Committee of Worcester, Mass., writes:

"Our High School is exceedingly popular with all classes, and in the school-rooms and on the play-grounds, the children of the richest and poorest mingle with perfect equality. No assumption,—no jealousy are seen among them. I have been charmed with this republican and Christian character of the school. I have seen the children of parents whose wealth was estimated by hundreds of thousands, in the same school-room with children (and those last among the best scholars of their class) whose parents have been assisted year after year by individual charity. The manners, habits, and moral sentiments of this school are as pure and high as in any academy, or female seminary of the same grade in the commonwealth.

"To the improvements of our public schools, which has been going steadily forward since 1825, does this town owe more of its prosperity, its large accession of families from abroad, especially of industrious and skillful mechanics, than to all other causes combined. As a mere investment of capital, men of wealth everywhere cannot do better with a portion of their property than to build elegant and attractive school-houses, and open in them free schools of the highest order of instruction. They will then see gathering around them men, it may be, of small means, but of practical skill, and moral and industrious habits; that class of families who feel that one of the great ends of life is to educate their children well."

A correspondent from Brattleboro', Vt., writes:

"In the same school-room, seated side by side, according to age and attainments, are eighty children, representing all classes and conditions in society. The lad or miss, whose father pays a school tax of thirty-five dollars, by the side of another whose expense of instruction is five cents *per annum*. They play cordially and happily on the same grounds, and pursue the same studies—the former frequently incited by the native superiority and practical good sense of the latter. While the contact corrects the factitious gentility and false ideas of superiority in the one, it encourages cleanliness and good breeding in the other."

The history of the High School in Providence is the history of almost every similar institution.

"The High School was the only feature of our system which encountered much opposition. When first proposed, its bearings on the schools below, and in various ways on the cause of education in the city, was not clearly seen. It was opposed because it was "aristocratic," "because it was unconstitutional to tax property for a city college," "because it would educate children above working for their support," "because a poor boy or girl would never be seen in it"—and for all such contradictory reasons. Before it became a part of the system, the question of its adoption, or rejection, was submitted directly to the people, who passed in its favor by a vote of two thirds of all the legal voters of the city. Even after this expression of popular vote in its favor, and after the building for its accommodation was erected, there was a considerable minority who circulated a petition to the City Council against its going into operation. But the school was opened, and now it would be as easy to strike out the whole or any other feature of the system as this. Its influence in giving stimulus and steadiness to the workings of the lower grade of schools,—in giving thoroughness and expansion to the whole course of instruction,—in assisting to train teachers for our city and country schools,—and in bringing together the older and more advanced pupils, of either sex, from families of every profession, occupation and location in the city, many of whom, but for the opportunities of this school, would enter on the business and duties of life with an imperfect education—has demonstrated its own usefulness as a part of the system, and has converted its opponents into friends."

Testimony of the same character might be adduced from Philadelphia, Lowell, New Orleans, and every place where a school of this grade has been established.

School Furniture.

Much attention has been devoted recently to the improvement of school furniture of every kind, with a view of securing convenience, comfort, durability and economy. In addition to the varieties already described and illustrated, we present the following to aid committees and builders in this important department of school architecture.

Primary School Bench.

A movable bench for more than two pupils is an objectionable article of school furniture; but if introduced at all,

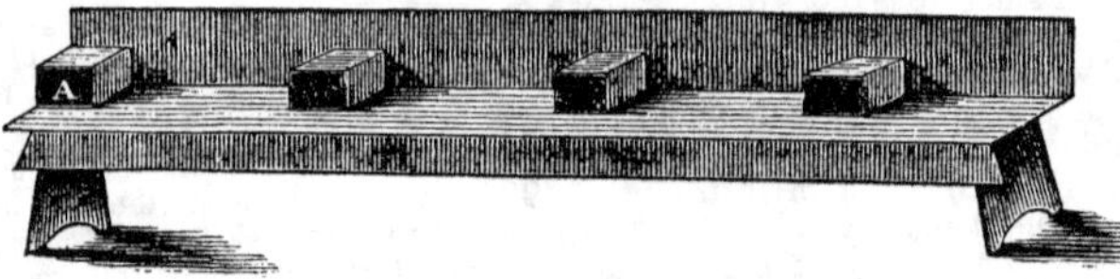

the above cut represents a style of this article which combines economy and convenience. The back is inclined slightly from a perpendicular, and the seat is hollowed. The scholars are separated by a compartment, or box, A, which serves as a rest for the arm, and a place of deposit for books.

Gallery and Sand Desk for Primary and Infant Schools.

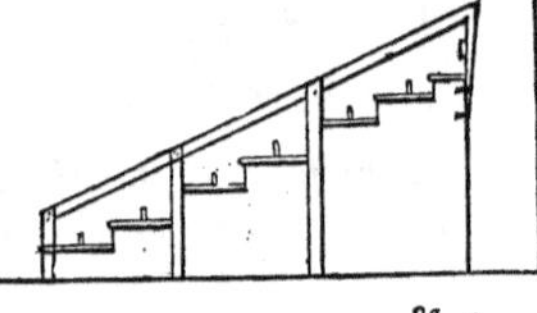

For very small children a *Gallery* consisting of a succession of seats rising above each other, varying in height from seven to nine inches, and provided with a support for the back. This arrangement, in large schools, affords great facility for instruction in music and all simultaneous exercises.

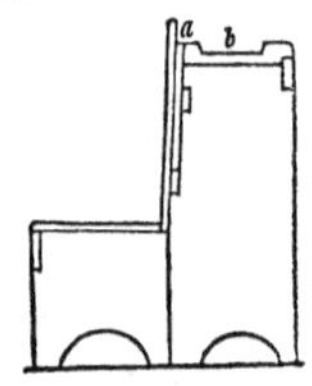

The *Sand Desk* having a trench (*b*) painted black, to contain a thin layer of sand, in which to trace letters and rude attempts at imitating forms, was originally much resorted to with the young classes, in schools educated on the Lancasterian or Mutual system. This style of desk is still used in the primary schools of the New York Public School Society, but very much improved by Mott's *Cast Iron Scroll Stanchions* and *Revolving Pivot Chair.* Every scholar is furnished with a slate, which is deposited in the opening (*a*) in the top of the desk.

The Boston Primary School Chair.

These chairs were got up by the late Joseph W. Ingraham, for many years chairman, and one of the most indefatigable members, of the Primary School Committee of Boston, and are now in very general use in the Primary Schools of Boston, and of that vicinity.

The first pattern is a Chair with a *Shelf* (*s*) under the seat, for the purpose of holding the Books, Slates, &c., of the scholars.

The second pattern differs from the first, in having, instead of the *Shelf*, a *Rack* (A) on the back of the chair, for the same use as the shelf in the preceding pattern. The third pattern is similar to the second, except that the *Rack* (A) is placed at *the side* instead of *the back*, of the chair. The latter pattern (with the Rack on the side) is that now adopted in the Boston Schools.

Other specimens of Chairs for Primary Schools will be found on pages 134, 135, and 139.

Range of Desks and Seats.

The following cut represents a range of new desks and seats, like that represented in school-room on page 53. The lowest seat (*d*) is nine inches

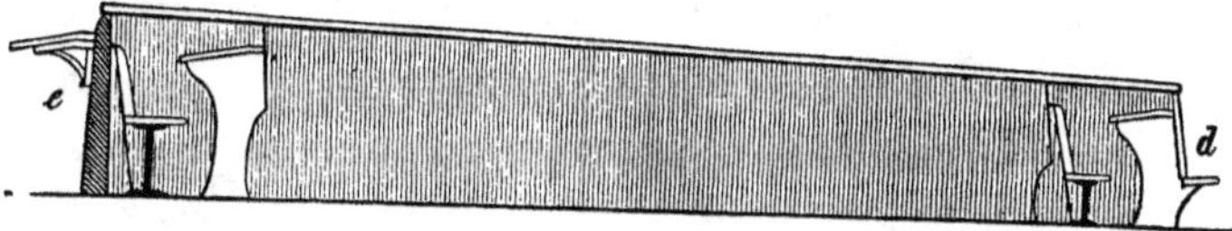

high, and the chair to the leaf-desk, (*e*,) is 17½ inches from the floor. The front edge of the lowest desk, is 19½ inches, and that of the highest desk, is 28½ inches from the floor. Each range of desk is divided by a partition of matched boards extending from the floor to three or four inches above the surface of the desk. This partition, to which the desks and seats, (if chairs are not used,) are attached, gives great firmness to each desk and seat, and at the same time effectually separates each scholar, as much as a single seat and desk, with greater economy of room. The desks in other respects are made like those described on page 47.

Boston Latin High School Desk.

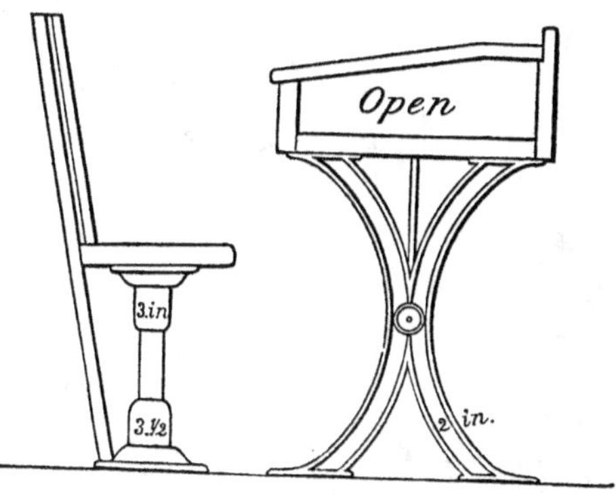

The above cut represents an end view of a new style of desk used in the Latin High School, in Bedford street, Boston, with a section of Wales' *Patent School Chair*. The standards of the desks are made of cast iron, and are braced in such a manner, that when properly secured to the floor, there is not the least motion. The curves in the standard facilitate the use of the broom in sweeping.

MOTT'S SCHOOL CHAIR AND DESK.

The following minute description of Mott's Patent Revolving Pivot Chair, and cast iron Scroll Stanchions for School Desks, is gathered from a circular of the patentee:

The seat of the chair is of wood: all the other parts, of cast iron. The desk stanchions are adjusted to the height of the chair—in the following scale, viz:

No. of the Chair.	Height of Chair Seat.	Height of front edge of Desk.	Width of Desk.	Length of Desk room for each scholar; (not less.)	Distance between the rows of Desks.
1	10 Inches.	17 Inches.	12 Inches.	17 Inches.	20 Inches.
2	12 "	19 "	12 "	18 "	22 "
3	14 "	22 "	14 "	20 "	24 "
4	16 "	24 "	15 "	22 "	25 "

The *first column* denotes the *number* of the chair, as also the number of the desk stanchions.

Second column, the height of the seat from the floor.

Third column, the height of the front edge of the desk from the floor.

Fourth column, the width of the top of the desk. The slope of the desk should rise 1¼ inch to the foot; the larger desks having 2½ to 3 inches level on top to accommodate inkstands.

Fifth column, the length of desk room required for each scholar. It should not be less than here given.

Sixth column, the distance that should be allowed between the desks, from the back of one to the front edge of the other. This space will allow a passage between the chair and the next rear desk. The number of scholars at a desk need not be limited.

The position of each chair, when screwed to the floor, should have two-thirds of the allotted desk room to the right of its centre, and be so near that the back of the chair, in its revolution, will barely clear the desk. By placing the chair as described, the body of the child is brought in close proximity to the desk, causing the back of the person to rest, at all times, and under all circumstances, against the back of the chair.

The chief peculiarity in the desk is, that in the place of straight wooden legs, there are substituted curved cast iron stanchions; the obvious advantages of which are, that they occasion no interference with the movements of the scholar seated opposite or near to them.

Two stanchions are necessary for a single desk. Two, also, will support a desk of sufficient length to accommodate three scholars; three, to accommodate six scholars; four, nine scholars; and so on for a greater number.

The expense of fitting up a room with this chair and desk, in the city of New York, varies from $1 50 to $2 00 a scholar, aside from the putting up of the desks.

Hartford School Desk and Seat.

The following cut (Fig. 1,) represents a style of school desk, with a seat attached, which has been extensively introduced into village and country districts in Rhode Island, and the neighborhood of Hartford, and is recommended wherever a rigid economy must be observed.

Fig. 1.

The end piece, or supports, both of the seat and desk, are cast iron, and the wood work is attached by screws. They are made for one or two scholars, and of eight sizes, giving a seat from ten inches to seventeen, and a desk at the edge next to the scholar, from seventeen to twenty-six inches from the floor.

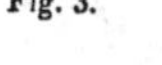
Fig. 3.

Fig. 2.

Each desk is fitted up with a glass ink-well (Fig. 2,) set firmly into the desk, and covered with a lid. The ink-well may be set into a cast iron box (Fig. 3,) having a cover; the box being let in and screwed to the desk, and the ink-well being removable for convenience in filling, cleaning, and emptying in cold weather.

Fig. 4.

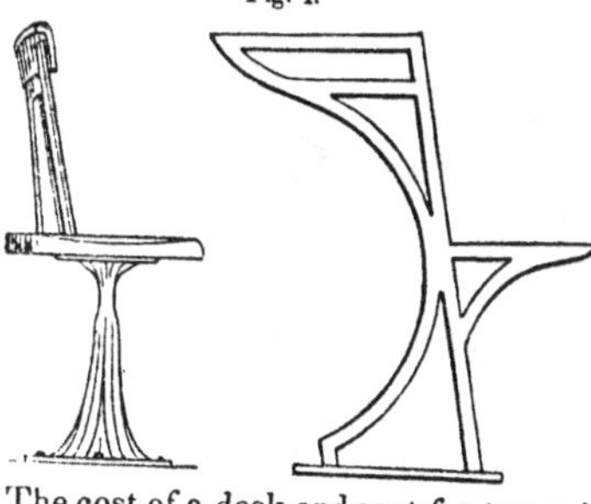

The desk can be used, by detaching the support for the seat, with a convenient school-chair, made in the style represented in cut (Fig. 4,) or in any other style.

The cost of a desk and seat for two scholars, perfectly fitted up, varies from $1 37½ to $1 50 per scholar.

Manufactured by Messrs. Allen & Reed, Nos. 37 and 38 Pearl street, Hartford.

Wales' Improved School Furniture.

The following cuts represent a large variety of improved school chairs, desks, and other furniture manufactured by Samuel Wales, Jr., at No. 14 Bromfield Street, Boston, Mass., from patterns of his own getting up, and with such facilities of experienced workmen, and ingenious machinery, as enables him to supply all orders for first-class work, with economy, precision, and promptness.

Wales' improved school chairs and desks embrace the following variety, and each variety is constructed on the following scale of height, so as to meet the varying proportions of scholars ranging from four years to twenty years of age:

No. 1.	Chairs,	10 inches high;	Desks, side next the scholar,	20	inches	high.
" 2.	"	11 " "	" " " " "	21	"	"
" 3.	"	12 " "	" " " " "	22	"	"
" 4.	"	13 " "	" " " " "	23	"	"
" 5.	"	14 " "	" " " " "	24	"	"
" 6.	"	15 " "	" " " " "	25½	"	"
" 7.	"	16 " "	" " " " "	27	"	"
" 8.	"	17 " "	" " " " "	28½	"	"

Wales' American School Chairs.

No. 1.

These chairs are plain and substantial. Each chair is based upon a single iron pedestal, which is secured to the seat of the chair at the top, and to the floor of the school-room at the foot. The center-piece of the chair-back descends directly into the foot of the iron pedestal, intersecting the back of the seat as it passes, in such a manner as to form a *back stay*, thereby producing in the chair, as a whole, the greatest possible degree of firmness and strength.

No. 2.

No. 2 represents an improved school desk for two scholars.

No. 3.

No. 3 represents an improved single desk for one scholar, on iron supports, with American school chairs to correspond. Each desk is furnished with an ink-well, and a metal cover of the best kind. The top is grooved, to accommodate pens, pencils, and other small articles, with a safe resting-place.

Wales' New England School Chairs.

No. 4.

Each chair is based upon a pedestal of iron, of great beauty and strength, which is firmly secured to the seat of the chair at the top, and to the floor of the school-room at the foot. An ornamental center-piece passes down into the base of the pedestal, forming the center of the chair-back and the *back stay*.

No. 5.

No. 6.

Cuts No. 5 and No. 6, represent an improved double school desk, the latter for one, and the former for two scholars, with the New England school chair to correspond.

Wales' Bowdoin School Chairs.

No. 7.

These chairs are constructed substantially like those already described, with a tasteful scroll top. The following diagrams, Nos. 8 and 9, represent the chair in connection with a desk, both for one and two scholars.

No. 8.

No. 9.

WALES' WASHINGTON SCHOOL CHAIRS.

No. 10.

Nos. 10, 11, and 12, represent the eight sizes of another variety of the chair, with the corresponding desk, both single and double

No. 11.

No. 12.

WALES' NORMAL SCHOOL DESKS AND CHAIRS.

No. 13.

No. 14.

The engraving represents a Normal School Double Desk, on iron supports, having two covers, with Washington School Chairs to correspond. Each cover opens a separate apartment in the desk, designed for the exclusive use of one scholar.

Wales' Improved Writing Stools.

No. 15.

For most educational purposes, chairs are highly preferable, and this seems to be the general opinion; but, in cases where writing is taught in a separate department, the writing-stool is preferred, as being less expensive, and occupying less room.

Wales' Primary School Chair.

No. 16.

The engravings No. 16 and No. 17, represent a series of *three sizes*, suitable for scholars from four years of age and upward, comprehending all the sizes needed in primary and intermediate schools, to wit:—

No. 1, . . 10 inches high.
" 2, . . 11 " "
" 3, . . 12 " "

Each chair is based on an iron pedestal, securely fastened to the seat at the top, and to the floor of the school-room at the foot; thus becoming a permanent article of furniture, and completely avoiding the confusion, irregularity and noise, which are the unavoidable accompaniments of movable chairs in a school-room.

Wales' Basket Primary School Chair.

No. 17.

The Basket Chair has a tastefully ornamented book basket of iron, into which the children can place their books, slates, and other utensils of study. As a whole, in view of their strength, comfort, beauty and adaptation to their object, these are regarded as the best Primary School Chairs extant.

WALES' IMPROVED SETTEES.

No. 18.

The engravings No. 18 and No. 19, represent an Improved Settee, eight feet in length, based upon iron supports, designed for that purpose. Such settees are well adapted for recitation-rooms, the walls of school-rooms, for the accommodation of visitors, or for any position where permanent settees are wanted. They are made of any required height, size, or length; often from forty to sixty feet in length, when placed on the walls of school-rooms; and, being without arms or other divisions, the whole length, in fact, forming a single settee, have been found to be very convenient, and of good appearance.

WALES' IMPROVED LYCEUM SETTEE.

No. 19.

The Improved Lyceum Settee is divided into five parts or seats, with fancy iron arms, made for that purpose.

WALES' TEACHERS' ARM-CHAIRS.

No. 20.

The engravings, Nos. 20 and 21, represent two substantial, well-made, and comfortable arm-chairs, having no other claim to novelty than may be due to the fact that they are constructed entirely of hard wood, and are finished without paint of any kind; they will therefore wear well, and retain their good appearance without soiling or defacement, for a long period.

WALES' TEACHER'S ARM-CHAIRS, WITH CUSHIONS.
No. 21.

WALES' TEACHER'S TABLE, WITHOUT DRAWERS.
No. 22.

WALES' TEACHER'S TABLE, ONE DRAWER.
No. 23.

WALES' TEACHER'S TABLE, TWO DRAWERS.
No. 24.

Movable Skeleton Desk.
No. 25.

Portable Desk.
No. 26.

Wales' Teacher's Desk.
No. 27.

Wales' Teacher's Desk, three Drawers and Table Top.
No. 28.

Wales' Teacher's Desk, three Drawers and Top Desk.
No. 29.

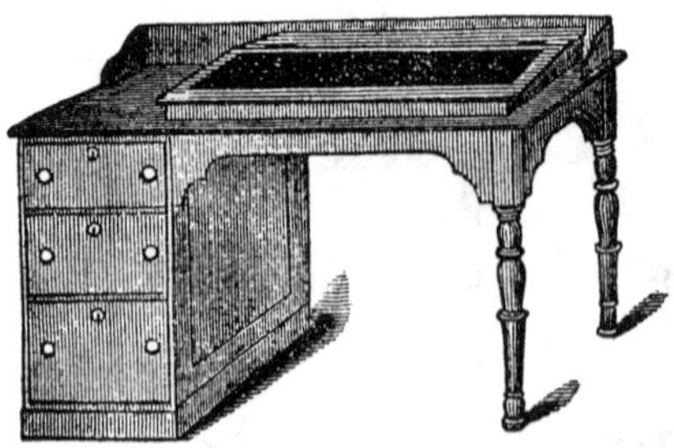

WALES' TEACHER'S DESK, TWO DRAWERS AND TABLE TOP.
No. 30.

WALES' TEACHER'S DESK, TWO DRAWERS AND TOP DESK.
No. 31.

WALES' TEACHER'S DESK, FOUR DRAWERS AND TABLE TOP.
No. 32.

WALES' TEACHER'S DESK, FOUR DRAWERS AND TOP DESK
No. 33.

WALES' TEACHER'S DESK, SIX DRAWERS AND TABLE TOP.

No. 34.

WALES' TEACHER'S DESK, SIX DRAWERS AND TOP DESK.

No. 35.

WALES' TEACHER'S DESK AND LIBRARY, FOUR DRAWERS, TABLE TOP AND BOOK-CASE.

No. 36.

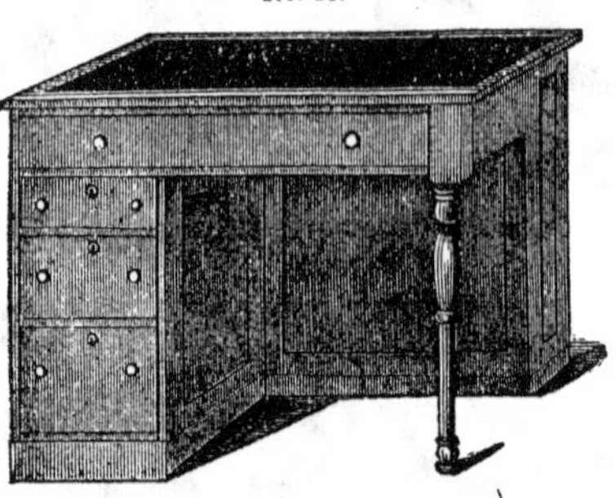

A.

A. The side occupied by the Teacher.

No. 37.

B.

B. The side facing the school, with a large drawer for maps, drawings, &c., and two doors which open a book-case, suitable for a school library.

WALES' TEACHER'S DESK AND LIBRARY, SIX DRAWERS, TABLE TOP AND LARGE BOOK-CASE.

No. 38.

A.

A. The side occupied by the Teacher.

No. 39.

B.

B. The side facing the school, with a large drawer for maps, drawings, &c., a small drawer for utensils of study, and three doors which open a large book-case, suitable for a school library.

Apparatus for Warming.

The thorough ventilation, the constant and regular change of the atmosphere of a school-room cannot be secured by simply providing flues or openings, however judiciously constructed and placed, for the escape of the air which has become impure from the process of breathing or other causes. These flues will not work satisfactorily, unless a mode of warming the room is adopted by which a large supply of pure fresh air, properly heated, is flowing in to supply the place of that which is escaping by means of the flues. Among the various modes of warming school-rooms and public halls, which we have seen in full and successful operation, we select a few, in addition to those described in other parts of the work, as worthy of the particular attention of committees and others, who are looking round for a heating apparatus. We shall use the cuts and description by which the patentees and venders have chosen to make their several modes of warming known to the public, without intending to decide on the relative merits of any one mode.

Double Fire-Place for Warming and Ventilation.

The following plan of warming and ventilating a school-room is recommended by Mr. George B. Emerson in the School and Schoolmaster. The position of the proposed fire-place may be seen in the Plans of School-rooms by the same eminent teacher, published on page 50 of this work.

Warming.—In a suitable position, pointed out in the plates, near the door, let a common brick fireplace be built. Let this be inclosed, on the back and on each side, by a casing of brick, leaving, between the fireplace and the casing, a space of four or five inches, which will be heated through the back and jambs. Into this space let the air be admitted from beneath by a box 24 inches wide and 6 or 8 deep, leading from the external atmosphere by an opening beneath the front door, or at some other convenient place. The brick casing should be continued up as high as six or eight inches above the top of the fireplace, where it may open into the room by lateral orifices, to be commanded by iron doors, through which the heated air will enter the room. If these are lower, part of the warm air will find its way into the fireplace. The brick chimney should

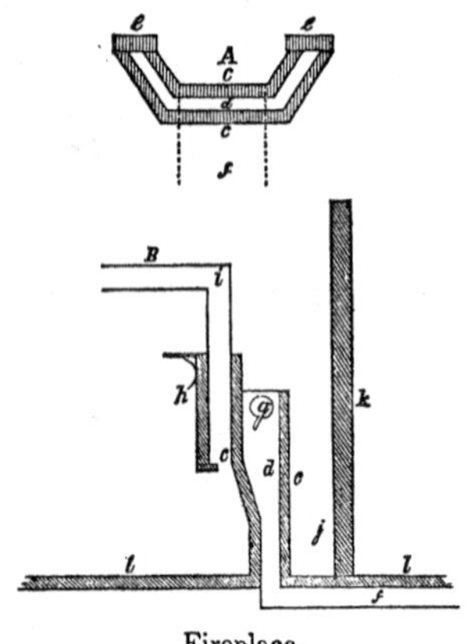

Fireplace.

A. Horizontal section. B. Perpendicular section. *c.* Brick walls, 4 inches thick. *d.* Air space between the walls. *e.* Solid fronts of masonry. *f.* Air box for supply of fresh air, extending beneath the floor to the front door. *g.* Openings on the sides of the fireplace, for the heated air to pass into the room. *h.* Front of the fireplace and mantelpiece. *i.* Iron smoke flue, 8 inches diameter. *j.* Space between the fireplace and wall. *k.* Partition wall. *l.* Floor.

rise at least two or three feet above the hollow back, and may be surmounted by a flat iron, soap-stone, or brick top, with an opening for a smoke-pipe, which may be thence conducted to any part of the room. The smoke-pipe should rise a foot, then pass to one side, and then over a passage, to the opposite extremity of the room, where it should ascend perpendicularly, and issue above the roof. The fireplace should be provided with iron doors, by which it may be completely closed.

The advantages of this double fireplace are, 1. the fire, being made against brick, imparts to the air of the apartment none of the deleterious qualities which are produced by a common iron stove, but gives the pleasant heat of an open fireplace; 2. none of the heat of the fuel will be lost, as the smoke-pipe may be extended far enough to communicate nearly all the heat contained in the smoke; 3. the current of air heated within the hollow back, and constantly pouring into the room, will diffuse an equable heat throughout every part; 4. the pressure of the air of the room will be constantly outward, little cold will enter by cracks and windows, and the fireplace will have no tendency to smoke; 5. by means of the iron doors, the fire may be completely controlled, increased or diminished at pleasure, with the advantages of an air-tight stove. For that purpose, there must be a valve or slide near the bottom of one of the doors.

If, instead of this fireplace, a common stove be adopted, it should be placed above the air-passage, which may be commanded by a valve or register in the floor, so as to admit or exclude air.

Ventilation.—A room warmed by such a fireplace as that just described, may be easily ventilated. If a current of air is constantly pouring in, a current of the same size will rush out wherever it can find an outlet, and with it will carry the impurities wherewith the air of an occupied room is always charged. For the first part of the morning, the open fireplace may suffice. But this, though a very effectual, is not an economical ventilator; and when the issue through this is closed, some other must be provided. The most effective ventilator for throwing out foul air, is one opening into a tube which incloses the smoke-flue at the point where it passes through the roof. Warm air naturally rises. If a portion of the smoke-flue be inclosed by a tin tube, it will warm the air within this tube, and give it a tendency to rise. If, then, a wooden tube, opening near the floor, be made to communicate, by its upper extremity, with the tin tube, an upward current will take place in it, which *will always act whenever the smoke-flue is warm.*

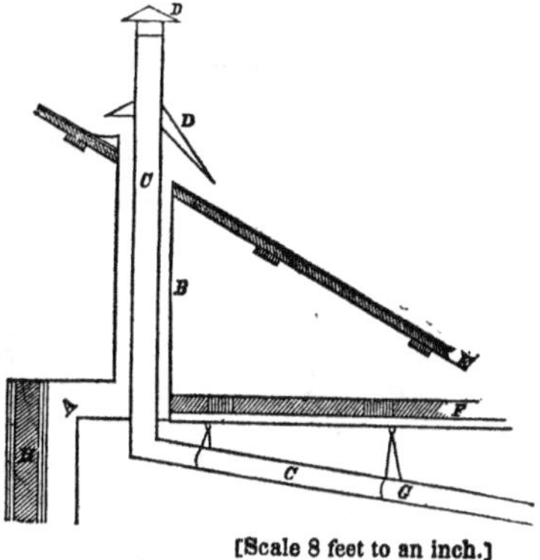

[Scale 8 feet to an inch.]

Ventilating Apparatus.

A. Air box, 1 foot square, or 24 inches by 6, covered by the pilaster, and opening at the floor, in the base of the pilaster. B. Round iron tube 15½ inches in diameter, being a continuation of the air box, through the center of which passes C. The smoke flue, 8 inches in diameter. D. Caps to keep out the rain.

It is better, but not absolutely essential, that the opening into the wooden tube be near the floor. The carbonic acid thrown out by the lungs rises, with the warm breath, and the perspirable matter from the skin, with the warm, invisible vapor, to the top of the room. There both soon cool, and sink towards the floor; and both carbonic air and the vapor bearing the perspirable matter are pretty rapidly and equally diffused through every part of the room.

MOTT'S VENTILATING SCHOOL-STOVE, FOR BURNING WOOD OR COAL.

Patented and Manufactured by J. L. MOTT, 264 *Water-street, N. Y.*

By this stove the room is warmed by conducting a supply of moderately heated pure air from without, as well as by direct radiation from the upper portion of the stove.

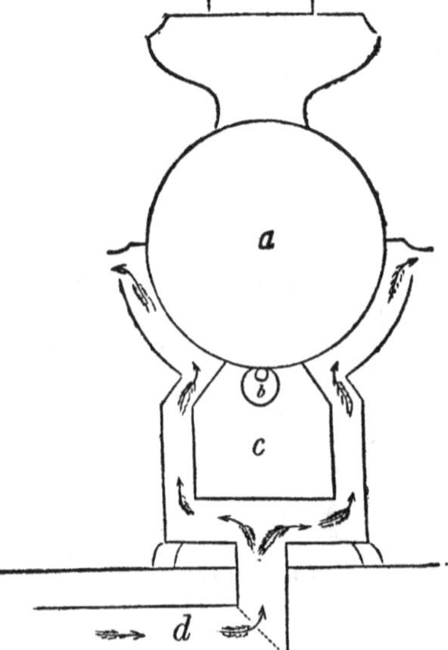

A. Air Chamber, for coal or wood.
B. A revolving grate with a cam process, by which the ashes are easily detached and made to drop into the ash-pit below.
C. Ash-Pit, by which also the draft can be regulated, and the stove made an air-tight.
D. Duct, or flue under the floor, by which fresh air from without is admitted under and around the stove, and circulates in the direction indicated by the arrows.

This, and all stoves designed to promote ventilation by introducing fresh air from without, will work satisfactorily only where a flue properly constructed is provided to carry off the air which has become impure from respiration.

The Boston Ventilating Stove and Portable Ventilating Furnace.

Patented March 10th, 1848, *by Henry G. Clark, M. D., and manufactured by Gardner Chilson, Boston.*

The Boston Ventilating Stove is composed of two cylinders, the inner (Fig. 1,) containing a fire chamber, which is lined with soapstone or fire brick, and is fitted with additional smoke-pipes to increase the radiating surface, while the outer (Fig. 2,) constitutes a chamber for warming the air, which is introduced into it beneath the inner cylinder by a flue from out of doors, and flows out at the top, to which there is a movable cap, or distributor attached, by which the opening is enlarged or diminished, and thus the supply and temperature of the air admitted can be easily regulated.

Fig. 1 Fig. 2.

The *dark* arrows show the course of the air in its passage from the opening underneath the stove, through the air-chamber, into the apartment. The light arrows show the circulation of the *smoke* through the various radiating pipes.

This stove is made of three sizes, varying in price from twenty-five to forty dollars. It received a *silver medal* at the Fifth Exhibition of the Massachusetts Charitable Mechanic Association, and has been introduced with signal success into many school-houses in Boston, Charlestown, and other places.

This stove can be advantageously used as a hall stove and as a portable furnace, under circumstances which will not admit of a brick inclosure.

Millar's Ventilating School Stove.

In Millar's Ventilating School Stove, manufactured at Worcester, Mass., and designed for burning wood, the air is introduced from outside of the building beneath the stove, by an air-box, and is warmed by circulating through cast-iron tubes around the fire, until it is discharged into the room. Stoves of this patent are much used in the country district in Worcester county, and other parts of Massachusetts.

CHILSON'S AIR-WARMING AND VENTILATING FURNACE.

Patented and Manufactured by Gardner Chilson, Boston.

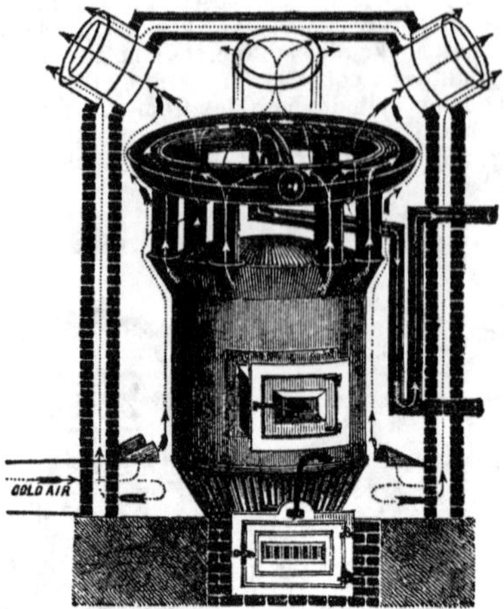

The advantages of the Furnace are—

1. The fire-pot is constructed on the most economical and philosophical principles. It is broad and shallow,—at least twice as broad and one third as deep as the common fire-pot;—is one third smaller at the bottom than at the top, and is lined with fire-brick or soap-stone. Thus the fire-bed is deep enough to keep the coal well ignited with a slow but perfect combustion, while the entire heat from the fuel is given out to act upon the radiating surface alone and the fire-pot can never become red-hot, and does not require renewal. This plan for burning coal is original with the inventor, and has met with universal approbation.

2. The radiating surface is large, and so placed that it receives the immediate and natural action of the heat, and at the same time imparts its heat in the most direct and uniform manner to the fresh air from without, without suffering waste by absorption from the outer walls of the air-chamber.

3. The air-chamber is large, and the fresh air is admitted and discharged so readily and uniformly that no portion of the radiating surface can ever become overheated; and a delightful summer temperature is maintained in the rooms.

4. The joints of the furnace are so constructed, that, even if the iron-work was liable, like other furnaces, to crack from extreme expansion, by being overheated, (which it is not,) the gas from the burning coal cannot escape into the air-chamber.

5. There are no horizontal inner surfaces on which dust and soot can gather, which do not, at the same time, clean themselves, or admit of being easily cleaned.

6. The grate in the fire-pot is so constructed, that the ashes can be easily detached, and the combustion facilitated.

7. It has stood all the test which sharp rivalry and the most severe *philosophical* practical science could apply to it, and has thus far accomplished all that its inventor promised, and when tried in the same building with other furnaces, has uniformly received the preference.

G. Chilson also manufactures an Open Stove for wood, or coal, and a Grate for coal, with an air-chamber on the sides and back of the fire, by which fresh air is warmed in its passage into the room, and the cheerful aspect of an open fire-place secured.

Bushnell's Patent Hot-air Furnace.

Manufactured by Ezra Clark, Jr., 61 Front street, Hartford, Conn.

Bushnell's Furnace is the only one constructed on strictly scientific principles, and bears any test either of theory or practice. Scientific gentlemen have endorsed its excellence, and successful practice approves and confirms their recommendation.

The radiating part of this furnace, being that portion which diffuses the heat, is distinguished from all others from the fact that the cold air is passed into the furnace chamber *between* horizontal cast iron pipes or tubes, *inside of which the hot gas of the fire is circulating*, and communicating its heat, as it passes off to the chimney; so that the cold air is brought in direct contact with the heated iron, and is actually heated before it reaches the inner chamber of the furnace. While the cold air is passing one way to be heated (between the heated iron pipes) the hot gas of the fire is passing the other way to be cooled, and thus the mean difference of temperature *is kept the greatest possible at every point*. The *greatest* amount of heat will be communicated in this way, by the *least* amount of iron surface; and as the radiator has a very large surface, it follows that *more* heat is extracted (from a given amount of fuel) *than by any other invention* yet offered to the public.

This furnace is so constructed that it *clears itself* of ashes and soot, never requiring to be disturbed, and consequently requires not as much care as an ordinary fire. A child can take care of it when in use, and it can stand from season to season, untouched, without trouble or expense, and be at any moment ready for immediate use.

Two kinds of pots are offered by the manufacturer, for use with this furnace; one similar to the most approved forms now in use, the other entirely different, and the invention of Dr. Bushnell. It differs from all others in allowing the fire to be *stirred above the grate*, and through the opening by which the coal is entered. This throws up the dead coals and cinders, which are then easily removed, and, as the grate *need never be dropped*, the dirty process of riddling is avoided. No ashes escape, and the cloud of dust which usually envelopes the tender in all other furnaces, is no where seen in this, and no uncleanliness results from renewing the fire. The fire may be stirred and cleaned when it is in full action, as well as at any other time; the coals will never rattle down to choke the fire, but will of necessity, by his method of stirring, *always* be thrown up into a light open cinder, giving free passage to the draft and facilitating combustion.

This furnace is offered in the entire confidence that it is *the best ever manufactured*, and this bold assertion is warranted and proved by the favorable testimony of those who have used it. A trial is all the proof required.

Three sizes of furnaces are made, viz.: No. 1 with 17 inch pot; No. 2 with 20 inch pot; No. 3 with 24 inch pot; which are now for sale in most of the larger cities and towns in the northern states.

Orders for Bushnell's Furnaces will be promptly attended to, on application by mail or otherwise, to Ezra Clark, Jr., Hartford, Conn.

Culver's Hot-Air Furnace.

Patented and Manufactured by Culver & Co., 52 Cliff-street, New York.

Culver's Hot-Air Furnace, as described in the following diagram and explanations, is intended for hard coal, to be set in double walls of brick masonry in cellar or basement, below the rooms to be warmed.

Figure 1.

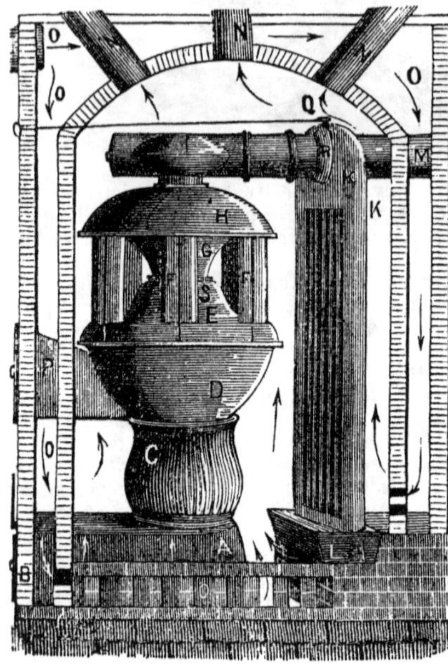

A. Iron or Brick Ash Pit.
B. Ash Pit door.
C. Pot, or coal Burner, with or without *soapstone* lining.
D. Fire Chamber.
E. Lower half of Tubular drum.
F. Elliptical tubes.
G. Upper half of Tubular drum.
H. Top of Tubular drum.
I. Cap and smoke pipe.
K. Flat Radiator.
L. Water bason or evaporator.
M. Smoke pipe to chimney.
N. Conductors of Hot Air.
O. Cold air conductor and chamber.
P. Feed door.
Q. Hot-Air chamber.
R. Damper in globe with rod attached.
S. Pendulum valve for cleaning.
→ Shows the direction of the currents of hot or cold air.

Figure 2.

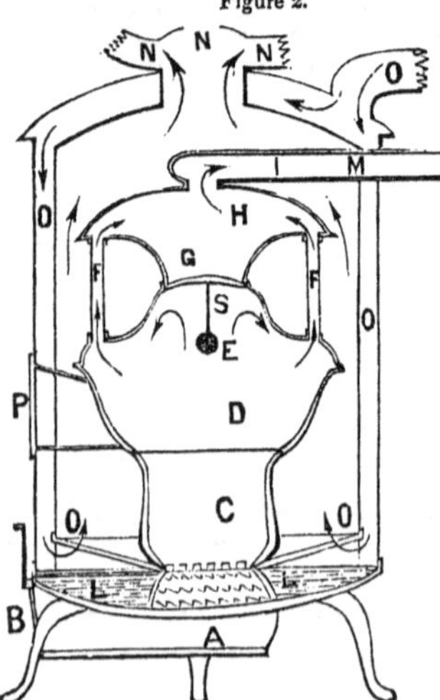

Fig. 2 represents a section of large size Portable Furnace with double casings of sheet iron or zinc. The same letters for reference are used as in Fig. 1.

Fig 3 represents a smaller size Portable Furnace, with two metal coverings and an evaporating dish standing upon the top of the drum.

Figure 3.

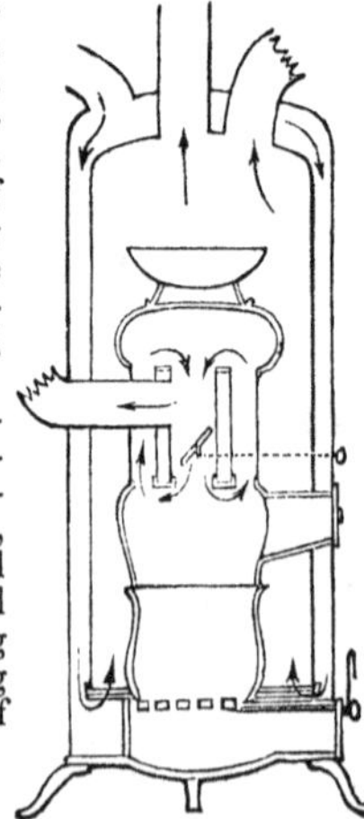

APPARATUS.

In addition to the necessary furniture of a school, such as seats, desks, and other fixtures and articles required for the accommodation of pupils and teacher, and the order and cleanliness of the premises, every school-room should be furnished with such apparatus as shall enable the teacher to employ the hand and eye of every pupil in illustration and experiment, so far as may be practicable and desirable in the course of instruction pursued in the school. It is therefore important, in the internal arrangement of a school-house, to have regard to the safe-keeping, display, and use of such apparatus as the grade of the school, for which the house is intended, may require. A few suggestions will therefore be made on these points, and in aid of committees and trustees in selecting apparatus.

1. In a large school, and in schools of the highest grade, there will be need of a separate apartment appropriated to the safe-keeping of the apparatus, and in some departments of instruction, for the proper use of the same. But in small schools, and as far as practicable in all schools, maps, diagrams, and other apparatus, should be in view of the school at all times.

This will not only add to the attractions of the school, and make the school-room look like a workshop of education, but will awaken a desire in the pupils to know the uses of the various articles, and to become acquainted with the facts and principles which can thus be seen, heard, or handled.

2. Such articles as are liable to be injured by dust, or handling, must be provided with an appropriate room, or a case of sufficient size, having glazed and sliding doors, and convenient shelves.

The doors should not be glazed to the floor, on account of liability to breakage, and also to admit of drawers for maps and diagrams, and a closet for such articles as may be uninteresting or unseemly to the eye, although useful in their place.

The shelves should be movable, so as to admit of additions of larger or smaller specimens of apparatus, and also of such arrangement as the varying tastes of different teachers may require.

3. There should be a table, with a level top, and capable of being made perfectly firm, unless the teacher's desk can be so, for the teacher to place his apparatus on, when in use.

4. The apparatus of every school-room should be selected with reference to the grade of schools to which it is appropriated, and in Primary and District schools in particular, should be of simple construction and convenient for use.

5. As far as practicable, the real object in nature and art, and not a diagram, or model, should be secured.

The following list of articles is necessarily very imperfect, but it may help to guide committees in their search after apparatus.

Articles indispensable in Schools of every Grade.

A clock.

The cardinal points of the heavens painted on the ceiling, or on the teacher's platform, or the floor of the recitation room.

As much blackboard, or black surface on the walls of the school-room, and the recitation rooms, as can be secured. A portion of this black surface should be in full view of the whole school, for passing explanations; and another portion out of the way, within reach of the smallest pupils. One or more movable blackboards, or large slate, with one or more movable stands or supporters.

All the appendages to a blackboard, such as chalk, crayons, and a rubber of soft cloth, leather, or sheepskin, and a pointer.

An inkstand, fixed into the desk, with a lid, and with a pen-wiper attached.

A slate, iron-bound at the corners, and covered with list, or India-rubber cloth, for every desk, with a pencil-holder and sponge attached. A few extra slates for the use of the youngest pupils, under the care and at the discretion of the teacher.

A map of the district, town, county, and state.

A terrestrial globe, properly mounted, or suspended by a wire.

The measure of an inch, foot, yard, and rod, marked off on the edge of the blackboard, or on the wall.

Real measures of all kinds, linear, superficial, solid, and liquid; as a foot-rule, a yard-stick, quarts, bushels, an ounce, pound, &c., for the exercise of the eye and hand.

Vases for flowers and natural grasses.

Apparatus for a Primary or District School.

The apparatus for this class of schools cannot be specified with much minuteness, because the ages of the pupils, and the modes of instruction vary so much in different localities. The following list embraces the articles purchased for Primary and District schools in Rhode Island:

Movable Lesson Posts. These are from three and a half to four feet high, and are variously made of wood, and of cast-iron. It consists, when made of wood, of an upright piece of plank from two to three inches square at the bottom, and diminishing regularly to the top, where it is one inch, inserted in a round or cross base broad enough to support the lesson board, or card, which is suspended by a ring on a hook at or near the top of the post.

J. L. Mott, 264, Water street, New York, manufactures for the Primary schools of the Public School Society of New York, a very neat *cast-iron* lesson stand.

Reading Lessons. Colored Prints, and Diagrams of various kinds, such as of animals, costumes, trades, &c., pasted on boards of wood or strong pasteboard; some with, and others without printed descriptions beneath; to be suspended at appropriate times on the lesson stands, for class exercises, and at other times, on the walls, or deposited in their appropriate places.

In this list should be included the numeration table, tables for reading arithmetical marks, easy lessons, geometrical figures, punctuation marks, outline maps, &c.

Allen's *Education Table* will be found very useful in teaching the Alphabet, Spelling, Reading, and Arithmetic, to little children at home, and in Primary Schools.

Allen's Education Table consists of a board or table, along the centre of which are horizontal grooves, or raised ledges forming grooves between them, that connect with perpendicular grooves or compartments on the sides, in which are inserted an assortment of movable blocks, on the face of which are cut the letters of the alphabet, both capitals and small, the nine digits and cipher, and all the usual pauses and signs used in composition and arithmetic.

The letters, figures and signs are large, so as to be readily recognized by all the members of a large class, and from even the extremity of a large school-room, and are so assorted and arranged as to be easily slid from the perpendicular grooves or compartments into the horizontal grooves, and there combined into syllables, words and sentences, or used in simple arithmetical operations. When the lesson in the alphabet, spelling, reading, composition, or arithmetic, is finished, the blocks can be returned to their appropriate places.

The experience of many teachers in schools of different grades, and of many mothers at home, (the God-appointed school for little children, next to which should be ranked the well organized Primary School, with a bright, gentle, affectionate and patient female teacher,) has demonstrated that by accustoming the child, either individually, or in a class, to select letter by letter, and move them from their appropriate case to the centre of the board, and there combining them into syllables and words, a knowledge of the alphabet, and of words, is acquired in a much shorter time and in a much more impressive and agreeable manner, than by any of even the best methods now pursued.

All of the advantages derived from the method of dictation, and the use of the slate and blackboard, in teaching children the alphabet, spelling, reading, and the use of capital letters and pauses, as well as the elementary principles of arithmetic, such as numeration, addition, subtraction, &c., can be secured by the introduction of this Table into our Primary and District Schools.

Manufactured by Edwin Allen *only, Windham, Conn., who will promptly attend to all orders for them.*

A *Moveable Black-board,* or prepared black surface of considerable extent, is indispensable.

The upper portion of the standing blackboard should be inclined back a little from the perpendicular, and along the lower edge there should be a projection or trough to catch the particles detached from the chalk or crayon when in use, and a drawer to receive the sponge, cloth, lamb's-skin, or other soft article used in cleaning the surface of the board.

Blackboards, even when made with great care, and of the best seasoned materials, are liable to injury and defacement from warping, opening of seams, or splitting when exposed to the overheated atmosphere of school-rooms, unless they are set in a frame like a slate, or the panel of a door.

By the following ingenious, and cheap contrivance, a few feet of board can be converted into a table, a sloping desk, one or two blackboards, and a form or seat, and the whole folded up so as not to occupy a space more than five inches wide, and be easily moved from one room to another. It is equally well adapted to a school-room, class-room, library or nursery.

f f Under side of the swinging board, suspended by rule-joint hinges, when turned up, painted black or dark chocolate.

a d Folding brackets, inclined at an angle of 75 degrees, and swung out to support the board when a sloping desk is required.

b c Folding brackets to support the swinging board when a bench or flat table is required.

e e e e Uprights attached to the wall.

g g Form to be used when the swinging board is let down, and to be supported by folding legs. The under side can be used as a blackboard for small children.

h A wooden button to retain the swinging board when turned up for use as a blackboard.

n Opening to receive inkstands, and deposit for slate, pencil, chalk, &c.

m Surface of swinging board when let down.

l Surface of form or bench.

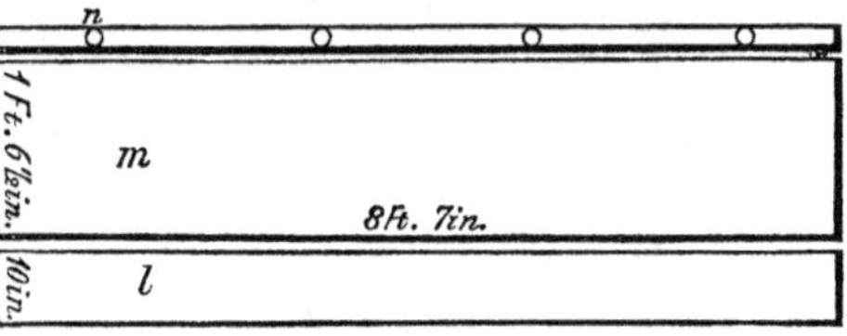

When not in use, or let down, the desk and form should hang flush with each other.

A cheap movable blackboard can be made after the following cut (Fig. 3.

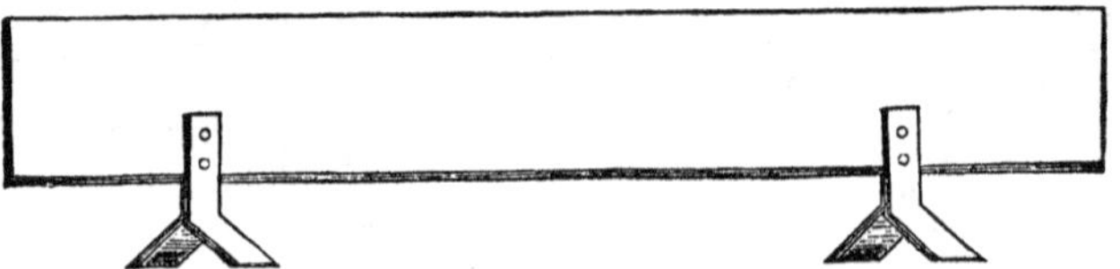

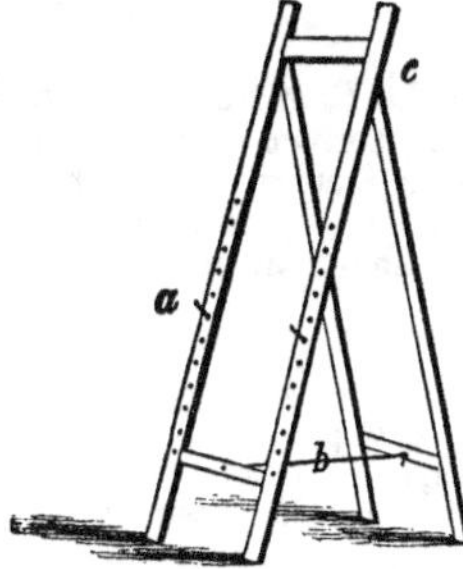

A movable stand to support a blackboard may be made like a painter's easel, as represented in the accompanying cut.

a, Pins for board to rest on. *c*, Hinge or joint to the supporting legs, which are braced by hook *b*, and may be folded up, and the stand put away in a closet. A stand of this kind is convenient to display outline and other maps, reading lessons and other diagrams.

A large movable blackboard may be made as represented in the accompanying cut. An upright frame, strongly braced by cross-pieces (*a*) is inserted into the feet (*b*,) or horizontal supports having castors, on which the whole may be rolled on the floor. Within grooves on the inside of this upright frame is a smaller frame (*c*) hung by a cord which passes over a pulley (*d*,) and is so balanced by weights, concealed in the upright parts, as to admit of being raised or lowered conveniently. Within this inner frame is hung the blackboard on pivots, by which the surface of the board can be inclined from a perpendicular.

A cheaper movable frame, with a blackboard suspended on a pivct, can be made as represented in the lower diagram. The feet, if made as represented in this cut, will be liable to get broken.

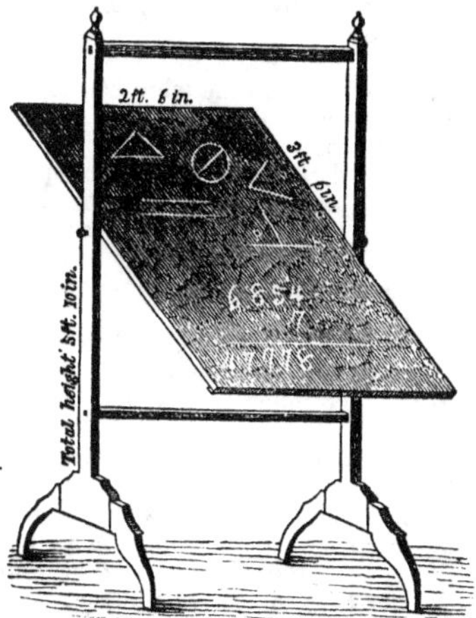

Composition for Blackboards.

Lampblack and flour of emery mixed with spirit-varnish.

No more lampblack and flour of emery should be used than are sufficient to give the required black and abrading surface ; and the varnish should contain only sufficient gum to hold the ingredients together, and confine the composition to the board. The thinner the mixture, the better.

The lampblack should first be ground with a small quantity of alcohol, or spirit-varnish, to free it from lumps.

The composition should be applied to the smoothly-planed surface of the board, with a common painter's brush. Let it become *thoroughly dry and hard before it is used.* Rub it down with pumice-stone, or a piece of smooth wood covered with the composition.

This composition may also be used on the walls.

Slate Blackboard.

In the class-rooms of the American Asylum for the Deaf and Dumb, and all similar institutions, where most of the instruction is given by writing, and drawings on the blackboard, large slates from three feet wide, to four feet long are substituted for the blackboard. These slates cost from $2 to $3, and are superior to any other form of blackboard, and in a series of years prove more economical.

Plaster Blackboard.

As a substitute for the painted board, it is common to paint black a portion of the plastered wall when covered with hard finish, (i. e. plaster of Paris and sand;) or to color it by mixing with the hard finish a sufficient quantity of lamp-black, wet with alcohol, at the time of putting it on. The hard finish, colored in this way, can be put on to an old, as well as to a new surface. Unless the lamp-black is wet with alcohol, or sour beer, it will not mix uniformly with the hard finish, and when dry, the surface, instead of being a uniform black, will present a spotted appearance.

Canvas Blackboard.

Every teacher can provide himself with a portable blackboard made of canvas cloth, 3 feet wide and 6 feet long, covered with three or four coats of black paint, like Winchester's Writing Charts. One side might, like this chart, present the elements of the written characters classified in the order of their simplicity, and guide-marks to enable a child to determine with ease the height, width, and inclination of every letter. Below, on the same side, might be ruled the musical scale, leaving sufficient space to receive such characters as may be required to illustrate lessons in music. The opposite side can be used for the ordinary purposes of a blackboard. When rolled up, the canvas would occupy a space three feet long, and not more than three inches in diameter.

Directions for making Crayons.

A school, or the schools of a town, may be supplied with crayons very cheaply, made after the following directions given by Professor Turner of the American Asylum for the Deaf and Dumb.

Take 5 pounds of Paris White, 1 pound of Wheat Flour, wet with water, and knead it well, make it so stiff that it will not stick to the table, but not so stiff as to crumble and fall to pieces when it is rolled under the hand.

To *roll* out the crayons to the proper size, two boards are needed, *one*, to roll them *on;* the *other* to roll them *with.* The first should be a smooth pine board, three feet long, and nine inches wide. The other should also be pine, a foot long, and nine inches wide, having nailed on the under side, near each edge, a slip of wood one third of an inch thick, in order to raise it so much above the under board, as, that the crayon, when brought to its proper size, may lie between them without being flattened.

The mass is rolled into a ball, and slices are cut from one side of it about one third of an inch thick; these slices are again cut into strips about four inches long and one third of an inch wide, and rolled separately between these boards until smooth and round.

Near at hand, should be another board 3 feet long and 4 inches wide, across which each crayon, as it is made, should be laid so that the ends may project on each side—the crayons should be laid in close contact and straight. When the board is filled, the ends should be trimmed off so as to make the crayons as long as the width of the board. It is then laid in the sun, if in hot weather, or if in winter, near a stove or fire-place, where the crayons may dry gradually, which will require twelve hours. When thoroughly dry, they are fit for use.

An experienced hand will make 150 in an hour.

The Gonigraph is a small instrument composed of a number of flat rods connected by pivots, which can be put into all possible geometrical figures that consist of straight lines and angles, as triangles, squares, pentagons, hexagons, octagons, &c.

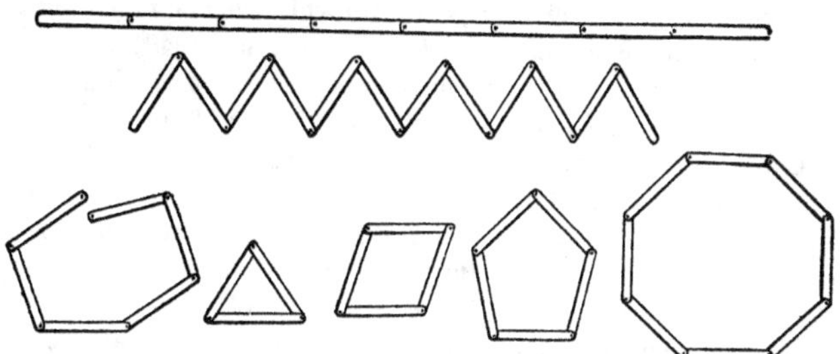

The Arithmeticon, represented in the annexed cut, is a most useful instrument. In an oblong open frame, twelve rows of wooden balls, alternately black and white, and of the size of a nutmeg or small walnut, and twelve in each row, are strung like beads on strong wires. The instrument, when fixed to a stand, is about four feet high, the frame being one-fourth part broader than it is high. It may be made much smaller, as in the cut. When it is used to exercise the children in arithmetic, the teacher or monitor stands behind, and slides the balls along the wires from his left to his right, calling out the number he shifts, as, twice two are four, thrice two are six, shifting first four balls, and then two more. As the children are apt to confuse the balls remaining with those shifted, a thin board covers half the surface on the side next the children, as marked by a line down the centre, so that they see only the balls shifted to the open side.

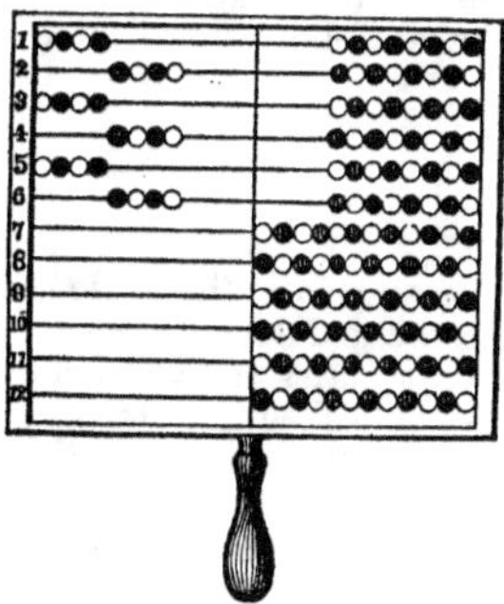

Holbrook's Scientific Apparatus embraces a variety of articles which will be found highly useful in the District school, in which both the older and younger pupils of the districts are ordinarily gathered at the same time, and under one teacher.

The following articles constitute a set which costs $14.75, including a neat box with lock and key:

Tellurian; Suspension Orrery; Gear or Wheel Orrery with metal wheels; Globe; Orbit Plain; Numerical Frame; Geometrical Forms and Solids; Twenty-five Geological Specimens; Geometry; Scale and Triangle; Block to illustrate Cube Roots; Geometrical Chart; Manuscript Letters: Text Book.

Mr. Josiah Holbrook of New York, whose name was originally connected with this set of apparatus, and with which, as manufactured under his direction, we are familiar, disclaims at this time (1848) any responsibility for the articles manufactured by Holbrook & Co., of Ohio.

This gentleman, so long and so favorably known from his connection with Lyceums, and elementary instruction, is now residing in New York, and has an office in the Hall of the Public School Society. There, in connection with Mr. Seton, and two very ingenious workmen, (Messrs. Riker,) he is now getting up apparatus "which shall be simple, easily used, readily understood, not liable to get out of order, and durable." The following is a list of articles already prepared for Primary Schools:

A Geological Cabinet, Geometricals, embracing plain figures, solids, models of crystals, illustrations of insect architecture and human mechanism, transposing and revolving figures, all illustrated with cuts and explanations; a globe with maps of the world and United States; numeral frame; a simple lever, with weights; a syphon and glass pump, showing the weight of the atmosphere in raising water; an air bulb, showing the expansive power of heat, simply by the hand; a simple permanent magnet; also an electro-magnet, a microscope, a simple orrery, and First Drawing Book for children, are among the instruments fitted to make clear, distinct, correct and lasting *first impressions* upon young minds, before reading-lessons or the letters of the alphabet can be rendered intelligible to them.

To teach Geography and History properly, the following maps are desirable:

Map or plan of the school-room, yard, &c.
Map or plan of the District or Village.
Map or plan of the Town, County, and State.
Map of the United States.
Map of North America.
Map of Europe.
Map of the World.
Map of Palestine.
Map of the countries mentioned in the Bible and in ancient history.
Map of Europe during the middle ages.
Fitch's Chirography, or plates and instruction in map-drawing.
Series of Outline Maps, published by J. H. Mather & Co., Hartford, Ct.
A selection from Borgaus & Johnston's *Physical Atlas*, published in Edinburgh in 1847, viz.

Rivers in America.
Rivers in Europe and Asia.
Mountain chains in North and South America.
Mountain chains in Europe and Asia.
Regions of Earthquakes and Volcanoes.
Geological Map of America.
Geological Map of Europe.
Distribution of Food-plants over the world.
Distribution of Animals.
Distribution of Man.

Colton's Historical Chart.
Willard's Map of Time.
Mattison's Astronomical Maps.
Page's Normal Chart of Elementary Sounds.

Fulton's Chirographic Charts.
Green's Analysis of Sentences.
Henry's Family and School Monitor.
Wickham's Drawing Tablets.

Apparatus for Grammar Schools.

The School Committee of Boston, in 1847, adopted the following articles as a set of Philosophical Apparatus for the Grammar schools, which was selected and classified by Mr. Wightman, whose long experience in manufacturing apparatus for schools of every grade, admirably qualified him for the work:

Laws of Matter.

Apparatus for illustrating Inertia.
Pair of Lead Hemispheres, for Cohesion.
Pair of Glass Plates, for Capillary Attraction.

Laws of Motion.

Ivory Balls on Stand, for Collision.
Set of eight illustrations for Centre of Gravity.
Sliding Frame, for Composition of Forces.
Apparatus for illustrating Central Forces.

Mechanics.

Complete set of Mechanicals, consisting of Pulleys; Wheel and Axle; Capstan; Screw; Inclined Plane; Wedge.

Hydrostatics.

Bent Glass Tube, for Fluid Level.
Mounted Spirit Level.
Hydrometer and Jar, for Specific Gravity.
Scales and Weights, for Specific Gravity.
Hydrostatic Bellows, and Paradox.

Hydraulics.

Lifting, or Common Water Pump.
Forcing Pump; illustrating the Fire Engine.
Glass Syphon Cup; for illustrating Intermitting Springs.
Glass and Metal Syphons.

Pneumatics.

Patent Lever Air Pump and Clamp.
Three Glass Bell Receivers, adapted to the Apparatus.
Condensing and Exhausting Syringe.
Copper Chamber, for Condensed Air Fountain.
Revolving Jet and Glass Barrel.
Fountain Glass, Cock, and Jet for Vacuum.
Brass Magdeburg Hemispheres.
Improved Weight Lifter for upward pressure.
Iron Weight of 56 lbs. and Strap
Flexible Tube and Connectors for Weight Lifter.
Brass Plate and Sliding Rod.
Bolt Head and Jar.
Tall Jar and Balloon.
Hand and Bladder Glasses.
Wood Cylinder and Plate.
India Rubber Bag, for expansion of air.
Guinea and Feather Apparatus.
Glass Flask and Stop-Cock, for weighing air.

Electricity.

Plate Electrical Machine.
Pith Ball Electrometer.
Electrical Battery of four Jars.
Electrical Discharger.
Image Plates and Figure.
Insulated Stool.
Chime of Bells.
Miser's Plate, for shocks.
Tissue Figure, Ball and Point.
Electrical Flyer and Tellurian.
Electrical Sportsman, Jar and Birds.
Mahogany Thunder House and Pistol.

Hydrogen Gas Generator.
Chains, Balls of Pith, and Amalgam.

Optics.

Glass Prism; and pair of Lenses.
Dissected Eye Ball, showing its arrangement.

Magnetism.

Magnetic Needle on Stand.
Pair of Magnetic Swans.
Glass Vase for Magnetic Swans.
Horseshoe Magnet.

Astronomy.

Improved School Orrery.
Tellurian, or, Season Machine.

Arithmetic, and Geometry.

Set of 13 Geometrical Figures of Solids.
Box of 64 one inch Cubes, for Cube Root, &c.

Auxiliaries.

Tin Oiler.
Glass Funnel.
Sulphuric Acid.
Set of Iron Weights for Hydrostatic Paradox.

Apparatus for High Schools.

The articles of Apparatus for a High School, will depend on the extent to which such studies as Natural Philosophy, Chemistry, &c., are carried, and to the amount of money which can be expended. We have drawn up several such lists, and in doing so have been governed by the circumstances mentioned. As the best guide to committees and teachers, we shall publish in another place, under the head of Priced Catalogues, &c., lists of such articles as can be purchased for sums of money varying from $50 to $1000.

LIBRARY.

Every school should be furnished with a Library which should include,

1. Books on schools and school-systems, for the use of school officers and parents; and on the theory and practice of teaching, for the professional instruction of teachers.
2. Books of reference, for the use principally of teachers.
3. Books for circulation among the pupils.
4. Books for circulation among the parents, and inhabitants of the District, or neighborhood.

In the arrangement, and furniture of a school-house, provision should be made for the Library.

The following catalogue may assist those who are charged with the purchase of books:

Rules for the Care and Preservation of School-Houses.

The following provisions are included among the Regulations for the Government of Teachers and Pupils of Public Schools, adopted by School Committees in most of the towns of Rhode Island:

For Teachers:

There shall be a recess of at least fifteen minutes in the middle of every half day; but the primary schools may have a recess of ten minutes every hour: at the discretion of the teacher.

It shall be the duty of teachers to see that fires are made, in cold weather, in their respective school-rooms, at a seasonable hour to render them warm and comfortable by school time; to take care that their rooms are properly swept and dusted; and that a due regard to neatness and order is observed, both in and around the school-house.

As pure air of a proper temperature is indispensable to health and comfort, teachers cannot be too careful in giving attention to these things. If the room has no ventilator, the doors and windows should be opened before and after school, to permit a free and healthful circulation of air; and the temperature should be regulated by a thermometer suspended, five or six feet from the floor, in such a position as to indicate as near as possible the average temperature, and should be kept about 65 degrees Fahrenheit.

The teachers shall take care that the school-houses, tables, desks, and apparatus in the same, and all the public property entrusted to their charge, be not cut, scratched, marked, or injured and defaced in any manner whatever. And it shall be the duty of the teachers to give prompt notice to one or more of the trustees, of any repairs that may be needed.

For Pupils:

Every pupil who shall, *accidentally* or *otherwise*, injure any school property, whether fences, gates, trees or shrubs, or any building or any part thereof; or break any window glass, or injure or destroy any instrument, apparatus or furniture belonging to the school, shall be liable to pay all damages.

Every pupil who shall any where, on or around the school premises, use or write any profane or unchaste language, or shall draw any obscene pictures or representations, or cut, mark, or otherwise *intentionally* deface any school furniture or buildings, or any property whatsoever belonging to the school estate, shall be punished in proportion to the nature and extent of the offence, and shall be liable to the action of the civil law.

No scholar of either sex shall be permitted to enter any part of the yard or buildings appropriated to the other, without the teacher's permission.

Smoking and chewing tobacco in the school-house or upon the school premises, are strictly prohibited.

The scholars shall pass through the streets on their way to and from school in an orderly and becoming manner; shall clean the mud and dirt from their feet on entering the school-room: and take their seats in a quiet and respectful manner, as soon as convenient after the first bell rings; and shall take proper care that their books, desks, and the floor around them, are kept clean and in good order.

It is expected that all the scholars who enjoy the advantages of public schools, will give proper attention to the *cleanliness* of their persons, and the neatness and decency of their clothes—not only for the moral effect of the habit of neatness and order, but that the pupils may be at all times prepared, both in conduct and external appearance—to receive their friends and visitors in a respectable manner; and to render the school-room pleasant, comfortable and happy for teachers and scholars.

In the "*Regulations of the Public Schools in the city of Providence,*" it is made the duty "of the principal teacher in each school-house, for the compensation allowed by the Committee, to employ some suitable person to make the fires in the same when necessary, and to see that this important work is properly and economically done;" also "for the compensation allowed, to employ some suitable person to sweep the room and its entries daily, and dust the blinds, seats, desks, and other furniture in the same, and to clean the same once a quarter, and to see that this work is neatly and properly done."

The teachers must also "take care that the school-houses, the apparatus in the same, and all the public property entrusted to their charge, be not defaced, or otherwise injured by the scholars, and to give prompt notice to the Superintendant of any repairs and supplies that may be needed."

Practical Suggestions respecting Ventilation, Fires, Sweeping and Dusting.

The following suggestions are taken from the *Manual of the System of Discipline and Instruction for the Schools of the Public School Society of New York:*

VENTILATION.

Strict attention should be paid to all the means provided for temperature and ventilation. During the season of fires, the thermometer should be watched,—and the ventilating flues, windows, doors, and stoves, should be constantly attended to,—and every precaution taken, to give as pure an atmosphere to the school-room, as circumstances will allow. This is not only necessary, for a proper and free exercise of the physical powers,—but it will be found greatly to influence every mental exercise; for, both will partake of either languor, or vigor, according as ventilation is neglected, or duly attended to. In warm weather, the upper sashes should be down during school hours, and allowed to remain open about four inches during the night,—except, that on occasion of a storm, the windows against which it beats, may be closed. In winter, excepting when the weather is exceedingly cold and piercing, it may be of advantage to have two or more of the upper sashes down about an inch during the night; but these as well as the doors should be closed before kindling the fires. Two or more of the upper sashes should be drawn down at the end of the first half hour after opening school,—and again, for a short time at each successive half hour,—and whenever the thermometer rises to 70 degrees. At all seasons, the windows and doors should be thrown wide open for a few minutes during each recess, while the scholars are in the yard. The teacher should be careful to require all the scholars to go out, except such as may reasonably be excused on account of infirmity or sickness; and even these should be required to change their places, and to exercise themselves by walking to and fro in the school-room. At all seasons, at the close of school, all the doors and windows should be opened for a few minutes, in order that a pure atmosphere may be admitted and retained during the noon-time recess, or at night. A thermometrical diary must be kept during the winter season, and the temperature of the room noted at the opening, middle, and close, of each daily session. Further directions on this point are given in the instructions for making fires. The window-blinds and curtains are for the purpose of guarding against the sunshine, or observation from without. They should, therefore, be so managed, as only to exclude the direct rays of the sun, and kept open or shut accordingly. When required as a screen from observation, they should extend no farther than necessary for that purpose. Attention to these rules will give an air of cheerfulness within, so congenial to the young. It is important that this fact be impressed on all—that air, and light, are grand essentials in a school-room: let the first be freely admitted, and the second never causelessly excluded.

FIRES.

The ashes should be taken from the stoves in the morning only, leaving a layer of one inch in depth: then to proceed to build with the materials after the following manner: Place one large stick on each side; in the space between them, place the kindling wood; and above it, the small wood, somewhat crosswise; then, set fire to the kindling, and close the stove door. See that the draught is cleared of ashes, or other obstructions; and that the dampers are properly adjusted; (these are generally so arranged as to open the draught when the handle is parallel with the pipe). If the materials have been laid according tc the foregoing directions, the combustion will be free. Should the temperature of the room be as low as 40°, fill the stove with wood. Under ordinary circumstances, in thirty-five minutes the temperature will be raised to 60 degrees,—at which point it should certainly be, at the time of opening school; when the stove may be supplied with one or two large sticks. At all times, before supplying wood, draw forward the brands and coals with the fire-hook. If there should be too much fire, open the stove door, and if necessary, turn the damper,—or, what may be better for economy, effectually close the draft at the stove door with ashes. By attention to all these directions,* the temperature may be maintained, the wood entirely consumed, and the thermometer stand at 60 degrees, at the close of the school; which is desirable in cold weather, so as not to subject the pupils to too sudden a change of temperature on going into the open air. The evaporating pan should be kept *clean*, and filled with water when in use. In damp rooms it is not needed,—nor in damp weather:—but it should be emptied, and wiped dry, before it is set aside.

DUSTING AND SWEEPING.

For a large room, or one department of a Public School building, six brooms will be found sufficient to be in use. When half worn, they will serve for sweeping the yard; and when well worn down in that service, will still be useful for scrubbing, with water or sand; and, if properly used by the sweepers, will be evenly worn to the last. Before sweeping, pull down the upper sashes, and raise the under ones. Let the sweepers be arranged, one to each passage between the desks,—and, beginning at the windward side, sweep the dirt before them, till it is carried forward to the opposite side of the room. The broom should rest square on the floor, and, with the motion used in raking hay, should be drawn towards the sweeper, without flirting it outwards, or upwards, which raises unnecessary dust, and wears the broom irregularly. The dirt, when taken up, should be carried into the *middle of the street*. The dusting is to be done in the same regular manner, allowing a suitable interval after sweeping. If at noon, dusting should be done shortly before school time; if at night, dust the next morning. In out-door sweeping, the same rule is to be followed—the sweepers going in ranks, and sweeping from the windward. Let the scrubbing be done by a similar method. When once acquainted with these methodical plans, the cleaners will do the work, not only more effectually, but with more satisfaction and ease to themselves—and being a part of domestic economy, it will be, so far, an advantage to understand how to do it well.

REGULATIONS OF CHAUNCY-HALL SCHOOL, BOSTON.

The following Regulations of one of the best conducted Private Schools for Boys in New England, will furnish useful hints to teachers in framing regulations for their own schools, especially in reference to the *good behavior* of the pupils, and to the care of the school-room, furniture, &c.

REQUISITION.

Boys are required to be punctual at school.

To scrape their feet on the scraper, and to wipe them on every mat they pass over on their way to the hall.

To hang their hats, caps, coats, &c., on the hooks appropriated to them respectively, by loops prepared for the purpose.

To bow gracefully and respectfully on entering and leaving the hall, and any recitation room when a teacher is present.

To take their places on entering the hall.

To make no unnecessary noise within the walls of the building, at any time of night or day.

To keep their persons, clothes, and shoes clean.

To carry and bring their books for study, in a satchel.

To quit the neighborhood of the school in a quiet and orderly manner, immediately after dismissal.

To bring notes for absence, dated, and signed by persons authorized to do so, and stating the duration of the absence; also, notes for tardiness, and for occasions when pupils are wanted at home before the regular hour of dismissal.

To study lessons at home, except when inconvenient to the family—in such cases to bring a certificate of the fact in writing.

To present a pen by the feather end; a knife, by its handle; a book, the right side upward to be read by the person receiving it.

To bow on presenting or receiving any thing.

To stand while speaking to a teacher.

To keep all books clean, and the contents of desks neatly arranged.

To deposite in desks all books (except writing books,) slates, pencils, rulers, &c., before dismissal.

To give notice through the school Post Office, of all books, slates, &c., missing.

To pick up hats, caps, coats, pens, slips, books, &c., found on the floor, and put them in their appropriate places.

To replace lost keys, books, &c., belonging to the school, and make good all damage done by them.

To write all requests on their slates, and wait until called.

To close desks and fasten them before quitting school for the session.

To raise the hand as a request to speak across the hall or any recitation room.

To show two fingers when a pen is wanted.

To put all refuse paper, stumps of pens, &c., in the dust box.

To be accountable for the condition of the floor nearest their own seats.

To fill all vacant time with ciphering, as a general occupation; and to give notice to the teacher, before dismissal, in case of omitting the exercise wholly on any day.

To be particularly vigilant, when no teacher is in the hall.

To promote as far as possible, the happiness, comfort, and improvement of others.

To *follow* every class-mate while reading, and correct all errors discoverer in pronunciation, emphasis, or inflection.

To point the fore finger of the left hand, at each letter or figure of the slip of copy, while writing, and the feather of the pen towards the right shoulder.

To keep the writing book square in front.

To rest the body on the left arm, while spelling, and keep the eye directed towards their own slates.

To sit erectly against the back of the chairs, during the singing lessons, and to direct their attention to the instructor.

Transferrers to show reports finished as early in the week as 3 o'clock on Tuesday, P. M.

PROHIBITIONS.

Boys are forbidden to buy or sell, borrow or lend, give, take, or exchange, any thing, except fruit or other eatables, without the teacher's permission.

To read any book in school except such as contain the reading lesson of his class.

To have in his possession at school any book without the teacher's knowledge.

To throw pens, paper, or any thing whatever on the floor, or out at a window or door.

To go out to play with his class when he has had a *deviation.*

To spit on the floor.

To climb on any fence, railing, ladder, &c., about the school-house.

To scrawl on, blot, or mark slips.

To mark, cut, scratch, chalk, or otherwise disfigure, injure, or defile, any portion of the building or any thing connected with it.

To take out an inkstand, meddle with the contents of another's desk, or unnecessarily open or shut his own.

To write without using a card and wiper.

To quit school without having finished his copy.

To use a knife, except on the conditions prescribed.

To remove class lists from their depositories.

To meddle with ink unnecessarily.

To study *home* lessons in school hours.

To leave the hall at any time without leave.

To pass noisily, or upon the run, from one room to another, or through the entries.

To visit the office, furnace room, or any closet or teacher's room, except in class, without a written *permit.*

To play at *paw paw* any where, or any game within the building.

To play in the play-ground before school.

To leave whittlings or other rubbish in the play-ground, on the side-walk, or around the building.

To go out of the play-ground in school hours.

To carry out his pen on his ear.

To use any profane or indelicate language.

To nick-name any person.

To press his knees, in sitting, against a form.

To leave his seat for any purpose, but to receive class instruction.

To go home, when deficient, without having answered to his name.

To indulge in eating or drinking in school.

To go out in class, after having been out singly; or going out singly, to linger below to play.

To waste school hours by unnecessary talking, laughing, playing, idling, standing up, turning round, teazing, or otherwise calling off the attention of another boy.

To throw stones, snow-balls, or other missiles about the neighborhood of the school.

To bring bats, *hockey* sticks, bows and arrows, or other dangerous play-things to school.

To visit a privy in company with any one.

To strike, kick, push, or otherwise annoy his associates or others.

In fine, to do any thing that the law of love forbids—that law which requires us To do to others as we would think it right that they should do to us.

These regulations are not stated according to their relative importance, but as they have been adopted or called to mind. They are intended to meet general circumstances, but may be waived in cases of necessity, by special permission, obtained in the prescribed mode.

Dedicatory Exercises.

The opening of a new school-house is an occasion which well deserves a public and joyful commemoration. Out of it are to be the issues of life to the community in the midst of which it stands, and like the river seen in the vision of the prophet, which nourished all along its banks trees whose leaves were for the healing of the nations, the well-spring of all its influences should be a spot consecrated by religion. In prayer, and in praise to the Giver of all good, and the Author of all being,—in song, and hymn and anthem, and in addresses, from those whose position in society will command the highest respect for any object in whose behalf they may speak, and in the presence of all classes of the community, of pupils, and teachers, of fathers and mothers, of the old and young,—the school-house should be set apart to the sacred purpose of the physical, intellectual and moral culture of the children who will be gathered within its walls. We rejoice to see that these occasions are thus improved, and that so many of our most distinguished teachers, scholars and statesmen take part in the exercises. We have before us a large number of addresses, at once eloquent and practical, which have been delivered at the opening of new school-houses, and we shall select a few, not for their superiority to the rest, but as specimens of the manner in which topics appropriate to the occasion are introduced, and as fitting testimony to the importance of School Architecture.

School Celebration at Salem, Mass.

On the first of March, 1842, the occasion of occupying several new school-houses, was marked by a variety of interesting exercises, an account of which will be found in the Common School Journal for that year. We copy the addresses of Mr. George B. Emerson, and of G. F. Thayer.

Mr. Emerson said,—

"I congratulate you, my young friends, on this happy event. This pleasant day is like a smile of Heaven upon this occasion; and I believe Heaven always smiles on events like this. Many of us whom you see here have come from a distance, on the invitation of your excellent friend the Mayor, to show the interest which we feel in you, and in what has been done here for your improvement. We have taken great pleasure in looking over the buildings prepared for your use, the admirable arrangements and apparatus, so much superior to what is usually enjoyed by children in your position. We have been pleased to hear of the faithful teachers that are provided for you, and the excellent plan of your studies, and the excellent regulations.

Your fathers and friends have spared no pains to furnish you with all the best means and opportunities for learning. They now look to you to do your part. All that they have done will be of no avail, unless you are excited to exert yourselves,—to prove yourselves worthy of these great advantages.

I was gratified, in looking over the regulations, to see the course marked out for you,—to see the stress laid upon the great substantials of a good education,—to see the prominent place given to that most useful art, that most graceful accomplishment, *reading*. You cannot, my young friends, realize the great and manifold advantages of gaining, now, in the beginning of your life, familiarly and perfectly, the single power of reading distinctly, naturally, intelligently, with taste and interest,—and of acquiring a *love* for reading. There is no situation in life, in which it will not prove to you a source of the purest pleasure and highest improvement.

For many years, and many times in a year, I have passed by the shop of a diligent, industrious mechanic, whom I have often seen busy at his trade, with his arms bare, hard at work. His industry and steadiness have been successful, and he has gained a competency. But he still remains wisely devoted to his trade. During the day, you may see him at his work, or chatting with his neighbors. At night, he sits down in his parlor, by his quiet fireside, and enjoys the company of his friends. And he has the most extraordinary collection of friends that any man in New England can boast of. William H. Prescott goes out from Boston, and talks with him about Ferdinand and Isabella. Washington Irving comes from New York, and tells him the story of the wars of Grenada, and the adventurous voyage of Columbus, or the Legend of Sleepy Hollow, or the tale of the Broken Heart. George Bancroft sits down with him, and points out on a map, the colonies and settlements of America, their circumstances and fates, and gives him the early history of liberty. Jared Sparks comes down from Cambridge, and reads to him the letters of Washington, and makes his heart glow with the heroic deeds of that godlike man for the cause of his country. Or, if he is in the mood for poetry, his neighbor Washington Allston, the great painter, steps in and tells him a story,—and nobody tells a story so well,—or repeats to him lines of poetry. Bryant comes, with his sweet wood-notes, which he learnt among the green hills of Berkshire. And Richard H. Dana, father and son, come, the one to repeat grave, heart-stirring poetry, the other to speak of his *two years before the mast*. Or, if this mechanic is in a speculative mood, Professor Hitchcock comes to talk to him of all the changes that have befallen the soil of Massachusetts, since the flood and before; or Professor Espy tries to show him how to predict a storm. Nor is his acquaintance confined to his own country. In his graver hours, he sends for Sir John Herschel from across the ocean, and he comes and sits down and discourses eloquently upon the wonders of the vast creation,—of all the worlds that are poured upon our sight by the glory of a starry night. Nor is it across the stormy ocean of blue waves alone that his friends come to visit him; but across the darker and wider ocean of time, come the wise and the good, the eloquent and the witty, and sit down by his table, and discourse with him as long as he wishes to listen. That eloquent blind old man of Scio, with beard descending to his girdle, still blind, but still eloquent, sits down with him; and, as he sang almost three thousand years ago among the Grecian isles, sings the war of Troy or the wanderings of the sage Ulysses. The poet of the human heart comes from the banks of Avon, and the poet of Paradise from his small garden-house in Westminster; Burns from his cottage on the Ayr, and Scott from his dwelling by the Tweed;—and, any time these three years past, may have been seen by his fireside a man who ought to be a hero with schoolboys, for no one ever so felt for them; a man whom so many of your neighbors in Boston lately strove in vain to see,—Charles Dickens. In the midst of such friends, our friend the leather-dresser lives a happy and respected life, not less respected, and far more happy, than if an uneasy ambition had made him a representative in Congress, or a governor of a State; and the more respected and happy that he disdains not to labor daily in his honorable calling.

My young friends, this is no fancy sketch. Many who hear me know as well as I do, Thomas Dowse, the leather-dresser of Cambridgeport,

V and many have seen his choice and beautiful library. But I suppose there is no one here who knows a neighbor of his, who had in his early years the same advantages, but who did not improve them;—who never gained this love of reading, and who now, in consequence, instead of living this happy and desirable life, wastes his evenings in low company at taverns, or dozes them away by his own fire. Which of these lives will you choose to lead? They are both before you.

Some of you, perhaps, are looking forward to the life of a farmer,—a very happy life, if it be well spent. On the southern side of a gently sloping hill in Natick, not far from the place where may be still standing the last wigwam of the tribe of Indians of that name, in a comfortable farm-house, lives a man whom I sometimes go to see. I find him with his farmer's frock on, sometimes at the plough-tail, sometimes handling the hoe or the axe; and I never shake his hand, hardened by honorable toil, without wishing that I could harden my own poor hands by his side in the same respectable employment. I go out to look with him at trees, and to talk about them; for he is a lover of trees, and so am I; and he is not unwilling, when I come, to leave his work for a stroll in the woods. He long ago learnt the language of plants, and they have told him their history and their uses. He, again, is a reader, and has collected about him a set of friends, not so numerous as our friend Dowse, nor of just the same character, but a goodly number of very entertaining and instructive ones; and he finds time every day to enjoy their company. His winter evenings he spends with them, and in repeating experiments which the chemists and philosophers have made. He leads a happy life. Time never hangs heavy on his hands. For such a man we have an involuntary respect.

On the other side of Boston, down by the coast, lived, a few years ago, a farmer of a far different character. He had been what is called fortunate in business, and had a beautiful farm and garden in the country, and a house in town. Chancing to pass by his place, some four or five years ago, I stopped to see him. And I could not but congratulate him on having so delightful a place to spend his summers in. But he frankly confessed that he was heartily tired of it, and that he longed to go back to Boston. I found that he knew nothing about his trees, of which he had many fine ones,—for it was an old place he had bought,—nor of the plants in his garden. He had no books, and no taste for them. His time hung like a burden on him. He enjoyed neither his leisure nor his wealth. It would have been a blessing to him if he could have been obliged to exchange places with his hired men, and dig in his garden for his gardener, or plough the field for his ploughman. He went from country to town and from town to country, and died, at last, weary and sick of life. Yet he was a kind man, and might have been a happy one but for a single misfortune; he had not learned to enjoy reading. The love of reading is a blessing in any pursuit, in any course of life;—not less to the merchant and sailor than to the mechanic and farmer. What was it but a love of reading which made of a merchant's apprentice, a man whom many of you have seen and all have heard of, the truly great and learned Bowditch?

Our friends the young ladies may not think this which I have said exactly suited to them. But to you, my young friends, even more than to your brothers, it is important now to acquire a talent for reading well, and a taste for reading. I say *more important*, for, looking forward to the future, you will need it more than they. They are more independent of this resource. They have their shops, and farms, and counting-houses to go to. They are daily on change. They go abroad on the ocean. The sphere of woman, her place of honor, is home, her own fireside, the cares of her own family. A well-educated woman is a sun in this sphere, shedding around her the light of intelligence, the warmth of love and happiness.

And by a well-educated woman I do not mean merely one who has acquired ancient and foreign languages, or curious or striking accomplishments. I mean a woman who, having left school with a firmly-fixed love of reading, has employed the golden leisure of her youth in reading the best English books, such as shall prepare her for her duties. All the best books ever written are in English, either original or translated; and in this richest and best literature of the world she may find enough to prepare her for all the duties and relations of life. The mere talent of reading well, simply, gracefully,—what a beautiful accomplishment it is in woman! How many weary and otherwise heavy hours have I had charmed into pleasure by this talent in a female friend. But I speak of the higher acquisition, the natural and usual consequence of this, a taste for reading. This will give a woman a world of resources.

It gives her the oracles of God. These will be ever near her;—nearest to her hand when she wakes, and last from her hand when she retires to sleep. And what stores of wisdom, for this world and for a higher, will she gain from this volume! This will enable her to form her own character and the hearts of her children. Almost every distinguished man has confessed his obligations to his mother. To her is committed the whole formation of the character,—mind, heart, and body, at the most important period of life. How necessary, then, is it that she should possess a knowledge of the laws of the body and the mind! and how can she get it but by reading? If you gain only this, what an unspeakable blessing will your education be to you!

I need not, my young friends, speak of the other acquisitions you may make,—of writing, which places friends in the remotest parts of the world side by side,—or of calculation, the very basis of justice and honesty.

The acquisitions you may make will depend chiefly on yourselves. You will find your teachers ready to lead you on to higher studies whenever you are prepared to go.

These excellent establishments are emphatically yours. They are raised for your good; and, as we your seniors pass away,—and in a few years we shall have passed,—these buildings will become your property, and your children will fill the seats you now occupy. Consider them yours, then, to enjoy and profit by, but not yours to waste. Let it be your pride to preserve them uninjured, unmarred by the mischievous knives and pencils of vulgar children. Unite for this purpose. Consider an injury done to these buildings as an injury done to yourselves.

There is another thing which will depend on you, of more importance than any I have spoken of. I mean the tone of character which shall prevail in these schools. Your teachers will be happy to treat you as high-minded and generous children. Show that you can be so treated; that you are such.

Let me congratulate you upon the happy auspices of the name of him under whom, with the zealous co-operation of enlightened and patriotic associates, this momentous change in your school system has been effected,—a name which is borne by the oldest and best school in New Hampshire, and by one of the oldest and best in Massachusetts. It will depend upon you, my friends, to make the schools of Salem, equally, or still more distinguished, among those of the State."

Mr. Thayer said,—

Children: I did not expect that I should have the privilege of addressing you, on this most joyful occasion; for it was not till I met your respected Mayor, an hour ago, at the beautiful school-house we have just left, that I received an invitation to do so. You will not, therefore, anticipate a studied discourse, or any thing particularly interesting. Devoted, however, as my life is, and has long been, to the instruction and guidance of the young in no inconsiderable numbers, I shall, without further preface, imagine myself in the midst of my own school, and talk familiarly to you as I would, and do, to them.

And allow me to add my congratulations to those of your other friends, for the ample, beautiful, and convenient arrangements that have been made for you, in the school-houses of this city; and especially in the new one we have just examined. I can assure you, it is superior in almost every respect to any public school-house in New England, if not in the United States. It, with others in the city, has cost your fathers and friends a great deal of money, which they have cheerfully expended as a means of making you wise and good. But you have incurred a great debt to them, which you can never repay while you are children, but must endeavor to do it to your children, when you shall become men and women, and take the place of your parents in the world. But before that period, you can do something. Now, immediately on entering upon the enjoyment of the precious privileges extended to you, you can acknowledge the debt, evince the gratitude you feel, not by *words*, but *deeds*;—by, (to use an expression well understood by all children,) '*being good*.' Yes,—by 'being good and doing good;'—by obedience to parents and teachers; by kindness to brothers and sisters, and all your young friends and companions; by fidelity in duty, at home and at school; by the practice of honesty and truth at all times; by refraining from the use of profane and indecent language; by keeping the mind and heart free from every thing impure. These are the means in your own hands. Fail not to use them; and although they will in fact be merely an acknowledgment of your obligation for the boon you possess, your friends will consider themselves well repaid for all they have done for you. It is from such conduct that the teacher's, as well as the father's, richest reward and highest satisfaction are derived. To see the beloved objects of our care and instruction appreciating our labors, and improving in all that is good and useful, under our management, affords the greatest happiness, lightens the heavy load of toil, relieves the aching head, and revives the fainting spirit.

There is, however, one great danger to which you,—to which all the young,—are especially exposed. I mean the influence of bad example. Example is omnipotent. Its force is irresistible to most minds. We are all swayed more or less, by others. Others are swayed by us. And this process is continually going on, even though we are entirely unconscious of it ourselves. Hence we see the importance of choosing good companions, and flying from the bad. Unless this is done, it will be in vain for your friends to give you wise counsel, or for you to form good resolutions. 'Who can touch pitch and be clean?' You will resemble those with whom you associate. You will catch their words, their manners, their habits. Are they pure, you will be pure. Are they depraved, they will corrupt you. Be it a rule with you, then, to avoid those who are addicted to practices that you would be unwilling your most respected friends should know, and regulate your own conduct by the same standard.

I would particularly caution you against *beginnings*. It is the *first step* that is the dangerous one; since it is obvious that, if you were to ascend the highest mountain, it could only be done by a step at a time, and if the first were not taken, the summit could never be reached. But, one successfully accomplished, the next follows as a matter of course. And equally and fatally sure is the *downward* track to crime and misery! If we suffer ourselves to be drawn in *that* direction, what human power can save us from destruction? This danger, too, is increased by the feeling of security we indulge, when we say, 'It is only a *little* thing; we shall never commit any great fault;'—not remembering that nothing stands still in life, in character, any more than in the material universe. We must be going forward or backward; up, towards improvement and glory,—or down, towards infamy and woe! Every thing accumulates, according to its kind; though it begins small, like the snowball you hold in your hand, it becomes, as you roll it on the ground before you, larger at every revolution, till, at last, it is beyond your power to move it at all.

I will illustrate this by a sad case which has recently occurred in Boston. But first, I wish to interest you in something of an agreeable nature, in connection with the faithful performance of duty.

I have spoken of some things that you should do, to show your sense of the benefits which have been conferred upon you, and I should like to dwell on each one of them separately; but I shall have time only to speak of one. It is, however, among the most important. I allude to *speaking the truth*,—the most substantial foundation of moral character. It has innumerable advantages, one of which is strikingly exhibited in the following story:—

Petrarch, an eminent Italian poet, who lived about five hundred years ago, secured the confidence and friendship of Cardinal Colonna, in whose family he resided in his youth, by his candor and strict regard to truth.

A violent quarrel had occurred in the family of this nobleman, which was carried so far, that resort was had to arms. The cardinal wished to know the foundation of the affair; and, calling all his people before him, he required each one to bind himself by a solemn oath, on the Gospels, to declare the whole truth. None were exempt. Even the cardinal's brother submitted to it. Petrarch, in his turn, presenting himself to take the oath, the cardinal closed the book, and said, '*As for you, Petrarch, your* WORD *is sufficient!*'

What more delightful reward could have been presented to the feelings of the noble youth than this, from his friend, his master, and one of the highest dignitaries of the church? Nothing but the peaceful whispers of his own conscience, or the approbation of his Maker, could have given him more heart-felt satisfaction. Who among you would not be a Petrarch? and, in this respect, which of you could not?

While, then, I would hold up for imitation this beautiful example, I would present a contrast as a warning to you.

There is now confined in the Boston jail a boy of fourteen years of age, who, for the previous six years, had been sinking deeper and deeper into vice and crime, until last October, when he was convicted, and sentenced to two years' confinement within the cold damp cell of a gloomy prison, for aggravated theft. In his own written account of his life, which I have seen, he says that he began his wretched course by playing truant from school. His second step was *lying*, to conceal it. Idle, and destitute of any fixed purpose, he fell in company with others, guilty like himself, of whom he learned to steal, and to use indecent and profane language. He sought the worst boys he could find. He became a gambler, a frequenter of the circus and the theatre, and engaged in various other corrupt and sinful practices. At length, becoming bold in his dishonesty, he robbed the post-office of letters containing very considerable sums of money, and was soon detected and condemned. If you were to visit that abode of misery, you might often see the boy's broken-hearted mother, weeping, and sobbing, and groaning, at the iron grating of his solitary cell, as if she would sink on the flinty floor, and die! 'And all this,' (to use the boy's own words,) 'comes from playing truant!'

Look, then, my young friends, on these two pictures,—both taken from life,—and tell me which you like best; and which of the two characters you propose to imitate. Will you be young Petrarchs, or will you adopt the course of the unfortunate boy in Boston jail? They are both before you. If you would be like the former, *begin right.* Resist temptation to wrong-doing, with all your might. Let no one entice you from the way which conscience points out.

Dedication of the Public High School in Cambridge, Mass.

After appropriate introductory addresses by the School Committee and Mayor of Cambridge, Hon. Edward Everett, President of Harvard College, responded to an invitation to address the audience, as follows:—

May it please your Honor:—

Connected as I am with another place of education, of a kind which is commonly regarded as of a higher order, it is precisely in that connection, that I learn to feel and appreciate the importance of good schools. I am not so ignorant of the history of our fathers, as not to know, that the spirit, which founded and fostered Harvard College, is the spirit which has founded and upheld and will continue to support and cherish the schools of New England. I know well, sir, that Universities and Colleges can neither flourish nor even stand alone. You might as well attempt to build your second and third stories in the air, without a first floor or a basement, as to have collegiate institutions without good schools for preparatory education, and for the diffusion of general information throughout the community. If the day should ever come, which I do not fear in our beloved country, when this general education shall be neglected and these preparatory institutions allowed to perish;—if the day should ever come (of which I have no apprehension) when the schools of New England shall go down, depend upon it, sir, the colleges will go with them. It will be with them, as it was with the granite warehouses, the day before yesterday in Federal street, in Boston; if the piers at the foundation give way, the upper stories will come down in one undistinguished ruin.

I anticipate no such disaster, Mr. Mayor, though it must be admitted that we live in an age of revolutions, of which every steamer brings us some fresh and astonishing account. But our revolutions are of a more auspicious character, and it occurred to me as I was coming down with your worthy associate (Mr. Whitney,) and your respected predecessor (Mr. Green,) to whom we have just listened with so much pleasure, that we were traversing a region, in which a more important revolution commenced no very long time since, and is still in progress,—far more important for us and our children,—than any of those which have lately convulsed the continent of Europe. I do not now refer to the great political and historical events of which this neighborhood was the theatre; of which the monuments are in sight from these windows, but to a revolution quiet and silent in its origin and progress, unostentatious in outward manifestations, but imparting greater change and warranting brighter hopes for most of those who hear me,—for our young friends before us,—than any of the most startling events that stare upon us in capitals in the columns of the newspapers, after every arrival from Europe. The Reverend Mr. Stearns has beautifully sketched some of the most important features of this peaceful revolution.

When I entered college, Mr. Mayor, (and I believe I shall not tell the audience quite how many years ago that is; you can do it, sir, but I will thank you not to,) there were a few straggling houses, shops, and taverns along the Main street at Cambridgeport. All back of this street to the north, and I believe almost all south of it to the river,—the entire district, in the centre of which we are now assembled, was in a state of nature; pretty equally divided between barren pasturage, salt-marsh, and what I must admit had no mean attraction for us freshmen, whortleberry swamp. Not one of the high roads had been cut, which now traverse the plain between Main street and the old road to Charlestown. East Cambridge did not exist even in the surveyor's imagination. There was not a church nor a public school east of Dr. Holmes' and Old Cambridge Common; and if any one had prophesied that within forty years a population like this would cover the soil,—with its streets and houses, and gardens, its numerous school-houses and churches, its conservatories breathing all the sweets of the tropics, its private libraries equal to the choicest in the land, and all the other appendages of a high civilization, he would have been set down as a visionary indeed. But this change, this revolution has taken place even within the life time of the venerable lady (Mrs. Merriam) introduced to us in such a pleasing manner by Mr. Stearns; and we are assembled this morning to take a respectful notice of what may be called its crowning incident, the opening of a High School in that primitive whortleberry swamp. I believe I do not over-state matters when I say, that no more important event than this is likely to occur, in the course of the lives of many of those here assembled. As far as our interests are concerned, all the revolutions in Europe multiplied tenfold are nothing to it. No, sir, not if the north were again to pour forth its myriads on central and southern Europe and break up the existing governments and states into one general wreck, it would not be an article of intelligence at all so important to us as the opening of a new school. No, my young friends, this is a day which may give an auspicious turn to your whole career in life; may affect your best interests not merely for time but for eternity.

There is certainly nothing in which the rapid progress of the country is more distinctly marked than its schools. It is not merely their multiplication in numbers, but their improvement as places of education. A school forty years ago was a very different affair from what it is now. The meaning of the word is changed. A little reading, writing, and ciphering, a very little grammar; and for those destined for college, a little Latin and Greek, very indifferently taught, were all we got at a common town school in my day. The range was narrow; the instruction superficial. In our modern school system, taking it as a whole composed of its several parts in due gradation,—viz. the primary, the district, and the High School,—the fortunate pupil not only enjoys a very thorough course of instruction in the elementary branches, but gets a good foundation in French, a good preparation for college, if he desires it, according to the present advanced standard of requirement; a general acquaintance with the applied mathematics, the elements of natural philosophy, some suitable information as to the form of government and political system under which we live, and no inconsiderable practice in the noble arts of writing and speaking our mother tongue.

It might seem, at first, that this is too wide a circle for a school. But the experience of our well conducted schools has abundantly shown that it is not too extensive. With faithful and competent teachers and willing and hearty learners, all the branches I have named and others I have passed over can be attended to with advantage, between the ages of four and sixteen.

Such being the case, our School Committees have done no more than their duty, in prescribing this extensive course and furnishing to master and pupils the means of pursuing it. I cannot tell you, sir, how much I have been gratified at hastily looking into the alcove behind us. As I stepped into it this morning, Mr. Smith, the intelligent master of the school, pointed out to me the beautiful electrical machine behind the door with the just remark that my venerable predecessor, President Dunster, would not have known what it was. No, sir, nor would the most eminent philosopher in the world before the time of Franklin. Lord Bacon would not have known what it was, nor Sir Isaac Newton. Mr. Smith reminded me of the notion of Cotton Mather (one of the most learned men of his day,) that lightning proceeded from the Prince of the Power of the Air, by which he accounted for the fact that it was so apt to strike the spires of churches. Cotton Mather would have come nearer the truth, if he had called it a shining manifestation of the power and skill, by which the Great Author of the Universe works out some of the mighty miracles of creation and nature. And only think, sir, that these newly discovered mysteries of the material world, unknown to the profoundest sages of elder days, are so effectually brought down to the reach of common schools in our day, that these young friends, before they are finally dismissed from these walls, will be made acquainted with not a few of the wonderful properties of the subtle element, evolved and condensed by that machine, and which recent science has taught to be but different forms of one principle, whether it flame across the heavens in the midnight storm, or guide the mariner across the pathless ocean;—or leap from city to city across the continent as swiftly as the thought of which it is the vehicle; and which I almost venture to predict, before some here present shall taste of death, will, by some still more sublime generalization, be identified with the yet hidden principle which thrills through the nerves of animated beings, and binds life to matter, by the ties of sensation.

But while you do well, sir, in your High School to make provision for these advanced studies, I know that as long as it remains under your instruction, the plain elementary branches will not be undervalued. There is perhaps a tendency in that direction in some of our modern schools: I venture to hope it will not be encouraged here. I know it is not to be the province of this school to teach the elements; but I am sure you will show that you entertain sound views of their importance. I hold, sir, that to read the English language well, that is with intelligence, feeling, spirit, and effect;—to write with dispatch, a neat, handsome, legible hand, (for it is after all, a great object in writing to have others able to read what you write,) and to be master of the four rules of arithmetic, so as to dispose at once with accuracy of every question of figures which comes up in practical life:—I say I call this a good education; and if you add the ability to write pure grammatical English, with the help of very few hard words, I regard it as an excellent education. These are the tools; you can do much with them, but you are helpless without them. They are the foundation; and unless you begin with these, all your flashy attainments, a little natural philosophy, and a little mental philosophy, a little physiology and a little geology, and all the other *ologies and osophies*, are but ostentatious rubbish.

There is certainly no country in the world in which so much money is paid for schooling as in ours. This can be proved by figures. I believe there is no country where the common schools are so good. But they may be improved. It is not enough to erect commodious school-houses; or compensate able teachers, and then leave them, masters and pupils, to themselves. A school is not a clock which you can wind up and then leave it to go of itself. It is an organized living body: it has sensibilities; it craves sympathy. You must not leave the School Committee to do all the work. Your teachers want the active countenance of the whole body of parents, of the whole intelligent community. I am sure you, Mr. Smith, would gladly put up with a little injudicious interference in single cases, if you could have the active sympathies of the whole body of parents to fall back upon in delicate and difficult cases, and to support and cheer you under the burthen of your labors, from day to day. I think this matter deserves more attention than it has received; and if so small a number as thirty parents would agree together, to come to the school, some one of them, each in his turn, but once a month, or rather if but 25 or 26 would do it, it would give your teacher the support and countenance of a parent's presence every day; at a cost to each individual of ten or eleven days in the year. Would not the good to be effected be worth the sacrifice?

I have already spoken too long, Mr. Mayor, and will allude to but one other topic. In most things, as I have said, connected with education, we are incalculably in advance of other days:—in some, perhaps, we have fallen below their standard. I know, sir, old men are apt to make unfavorable contrasts between the present time and the past; and if I do not soon begin to place myself in that class, others will do it for me. But I really think that in some things, belonging, perhaps, it will be thought, to the minor morals, the present promising generation of youth might learn something of their grandfathers, if not their fathers. When I first went to a village school, sir, I remember it as yesterday;—I seem still to hold by one hand for protection, (I was of the valiant age of three years) to an elder sister's apron;—with the other I grasped my primer, a volume of about two and a half inches in length, which formed then the sum total of my library, and which had lost the blue paper cover from one corner, (my first misfortune in life;) I say it was the practice then, as we were trudging along to school, to draw up by the road-side, if a traveller, a stranger, or a person in years, passed along, "and make our manners," as it was called. The little girls courtesied, the boys made a bow; it was not done with much grace, I suppose: but there was a civility and decency about it, which did the children good, and produced a pleasing impression on those who witnessed it. The age of village chivalry is past, never to return. These manners belong to a forgotten order of things. They are too precise and rigorous for this enlightened age. I sometimes fear the pendulum has swung too far in the opposite extreme. Last winter I was driving into town in a carriage closed behind, but open in front. There was in company with me, the Rev. President Woods, of Bowdoin College, Maine, and that distinguished philanthropist and excellent citizen, Mr. Amos Lawrence. Well, sir, we happened to pass a school-house just as the boys (to use the common expression) were "let out." I suppose the little men had just been taught within doors something about the laws, which regulate the course of projectiles, and determine the curves in which they move. Intent on a practical demonstration, and tempted by the convenient material, I must say they put in motion a quantity of spherical bodies, in the shape of snow balls, which brought the doctrine quite home to us wayfarers, and made it wonderful that we got off with no serious inconvenience, which was happily the case. This I thought was an instance of free and easy manners, verging to the opposite extreme of the old fashioned courtesy, which I have just described. I am quite sure that the boys of this school would be the last to indulge an experiment attended with so much risk to the heads of innocent third persons.

Nothing remains, sir, but to add my best wishes for teachers and pupils;—You are both commencing under the happiest auspices. When I consider that there is not one of you, my young friends, who does not enjoy gratuitously the opportunity of obtaining a better school education, than we could have bought, Mr. Mayor, when we were boys, with the wealth of the Indies, I cannot but think that each one of you, boys and girls, will be ready to say with grateful hearts, the lines have fallen to me in pleasant places; yea, I have a goodly heritage.

www.ingramcontent.com/pod-product-compliance
Lightning Source LLC
LaVergne TN
LVHW021359110826
845150LV00007B/1708

* 9 7 8 1 4 2 5 5 1 3 4 5 0 *